FORWARD!
Labour Politics in Scotland 1888–1988

A SHADOW CABINET FOR THE SCOTS

The Rev. James Barr " provides for the better Government of Scotland "

(1) Mr. G. D. Hardie.   (4) Mr. Neil Mclean.
(2) Mr. David Kirkwood.   (5) Mr. Campbell Stephen.
(3) Mr. George Buchanan.   (6) Mr. James Maxton.

By permission of the Proprietors of Punch.

FORWARD!

Labour Politics in Scotland 1888–1988

EDITED BY

Ian Donnachie
Christopher Harvie
and
Ian S. Wood

POLYGON
determinations›

© 1989 Polygon
22 George Square, Edinburgh

Typeset using the Telos Text Composition
System from Digital Publications Ltd
and printed in Great Britain by
Redwood Burn Limited, Trowbridge

British Library Cataloguing
  in Publication Data
Forward! Labour politics in Scotland
  1888-1988 – (Determinations)
Fig. 1. Scotland. Political parties. (Great
Britain) Labour Party, 1888-1988
I. Donnachie, Ian, *1944*– II. Harvie,
Christopher III. Wood, Ian S. IV. Series
324.24107'09411

ISBN 0 7486 6001 1
     0 7486 6010 0 pbk

Contents

Series Preface

CAIRNS CRAIG

Scotland's history is often presented as punctuated by disasters which overwhelm the nation, break its continuity and produce a fragmented culture. Many felt that 1979, and the failure of the Devolution Referendum, represented such a disaster: that the energetic culture of the 1960s and 1970s would wither into the silence of a political waste land in which Scotland would be no more than a barely distinguishable province of the United Kingdom.

Instead, the 1980s proved to be one of the most productive and creative decades in Scotland this century—as though the energy that had failed to be harnessed by the politicians flowed into other channels. In literature, in thought, in history, creative and scholarly work went hand in hand to redraw the map of Scotland's past and realign the perspectives of its future.

In place of the few standard conceptions of Scotland's identity that had often been in the past the tokens of thought about the country's culture, a new and vigorous debate was opened up about the nature of Scottish experience, about the real social and economic structures of the nation, and about the ways in which the Scottish situation related to that of other similar cultures throughout the world.

It is from our determination to maintain a continuous forum for such debate that *Determinations* takes its title. The series will provide a context for sustained dialogue about culture and politics in Scotland, and about those international issues which directly affect Scottish experience.

Too often, in Scotland, a particular way of seeing our culture, of representing ourselves, has come to dominate our perceptions because it has gone unchallenged—worse, unexamined. The vitality of the culture should be measured by the intensity of debate which it generates rather than the security of ideas on which it rests. And should be measured by the extent to which creative, philosophical, theological, critical and political ideas confront each other.

If the determinations which shape our experience are to come from within rather than from without, they have to be explored and evaluated and acted upon. Each volume in this series will seek to be a contribution to that *self*-determination; and each volume, we trust, will require a response, contributing in turn to the on-going dynamic that is Scotland's culture.

1

Introduction

THE EDITORS

Given the plethora of books on Scottish politics and government —
especially on Scottish nationalism and devolution — it is perhaps
surprising that no single assessment exists of the history and role
of the Labour Party in Scotland. This gap is even more difficult
to understand given Labour's hegemony nationally and locally in
much of urban-industrial Scotland during the past fifty years.[1] It
may be explained by the fact that there are still very few studies of
Labour politics at the local level and by the relative inaccessibility
of such historical records of local parties as do survive. Yet there is
a growing if somewhat random historiography, admittedly weightier
on the early history and on biographies of Labour leaders. Some
important ground has been broken by Tom Gallagher's work on
sectarianism in modern Scotland and by John Holford's study of
Labour politics in Edinburgh during and after the First World War.[2]
The contributors to this present volume have drawn upon much of
this original research to piece together the story of Labour's fortunes
north of the Border from the early days of the Scottish Labour Party
in 1888 to the Devolution debate of the 1970s and 80s.[3]

How distinctively Scottish was the Labour Party in Scotland
over the last century? The problems posed by this question, as
we see it, are the products of the Scottish national question in
the forms of Home Rule or Devolution, of Scotland's continuing
allegiance to Labour in contrast to the apparent erosion of the
party's vote in much of England, and of such differences as
can be shown to have existed in Labour's recruitment of leaders
and activists in Scotland. These questions are addressed by the
contributors, though we recognize that an adequate treatment of
the changing characteristics of Scottish MPs — their social, religious
and educational backgrounds — requires much more detailed study.
However, the distinctiveness of Scottish Labour was not always

attractive to English incomers in search of safe parliamentary
havens. For example, John Strachey represented Dundee from
1945 till his death in 1963, during which time he had a generally
uneasy relationship with the local party. No doubt it must have
been a relief each time his train headed south over the Tay Bridge!
He himself was a major figure in the British Labour movement
and should perhaps have been more grateful to Dundee and to
Scotland. His attitude, and that of others like him, did less than
justice to the ability of Scottish Labour to respond generously to
international issues. For example, Anti-Fascism and the cause of the
Spanish Republic were not the monopoly of the Communist Party in
Scotland during the 1930s. Labour through its own efforts, and often
in cooperation with the Communist Party, contributed significant
support. More recently Scottish Labour was at the forefront of major
campaigns against apartheid, the war in Vietnam and the nuclear
arms race.

While each contribution reflects the background and concerns of
its period the treatment here is consistent throughout. Our checklist
of contents for the seven chronological chapters includes a range
of common elements designed to show Scottish Labour's progress
during the particular era under review, enabling comparison and
contrast with other periods. Each of the chronological chapters
therefore reviews the following themes:

1.   'Framework treatment' of
   (i)   general British historical developments;
   (ii) economic fluctuations, unemployment, etc;
   (iii) political and constitutional changes — size of
         electorate, redistributions, party splits,
         reorganisations.

2.   Specifically Scottish versions of above, deviations
     from the national norm, dominant issues.

3.   Electoral politics
   (i)   Parliament — general election performance,
         comparative swing issues, etc, costs.
   (ii) Municipal and county elections: as above,
         where ascertainable.
   (iii) Nature of candidates, MPs, councillors.

4.   Party organisation
   (i)   trends of income, relations with unions,
         membership.

   (ii)   agents and organisers, major problems.
   (iii) relations with British Labour party and TUC.

5.   Controversies and deviations
   (i)   leading personalities.
   (ii)   rival left-wing groupings.
   (iii) important conferences, negotiations.

6.   Generalisations as to political changes, Scottish
       Labour's success or failure.

First, then, Christopher Harvie examines the turbulent pioneering years before Scottish Labour's breakthrough at the 1922 General Election. He argues that Scottish Labour made a significant contribution to the nature of the British Labour Party, its leadership, language and ideology, notably through the efforts of James Keir Hardie, Ramsay MacDonald, John Wheatley, Patrick Dollan and James Maxton. Much of the complex history of Scottish Labour's relationship with the British Labour Party, the Independent Labour Party and other factions is revealed. While many at the time saw the victory of November 1922 as a reward for wartime struggles Harvie sees the breakthrough being more the result of a deteriorating post-war economic situation married to successful street politics and propaganda. For all that they were hardly archetypal proletarians, the Clydesiders and their associates set off for Westminster full of Socialist principles and a determination to improve the lot of the Scottish working class.

But how was this to be done? Could the despair that Shinwell saw in the eyes of the poor be replaced by the hope that shone from the faces of the crowd that night at St Enoch Station? Ian Wood takes the view that despite the gloom and doom of the twenties Scottish Labour made substantial gains and had considerable impact locally and nationally. Men like Dollan and Wheatley sharpened their skills in administration and debate through practical politics at the grass roots of local government and nationally at Westminster in the short-lived first Labour government of 1924. But for many — especially the agitators from Clydeside — disillusionment with MacDonald's gradualism and lack of imaginative policies soon set in, leading to the increased alienation of the ILPers. Prominent among them were Wheatley and Maxton, and certainly the former's death in 1930 robbed Scottish Labour of its most powerful intellect and skilled practical politician.

If hope had been deferred through force of economic circumstance in the twenties, what of Scottish Labour's fortunes in the 1930s? Ian

Donnachie emphasises that the major domestic issue remained the economy, and coping with the Slump was the most critical problem of governments — including the second Labour administration of 1929 - 31. He argues that within the constraints of the period Labour's record in Scotland added up to more than might have been expected, notably in the alleviation of unemployment, the development of agriculture and social welfare. The General Election of 1931, however, was an unmitigated disaster for Labour in Scotland, with some disastrous defeats even in traditional strongholds. But as early as 1932 there were some signs of Labour's electoral recovery in Scotland and this was sustained throughout the decade — not only nationally in 1935 but also in local government, where major successes were recorded after the famous Glasgow victory in 1933. As Gallagher shows, this was partly due to sectarianism — Protestant League candidates effectively splitting the anti-Labour vote — but was as significant as Labour's capture of London in the following year. The successes of the later thirties, says Donnachie, were owed in some measure to a new dynamism and professionalism in party organisation, coupled with a more precise programme designed to get to grips with Scottish problems. This was forced on the party after the ILP disaffiliation and owed much to the energy of Arthur Woodburn, later Secretary of State for Scotland.

During the period bridging the dark days of the Second World War and the immediate post-war era Labour consolidated its position and re-established a firm grip on the politics of urban-industrial Scotland. During the war itself party politics took a back seat and Scotland's resources were harnessed to the war effort. Despite these constraints, as Christopher Harvie again indicates, much of longer term significance was achieved by the Coalition's Labour Secretary of State, Tom Johnston, a man of determination and vision. Scotland contributed less than England to the great General Election victory of 1945 and hence Scottish problems, as Harvie shows, were not top of the agenda. Labour's performance in Scotland was hardly sparkling, though it at least persisted with some of its own preoccupations — housing, social policy, and the Highlands. Under Johnston and his successors administrative devolution was seen to work — so that St Andrew's House rather than Westminster became the terminus for many Scottish political issues. With the benefit of hindsight it is possible to see how this would pose problems for Labour once its centralist policies came under attack from the Scottish Nationalists.

Although Scotland was the great bastion of Labour in the fifties, says Michael Keating, there is at this time perhaps less that is distinctive from the United Kingdom experience than at any other time in the history of Scottish Labour. This he explains by the almost complete organisational integration of the parties and priorities. So much so that in the 1950s Scotland was something of a backwater in the Labour Party, her MPs generally home-bred and parochial in outlook. Home Rule had remained a hardy annual for many years, but its abandonment in 1958 was entirely consistent with the leadership's line of tying Scotland closely to the UK and using this position to argue for more material rewards. There was much that was positive, however: in municipal politics, Highland policy, the impact of radical protest from a new generation in the early 1960s.

How did the record of Scottish Labour stand during the 'white heat of the technological revolution' in the sixties, when planning seemed to be the answer to economic decline and regional disparities? As Frances Wood shows, regional economic policy at first favoured Scotland with new industries, but events in the early seventies nationally and internationally undid much that had been achieved before the early seventies. Continuing economic and social problems — apparently beyond the means of solution by either Labour or Tory governments — served to revive the Scottish nationalist movement and Labour performed an about-turn in a panic reaction to the electoral threat it posed. In the inevitable shambles of the Referendum campaign Scottish Labour earned little credit and an opportunity for Devolution was therefore lost.

In a chapter based on pioneering research Jim Craigen assesses the history and functions of the Scottish Trade Union Congress — what he calls 'Scotland's Assembly of Labour'. Inaugurated in 1897, nearly thirty years after the TUC, the STUC was a direct response to increasingly powerful and hostile employer's organisations. All the major unions soon affiliated. From its beginnings the STUC had a paramount political role, while in its more recent history has also been highly influential in economic affairs. Significantly, the STUC, from its creation, has been more consistent than the Labour Party in its support for Home Rule.

Finally, James Naughtie shows how in 1979 the Labour Party in Scotland sustained a threefold defeat. It lost the devolution referendum, it lost the general election (although its vote and number of seats rose) and it was humiliated in the first Euro-elections in June, when it won only two of the eight seats.

As he indicates, the next nine years were to prove paradoxical in that the assaults of a determined right-wing Conservatism shattered in Scotland where they struck home south of the border. Although Labour's vote changed little over this period, rising from only 42 per cent to 42.4 per cent — while union and party membership fell — the party became completely dominant in Scottish parliamentary and local politics at the expense of the Conservatives and the Alliance.

Had Scotland broken the 'British' mould to evolve a politics even more distinctive than those of the 1970s, or had it stuck, at any rate on the left, to the voting patterns of the 1950s? Conservatives, after successive electoral humiliations, tended to take the latter view, and by 1988 were demanding that the 'dependency culture' of Scotland be destroyed. But at the same time, they had to admit that local Labour administrations had been flexible and undogmatic, and had contributed to the country's relatively good economic performance.

On the other hand the Scottish National Party had re-emerged by 1988 as Labour's chief competitor. Polls regularly showed that independence was creeping close to devolution as the preferred option of Scottish voters. This, along with Conservative assaults on the state sector and local authorities, and deeply unpopular taxation policies, created a dilemma for a talented labour generation: the choice between trying to secure a Scottish future, or using a powerful position in the parliamentary party to revive the British Labour Party.

While there is much to criticise in the role of the Labour Party in Scotland its record nationally and in local government over a century or so has been a formidable one. Together with organised labour and the trade union movement it has helped immeasurably to advance living standards and levels of social welfare. Ideology has often had to give way to pragmatism in the real world — invariably at the cost of friction and the shattering of party unity. If this was a problem for Scottish Labour in the twenties and thirties it remained as potentially divisive in the post-war era and forward into the seventies and eighties. An exercise of this kind has run some risk of generalisation but nevertheless we hope this book can be read and enjoyed objectively as the record of a movement which has done much to advance the lot of the Scottish people over the last century.

2

Before the Breakthrough, 1886-1922

CHRISTOPHER HARVIE

The Scottish Labour Party was founded in 1888. In the December 1910 election, the last before World War I, Labour took 3.6 per cent of the Scottish vote and returned three MPs, in Dundee, Glasgow Gorbals and West Fife. This was modest progress compared with the next 13 years. In December 1923 Labour won 35.9 per cent of the Scottish vote and returned 34 MPs.[1] A Scottish socialist, James Ramsay MacDonald, became Britain's first Labour prime minister. Labour had moved, quite suddenly, into the political limelight, while the once-great Liberal party fell off the stage.

Despite the disproportionate presence of Scots at the head of the Labour movement, Labour's rise was not the outcome of the democratic ideals which marked their speeches and journalism but of sweeping changes in British society and politics, of which Labour was able to take advantage but never to control. Arguments about these still continue. Before 1914, was Labour becoming a mature expression of working class interests, a competent alternative to a Liberal party whose cohesion — rooted in sectional and religious loyalties — was breaking down? Or was a 'new' — socially concerned — Liberalism already pre-empting this possibility? Was the split in the Liberal party under pressure of the war inevitable? Could a united party have coped with the prospective threefold increase in the electorate, ultimately carried by the Reform Act of February 1918?[2] And what of the war itself? Setting the fate of the Liberals apart, how much did it validate collectivist approaches to social policy and enhance the political role of the trade unions? What contribution was made by the Russian revolution and the post-war remodelling of Europe to the ending of any prospect of recovering the old order? In these great issues the role of Scots radicals, socialists and trade unionists could only be a marginal one. Like their comrades in the rest of Britain they knew they were being sucked into a political vacuum, rather than, as a mature party, entering into an inheritance — an awareness that the two anguished decades which followed enhanced rather than diminished. Still, Scottish Labour made a significant contribution to the nature of the British Labour Party — its leadership, its language and its ideology — and its history should throw light on the circumstances of Labour's coming to power.

There was nothing new in working class electoral activity when Keir Hardie stood for Mid-Lanark in April 1888. The trades councils of Glasgow (1858) and Edinburgh (1859) had intervened almost from the start to help elect Liberals favourable to trade union legislation, and the first 'Lib-Lab' MP was a Scot, the miners' leader, Alexander Macdonald, who won Stafford in 1874. The miners subsequently expanded their representation to six out of the eleven 'Lib-Labs' elected after the Reform Act of 1884. But no 'Lib-Lab', then or indeed ever, was returned for a Scottish seat. Scots Liberal caucuses selected more and more English professional men, until by 1906 most Scottish MPs lived permanently in England. As a result Scottish trades councils were pressing for independent working class MPs even before the British Trades Union Congress endorsed this aim by creating in 1887 the Labour Electoral Association.[3]

Until the mid-1880s Scottish radicalism was geographically extensive. Toryism was limited to only a few, mainly south-western constituencies. But radicalism was ideologically vague, deferential to Gladstone and his plutocratic lieutenant Rosebery (who lived to denounce the 1909 budget as 'inquisitorial, tyrannical and socialistic'), and redolent of the dreich religious dispute which obsessed the Scots middle classes in the post-Disruption years. Socialism was, in part, the reaction to this of secularised intellectuals. London Scots, notably Dr Gavin Clark and the shadowy Tory radical Maltman Barry, had taken part in Karl Marx's International Working Mens' Association in the late 1860s. When, in 1884, the first Scottish branches of the avowedly Marxist Social Democratic Federation were set up, the members whom Martin Haddow quotes in his memoirs were likewise largely middle class. The SDF's leader, H M Hyndman (whose foreign-sounding name was actually Scots) soon lost control of many of his Scottish members, who joined William Morris's Socialist League, and founded branches in the major towns, especially after his visits and speeches.[4]

The SLP formally stood aloof from attempts at electoral action, but four factors quickened this and brought socialist and working class activists together: the depression of the mid-1880s, the 'land war' in the Highlands, the 1884 Reform Act, and Gladstonian home rule. The first may only have been a hiccup in otherwise improving standards of working class life, but it induced a general disquiet about the nostrums of *laissez-faire* and put pressure on working class organisations. The threat of more expulsions from the Highlands — and so more cheap labour in industrial areas — worried urban workers, while the theory of Henry George and practice of the Irish Land League gave weapons to such radical groups as the Scottish Land Restoration League and the Scottish Land and Labour League, led respectively by the ex-SDFers Bruce Glasier and Andreas Scheu. The extension of the vote to workers in county seats emphasised this, when five Crofters' MPs were returned in 1885, among them Gavin Clark in Caithness.

Home rule had a catalytic effect. Gladstone, the old elitist, used this 'great moral issue' to beat off the provincial radical challenge of Joseph Chamberlain, but it was Chamberlain's former Scottish allies who not only extended the principle to embrace Scottish home rule, but used the whole rationale of autonomous decision making to sanction their withdrawal from the traditional hierarchy of parliamentary Liberalism — and a truce in the old war between radical and Catholic in Scotland.

The numbers of such 'socialistic radicals' were small in comparison with those active in Liberal caucuses (themselves only a fraction of Scottish church members). But they represented a wide variety of background, deep convictions, and remarkable articulacy. John Ferguson came out of Irish nationalism, the electrician Martin Haddow from a new race of technologists. There was the elegant literary stylist and horseman 'Don Roberto' Cunninghame-Graham, the socialist novelist 'John Law' (Margaret Harkness). And above all there were the Christian socialists, reacting against the rigidity of fundamentalist Calvinism. A reconciling and (usefully in this respect) fairly well-heeled group, they included the Rev. John Glasse, J. Bream Pearce, David Lowe and Keir Hardie himself.

James Keir Hardie was thirty-two when he stood at Mid-Lanark, a former miner, journalist and official of one of the revived miner's unions involved in the campaign for an eight-hour day. He provoked contradictory reactions. Some saw him as vain and injudicious, others as courageous, far-sighted and quick of sympathy. He was, in fact, most of these things; given his moment in history, it is difficult to see how he could have been anything else. As the leader of the 'gathered church' of what became the Independent Labour Party, he had to embody the conviction of a small minority — the socialists — that they represented the political future: a role which, badly played, whittles a prophet down to an obsessed sectarian.

He had also to negotiate the compromises with the unions and the Liberals which allowed the successes of independent working-class representation to be registered in incremental terms. In the circumstances his success was remarkable. The Scottish Labour Party, the ILP and ultimately the Labour Representation Committee bore the mark of his personality. But it required an effort which was sapping him by the time he was fifty, and contributed to his early death. Some of his enthusiasms — his feminism, for example, or his anti-racism — were advanced for his day, but his deeply religious, sentimental mysticism, his veneration of superman-sages like Carlyle and Tennyson, were quintessentially late-Victorian. He preached and talked in parables — this was what a chapel-going generation understood and expected — but he was also adequate to the task of creating the necessary political institutions.

Mid-Lanark, in April 1888, was not an impressive result. Hardie polled only 617 votes against the 3,847 gained by Wynford Phillips, a carpet-bagging Welsh barrister. But it showed that Hardie and other Scottish radicals were in earnest about independent action, and it led directly to the formation in Glasgow on 19 May of the Scottish Labour Party. The SLP had a troubled career of five years. It was certainly more 'socialistic' than socialist in its programme, and with Cunninghame-Graham and Clark on its committee, Hardie had to resist too close an alignment with the Liberals. The election of 1892, when the SLP ran seven candidates in three-cornered contests, showed the penalty of independence. They performed disastrously. Equally ineffective was its federative constitution, although it anticipated the eventual structure of the Labour party. Still, it managed to build up lectures and propaganda work and sustain (though not without controversy) Hardie's *Labour Leader*. Martin Haddow records 150 delegates from 23 branches at its fourth annual conference on 3 January 1893. A few months before, in September 1892, SLP members were prominent at a conference held in Glasgow which decided on a meeting to be held in Bradford early in 1893 to consider setting up a Britain-wide party. As a result, the Independent Labour Party was set up, although a year was to pass before the SLP merged with it. Despite the leading role that Hardie was to take in it, its centre of gravity lay in Yorkshire rather than in Scotland, and it eschewed the attempt at a federal structure in favour of branches composed of convinced activists.

The Liberals were the main Scottish party but the 1886 home rule split and dissension over disestablishment lost them ground until, in 1900, the Unionist alliance took a majority of Scottish seats. Deserted by Protestants and mistrusted by Catholics, the

Liberals were driven into their strongholds in the eastern burghs and counties, only to spring back in the 1906 election. Their vote rose only by 6.2 per cent to 56.4 per cent, but they took 58 seats to the Unionists' 12, retaining these gains in the two 1910 elections while losing heavily in England.

The 'new liberalism' appears to have made little impact in the north. Party activity was limited, doctrine stagnant, and the electorate seemingly uninterested in positive legislation. Scots manufacturers, mostly exporters, held by free trade; the disestablishment crisis fizzled out in the toils of litigation which accompanied the creation of the United Free church in 1900 and a settlement with the Auld Kirk was even in sight; the old radical cause of land reform still echoed in the rural burghs and counties which accounted for a third of Scots constituencies. There was some movement after the Boer War when the Young Scots' Society, founded by pro-Boers in 1900, promoted the causes of home rule and 'real Scottish' (as opposed to carpet-bagging) MPs. 'The spearhead of the Liberal attack in Scotland',[5] it had many branches and several members with socialist links such as Roland Eugene Muirhead and Daniel Stevenson, but its strength was insufficient to prevent the Scottish Liberal Federation rejecting, by 55 to 34, a pact with Labour before the 1906 election.

In 1910 the Scottish electorate, at 16 per cent of the total population, was actually 7 per cent smaller, proportionately, than that of England. This was probably accounted for by the annual migrations of many Scottish landworkers from farmtoun to farmtoun and the equally rapid shifts of many urban families, given the peculiar nature of Scottish house-letting. Franchise extension, for which the labour movement as well as the women's suffrage organisations campaigned, would enfranchise a disproportionately large number at the lower end of the social scale and the Liberals were believed to be dragging their feet over it, fearful that their traditional electorate would be swamped.

Labour, too, was somewhat uncertain of its support. The moves towards independent representation in the 1880s had owed at least emotional force to the 'new unionism' of unskilled workers such as dockers and gasworkers. Their organisers were often convinced socialists, drawn from the ranks of the skilled. Yet this had hierarchical implications. General unions were less democratic than craft unions, and gave more power to officials. *Forward* reflected this, priding itself that it was *not* read in the slums. The 'democracy' of the skilled men was a neutral rather than, for socialists, a positive force. 'James Hamilton Muir' (a nom de plume for the brothers

Muirhead and David Bone) caught it brilliantly in a 1900 sketch
of a Glasgow fitter:

> When his time was served he became a Union man, and
> thought all the world of his District Delegate. He is a very good
> workman, who could turn his hand to many things, and "make
> a job o them a". He is intelligent, and has a clear perception of
> injustice. But according to his lights he is a reasonable man. He
> stands up for himself not only against the common enemy, his
> employer, but also against his comrades in allied trades if they
> invade his frontiers. He is gruff, intractable and independent,
> and his latent irritability takes fire if his rights are infringed.
> Of servility he has not a trace.[6]

There was no necessary reason why this 'perception of injustice'
should take a socialist form. At the turn of the century it was
as likely to show itself as hostility to Catholics. As late as 1900
Unionists had occupied every seat in the Glasgow area, and must
have gained majority support from a local working class, 70 per cent
of whose men could claim to be skilled. Harry McShane noted that
certain skilled groups, notably boilermakers, were strongly Orange
in inclination, something which could still coexist with loyal union
membership. At Mirlees Watson's engineering works in 1912 he
found that the Tory foremen

> were also members of the ASE and liked to see that the union
> was being organised properly; the ASE was a sort of religion
> to them.[7]

Under pressure from the employers' counter-attack, which culminated in the lock-out of the ASE in 1897-8, this union loyalty
led, however, to socialists such as George Barnes being given
positions of influence. Parallel setbacks suffered by the miners and
the railwaymen strengthened the hands of those within the TUC who
favoured an independent parliamentary presence. Their advocacy,
discreetly seconded by the ILP, led to the conference in London
on 27-8 February 1900, which set up the Labour Representation
Committee. Less memorable, because ultimately less successful, was
the initiative of the Scottish Trades Union Congress, which had
resulted in the setting up of the Scottish Workers' Parliamentary
Elections Committee six weeks earlier on 6 January 1900.

Turn of the century Scottish socialism was a paradox. Hardie,
MacDonald, Glasier, Henderson, Barnes and Smillie gave the
Labour 'establishment' a marked Scottish air, but organisation in
Scotland was relatively weak. Scottish Trades Councils, barred by
the 'Lib-Labs' from the TUC, set up the Scottish Trades Union
Congress in 1896 to reflect their more committed attitudes, but the

STUC limited itself to passing resolutions, and its affiliates in 1898 covered only about half the trade unionists in Scotland. There were energetic local groups of enthusiasts — not only on Clydeside but in Aberdeen, where the dominant SDF included James Leatham and H H Champion — but party membership was generally low. In 1900 the ILP affiliated 13,000 members to the new Labour Representation Committee, an inflation of perhaps fifty per cent compared with its own annual report. Twenty-two Scottish branches were noted, of which fifteen reported their membership. Averaging out at fifty-eight per branch, and calculating from this, Scotland had around 1,250 members out of a British total of around 9,500. Half the branches were in the cities; most of the others were in the larger towns. Only three were in colliery districts. Half a dozen Fabian Societies existed. The first had been founded by the Rev. John Glasse in Edinburgh in 1892, and two fairly important university societies followed, at Glasgow in 1896 and Edinburgh in 1898. The aggregate membership, can, however, scarcely have exceeded 150.

Nor did electoral performance improve much after 1892, when the average vote was only 5 per cent. In 1895 eight candidates (seven ILP and one SDF) averaged 5.3 per cent. There was a very good result for Tom Mann in a straight fight with a Liberal in Aberdeen in 1896, but in 1900 funds were so low that the ILP did not contest at all. An ILP member, A.E. Fletcher, and the Co-operator, William Maxwell had free runs against Tories in Camlachie and Tradeston, but were still unsuccessful. By 1900, however, the ILP had elected thirteen town councillors in Scotland, including five in Glasgow and three in Paisley, and in September 1901 Bob Smillie, standing as in independent miner's candidate in North East Lanark, performed well, split the Liberal vote, and let a Tory in. The LRC's secretary, Ramsay MacDonald, was thus fortified for his confidential negotiations with the Liberal Chief Whip.

The MacDonald-Gladstone pact, which only Hardie in the Labour party knew about, did not apply in Scotland, and in 1906 nine Labour candidates (4 LRC, 5 SWPEC) stood in three-party contests. All the SWPEC candidates lost, as the miners still stuck to their Liberal affiliation, but two LRC candidates won, at Dundee and Glasgow Blackfriars. The four LRC men had got 16,897, or 2.3 per cent of total vote. This worked out at 4,224 in every contested seat, and was a considerable improvement on the 1890s, especially when the hostility of the Liberals is taken into account. Alexander Wilkie, successful against a Liberal in the two-member constituency of Dundee, was general secretary of the Shipwrights Association, George Nicoll Barnes of the Amalgamated Society of Engineers:

both substantial figures in the union world who could demonstrate a prestige sufficient to cow the average Liberal candidate. Dundee, anyway, had a long tradition of political in-fighting on the left, into which the all-but-Lib-Lab Wilkie fitted. Barnes, who had been active in many left-wing groups during his youth in London, and was a member of the ILP, had more of the credentials of a socialist, but became much less militant once he entered the Commons.

But 1906 was no augury, with the reform of the unions' legal position in sight, and the prospect of a hard battle with the forces of constitutional privilege, one which many of the new Liberal MPs had little stomach for — or so many Scots radicals thought. This critical radicalism, from the Young Scots as well as from the ILP, went into the founding later that year of the weekly *Forward*. It could have been simply another of the struggling tadpoles of the socialist press, but fortunately the flair and downright business ability, in the shape of a young journalist, Thomas Johnston, was there to make it into a hard-hitting and effective paper. Within a couple of years, not only had it taken on the authority of its great German namesake and predecessor, but like Blatchford's *Clarion* a decade earlier, political organisation had started to coalesce round it. Journalism was as important a unifying factor in the radical movement as it had been when Feargus O'Connor's *Northern Star* focussed Chartist ideas in the 1840s. *Clarion* had spawned its choirs and cycling groups and lecturers, but Blatchford's increasingly jingoistic line was beginning to alienate many ILPers, while the *Labour Leader*, which had done a lot of effective muck-raking in the 1890s, became London-based, and rather dull, after Hardie lost control of it to the ILP in 1904. *Forward* provided a platform for Glasgow's multiplicity of radical groups, as well as the expanding ILP, whose membership, static between 1900 and 1904, grew 60 per cent between 1904 and 1908.

The expansion of the ILP was aided by the severe slump of 1906-8, when order books fell by over fifty per cent to 1870s levels, and unemployment in shipbuilding rose from 11.6 per cent in 1905 to 28.5 per cent in 1908. Matters were little better in engineering. This, the first intimation of mortality in Scottish industrial capitalism, increased the plausibility not only of socialist principles but of the remedies advanced by the ILP for unemployment and poverty, which were in great measure connected with the appalling problem of Glasgow's housing. The slump ended in 1909 and gave way to a spectacular boom which carried Scottish shipbuilding to its zenith in 1913. Although it unquestionably detracted from radical commitment, the boom still meant that the left kept its gains and did not seem demoralised by prolonged unemployment, as in the inter-war years.[8]

Subsequent events must, however, have been frustrating to the idealists. The New Liberalism, in the emphatic person of David Lloyd George, proved particularly attractive in Scotland, where calls for land reform and energetic abuse of the aristocracy could still enthuse radicals. *Forward* joined in. Johnston's famous series on 'Our Scots noble families' is a fair example, taking as its text Carlyle's description of the aristocracy as

> a selfish, ferocious, famishing, unprincipled set of hyenas, from whom at no time and in no way has the country derived any benefit whatsoever.[9]

But, on the present writer's grandfather's bookshelf, Johnston's subsequent book stood next to the Cobden Club's *Fallacies of Protection* and a book of Lloyd George's speeches, *Better Times*. He voted Liberal, as did 53.6 per cent of Scots voters in December 1910 — a decline of only 2.8 per cent from the *annus mirabilis* of 1906 and almost 10 per cent above the party's UK percentage. Labour, having risen to 5.1 per cent in January 1910, fell back in December to 3.6 per cent, although it won another seat, West Fife, which fell to the miner's leader William Adamson, whose union had only affiliated to Labour in the previous year. Relations with the Liberals were still somewhat edgy. It was partly in an attempt to detach the miners from Labour that the government in 1912 set up the Royal Commission into Scottish housing, in response to their expressions of concern. Both parties were under increasing pressure from the Unionists, who won five of the fourteen by-elections which occurred between 1911 and 1914.

Economic difficulties in the pre-war years did, however, mean that trade unions grew, by about 25 per cent between 1911 and 1913, and that the number of unionists affiliating to Labour increased. What effect did this have on the party? Ross McKibbin in his *Evolution of the Labour Party* is self-contradictory here. Although he argues that 'unions and their officials made up the deficiency of individual members. They provided the volunteer workers, the local party officers, and the money',[10] he notes that affiliation in Scotland was often the result of very hard-fought contests, and that organisation was particularly bad in seats whose candidates were sponsored by the miners, after 1909 Labour's most substantial union supporters. On the other hand, Scotland did have a disproportionate number — 31 out of 150 — of local trades councils which were affiliated to Labour, and a Scottish Trades Union Congress which, unlike the TUC, encouraged this.[11] There was probably more opportunity here for the socialist tail to wag the trade unionist dog.

The economy also had implications for municipal politics. The depression of 1905-8 caused a permanent downturn in the building industry, particularly in Glasgow. Dr David Englander has seen this as the result, at least partially, of shrewd use by the tenants of legal powers to restrain their landlords from evicting them (under Scots Law the only way of the latter recovering rent due under a yearly tenancy). In 1911 the powers of the landlords were strengthened by the House Letting (Scotland) Act and Labour, hitherto the party of the respectable working class, began to bid for wider support through a general programme of municipal housebuilding and controlled rents — the '£8 cottage' publicised effectively by John Wheatley. By 1914 this was taking modest effect. Labour now controlled 14 per cent of seats on Glasgow Corporation.

How many, and who, were the Scottish socialists? Accuracy is very difficult to achieve, but the ILP's national affiliation fees in 1910 indicate around thirty thousand members, and the Scottish proportion was probably around five thousand, grouped in some 125 branches. Over half of these were now in colliery districts (50) or textile centres (20). North and west of a line from the Vale of Leven to Montrose there were only eight branches, although Aberdeen remained a centre of the SDF, which had perhaps a thousand of its eight thousand members (1911) in Scotland.

Who were the party members? Our evidence is fragmentary, and distorted by the testimony of articulate members of the labour aristocracy and the middle class. But it was changing and becoming more working-class, as the growth in branches would indicate. John Paton, later secretary of the National Guilds League and General Secretary of the ILP, 1926-34, recollected a socialist demonstration in Partick about 1904 in which the participants were 'almost to a man. . .of the shop assistant or clerk type' (they were scattered by hulking Orange shipyard workers).[12] The ILP branch he joined in Springburn in 1906, however

> was typical of the rest of the ILP at that time and for a long time after. Except for an odd teacher and a few shop assistants, the members were all workmen and their wives. For the most part the men belonged to the skilled trades like engineering and were nearly always known as exceptionally good and steady workmen. They were active trade-unionists to a man.[13]

Socialist convictions even so were slow to take deep roots in the unions. Arthur Henderson, the Glasgow-born official of the Foundryman's union who later became the chief architect of the

Labour Party constitution in 1918, was still a Liberal in 1902, joining Labour only indirectly, through the Fabian Society, in the following year. Barnes of the Engineers had been fairly active in the socialist movement in London, but seems to have become a fairly orthodox Lib-Lab after his election to Parliament. Harry McShane knew his agent, Jock McVey, and found him almost completely lacking in political interests. Even Bob Smillie, the only prominent figure of the Mineworker's union to profess an unqualified socialist commitment, was deeply marked by his Liberal past. In *My Life for Labour*, 'the greatest man I met' turned out to be W E Gladstone, followed by Sir Henry Campbell-Bannerman. Liberal loyalty among the rank-and-file died even harder. Although the Miner's Federation of Great Britain balloted in 1908 to affiliate to the Labour Party by 32,000 to 25,000 (only about 10 per cent of the members having troubled to vote) an attempt to run a Labour candidate in the mining constituency of Midlothian in 1912, when the Liberal Master of Elibank went to the Lords, was a humiliating failure. The Labour candidate polled only 16 per cent and let the Unionist in.

The ILP received a fair amount of support from wealthy men: the landowner Cunninghame-Graham, the shipowners Thomas Allan and Algernon Henderson and the coal exporter Sir Daniel Stevenson all played some part in financing, and in the case of Allan, even organising the party, while the owner of the Greenock Ropework Company, Adam Birkmyre, bought Keir Hardie his substantial house, Lochnorris in Cumnock. A few of middling Glasgow business and professional men played more active roles. Was it calculation, philanthropy or conviction that moved them to this commitment? Because the ILP was scarcely militant, the first explanation has some plausibility. Supporting the ILP was a means of socialising the working class. Any sort of organisation, even one theoretically socialist, was better — so a far-sighted Glasgow bourgeois may have calculated — than the anomic violence which had hit the west end of London in 1886, and had caused death and destruction in Glasgow in 1848.[14] On the other hand middle-class hostility to socialism remained implacable, particularly on the part of the major business groups and the churches. It was more likely the absence of a commitment to social reform within such bodies, evidenced in the weakness of the new Liberalism in Scotland and the continuing vitality of religious politics, which drove the Scottish equivalent of the chocolate cousinhood — Rowntree, Cadbury, Fry — to put some of its money in the way of the socialists. And some, of course, like Allan and later on the tanner Roland Muirhead, believed deeply in the cause and sacrificed effort as well as money on its behalf. This blend of paternalism and cooperation is well caught in the one utopian novel which the Scottish Labour movement produced, Findlay Watt's *Allanforth Commune: the Triumph of Socialism*, published by the National Labour Press in 1913.

Straining socialist conviction out of the soup of turn of the century radical belief is difficult, especially given the nature of its adherents and publications. In his *Labour Leader* in 1894 Keir Hardie recommended 'as a basis on which to develop a Socialistic system of thought'

> the first four books of the New Testament, Carlyle's *Sartor Resartus* and *Past and Present*; Ruskin's *Crown of Wild Olive* and *Unto This Last*; Mazzini's *Thoughts on Democracy* and *Faith into the Future*. . . As textbooks take Nunquam's (Robert Blatchford's) *Merrie England*, Hobson's *Problems of Poverty* and Morrison Davidson's *The Old Order and the New*.[15]

As remote from specific political issues as from the classic texts of scientific socialism, this eclecticism flourished. Clerks like Edwin Muir or journalists like Christopher Grieve and William Graham existed in an atmosphere of progressive, not to say apocalyptic conviction — syndicalism, nationalism, the women's struggle — which were still pervaded by religious impulses, some inherited from the recent Scottish past (Arthur Woodburn, for instance, began his career as a propagandist for the Free Church) others stemming from a more general turn of the century crisis. Social Darwinism, eugenics, the 'scientific elitism' of such as H.G. Wells coincided, and frequently overlapped, with language reform, eurythmics, spiritualism and theosophy. Marxism was not overborne by methodism as it may well have been in English trade union circles, but by this heady brew, which made Scottish socialism both more original and articulate, and also much more difficult to organise.

Ideological richness explains to some extent the political extremism. Because of its social, and even geographical position, the Scottish left was open to a wide variety of cosmopolitan influences. In 1900 James Hamilton Muir described the Clyde as part of an international system, closer, perhaps to New York or Chicago than to Edinburgh.[16] Along the shipping lanes steamed ideas as well as cargo and an import particularly attractive in the 1900s was the idea of industrial rather than political action, whether derived from American industrial unionism or French syndicalism.

The SDF split in 1903, when a group of its Scottish members, strongly influenced by the philosophy of industrial activism formulated by the American Daniel De Leon, left to form the Socialist Labour Party. These included, at least for a time, the future

Labour MPs Neil MacLean, John Muir and David Kirkwood, but the rigidity of SLP discipline repelled both the industrial rank and file and, indeed, any sort of long-term membership. As one of its leaders, Tom Bell, later wrote

> The worker's wouldn't join. They thought we were terribly intellectual . . .Over three years we gained 350 members and lost 350.[17]

The SLP secession allowed a new and more militant group to influence the SDF. Prominent among its members was the Govan schoolteacher John Maclean, whose expositions of orthodox Marxism (something almost unknown in the ILP) drew audiences of hundreds on Sunday evenings, especially after 1911. In that year the campaign for 'socialist unity' inaugurated by Victor Grayson resulted in the creation of the British Socialist Party out of the SDF and some dissident ILPers. Hyndman and his group however remained in charge, and Glasgow became a centre of resistance to him. Maclean posited working-class education as the BSP alternative to the purely industrial militancy of the SLP and the ILP's compromises with bourgeois politics. But even the BSP was losing out. The SDF had claimed 40 branches in Scotland to the ILP's 50 in 1909, but many of these were nominal. The BSP claimed only 500 members in Glasgow in 1914, while the number in the SLP must have been much less, possibly only about 150.

Dr Iain Maclean has drawn attention to the Covenanting imagery with which the Scottish left surrounded itself. This did not only reflect the predominantly Protestant nature of the skilled workmen and their organisation, but a doctrinal exclusiveness and disputatiousness which was fundamental to the Scottish Calvinist tradition, and had been earlier evident in the attachment of educated workmen to 'questions of controversial divinity'.[18] Harry McShane noted that religious issues, often argued with considerable dialectical ability, still predominated among Sunday evening speakers on Glasgow Green in 1904.[19] It is arguable that besides the Depression, a relatively sudden loss of interest in religion (we know little enough about this but Scotland, unlike Wales, had no great revival in 1904-5) between about 1906 and 1912 underlay the transfer of this casual enthusiasm (there was, after all, nothing else to do in Glasgow on Sunday evening) from religion to politics.

There was certainly a change in what the working-class autodidact read. The first generation of Scots Labour MPs and candidates were reared, like Hardie, in the tradition of 19th century cultural criticism — Bunyan reflected through Carlyle and Dickens. Their ethos, though not rigid or fundamentalist, was pervasively religious, possibly affected by the ecumenicism of the Moody and Sankey mission of 1873-4. For those who came to maturity in the 1900s the leading themes were, on the other hand, secularism, materialism and rationalism: not just Marx but Darwin, Feuerbach and Dietzgen. An alternative, which gained a strong English following, was 'idealist reform' derived from T.H. Green, mediated through the University settlement and adult education movements. Elements of this existed in Scotland, with Edward Caird and Thomas Jones at Glasgow University, where the latter founded the Fabian Society. But (probably because of the churches' lack of interest) the Workers' Education Association did not get off the ground until 1919. By then the work of John Maclean had given working class education a quite different resonance.

More significant in the long run was the political organisation of Irish Catholicism, although most Catholics did not join the voters' rolls until the 1918 Reform Act. The United Irish League, formed in 1900, had branches all over western Scotland, and was particularly strong in Glasgow itself. It had succeeded the Parnellite Irish National League, formed in 1882 as the fund-raising and propaganda arm of an increasingly determined and disciplined Irish parliamentary party, whose most important organiser was John Ferguson, a stationer and publisher of Ulster Protestant stock. Ferguson, who backed Hardie's Mid-Lanark candidature, entered Glasgow Corporation as a Labour member and tried to push exile political organisations towards cooperation with Scottish democrats over land reform and the struggle for trade union rights.

The formation of the UIL indicated a recovery from the traumatic aftermath of Parnell's divorce case and resulting downfall. In Scotland most branches of the Parnellite league had kept going and by 1900 were expanding rapidly, aided in part by widespread commemorations of the centenary of the 1798 uprising. A further commemoration, of Robert Emmet's execution in 1903, brought to the fore the young John Wheatley, president of the Shettleston Daniel O'Connell branch. Born in County Waterford in 1869, Wheatley had emigrated with his parents to Scotland and began as a miner, moving later into printing and journalism. Irish home rule politics were his apprenticeship, but in the early 1900s he convinced himself that socialism was both desirable and compatible with Catholic belief, and resolutely defended this against the hostility of the church and traditional Liberal-inclined politicians. In 1906 his cause gained a fillip, when the UIL bosses, faced with an anti-home-rule Liberal and Andrew Bonar Law in Glasgow Blackfriars, instructed their members to vote for George Barnes. Later that year, he founded the Catholic Socialist Society.

Wheatley's commitment to Labour — he joined the ILP in 1907 — was one which had to be fought for. With a Liberal party dragging its feet on home rule such a move was seen as something near to treachery by the RC community and parish priests. More than once Wheatley had to face threats of violence from his Liberal-voting co-religionists, and elsewhere in Scotland ILPers within nationalist organisations were put under pressure. The president of the Dundee branch of the UIL had to resign in 1908 when his membership of the ILP became known — although the decision was carried only by a small majority. But the Irish political tradition of nearly a century of organised mass popular action was as valuable an inheritance as Scottish sectarianism was troublesome, and Wheatley and his lieutenant Patrick Dollan, another miner turned journalist, fought their way not only to a dominant position with their community but within West of Scotland politics.

The outbreak of war on 4 August 1914 divided Labour. The Second International had committed its members by resolution to oppose the war by a general strike, but nowhere was there any such action. The German Social Democrats voted overwhelmingly for war credits; in France and Britain most trade union MPs were fiercely pro-war, mirroring enthusiasm in their constituencies. This was particularly strong in industrial and mining areas; in Western Scotland 25 per cent of the male workforce had volunteered by December 1914. Why? It is still difficult to assign precise motives, but the fear of unemployment was probably as great as patriotic enthusiasm and solidarity with 'Brave Little Belgium'. In the Ayrshire coalfield, which had a secure domestic and Irish market, affected little by wartime disruption, only 20 per cent of miners volunteered, compared with over 36 per cent in the Lothian field, whose exports to East Europe collapsed. This being so, the herd instinct — 'following one's pals' — and the expectation of a short war were probably crucial.

Socialist legend has associated the Clyde with early and sustained opposition to the war, right from the engineers' strike of February 1915. This, according to John MacNair: 'bringing as it did the workers into open conflict with the employers and the government, lined the great majority against the war and made Glasgow a centre where so-called Patriots were on the way out.'[20] Opposition to the war, the sincerely held conviction of perhaps a majority of Scots socialist activists, has however to be distinguished from hostility to the way in which wartime measures of economic reorganisation were imposed. The reactions of a worried, and occasionally outraged, skilled working class could be claimed as revolutionary both by political enthusiasts and by a panicked government. Whether this was true was another matter.

For any revolutionary hypothesis to work, the drive for 'dilution' — the replacement of skilled by unskilled, often female, labour — would have to be confronted by positive resistance by working-class leaders, going far beyond the skilled men to mobilise the expanded labour force, and government would have to cave in to the political threat. None of this seems to have happened. The engineer's strike was a logical response to the 50 per cent plus inflation of the early months of the war; the Fairfield strike — the only one in the shipyards throughout the war — was a similarly straightforward reaction to the interference of the Munitions Acts in the traditional work practices of the skilled men. The Amalgamated Society of Engineers, which condemned the strikes, may also have been hedging on its initial commitment to the Treasury agreements of 17-19 March 1915 — its new advisor, the Oxford don and guild socialist, G.D.H. Cole, certainly tried to throw as many spanners in the works as he could — but the inquiry conducted by Balfour of Burleigh (former Unionist Secretary for Scotland) found the imprisoned shop stewards to be furious but indubitably respectable and patriotic men. By September 1915 the government's munitions directorate had burnt its boats. Under pressure from its gifted but far from tactful Scottish director, William Weir, it had abolished the management-union Clyde Armaments Output committee, and now had to impose agreements on dilution in time for Weir's factory conversion programme. The Balfour inquiry may in fact have helped here, as it demonstrated the gulf between the skilled men and the anti-war political activists. The rent strike of October to November 1915 definitely was helpful to the munitions drive, as it enabled munitions managers to come out on the side of their workers against the private landlords — the greatest losers of the war period — and secure rent control. In early 1916, with the battle of the Somme less than six months away, the Munitions Directorate and its Dilution Commissioners stepped up the pressure. They invested the Clyde Workers' Committee and its bowler-hatted, blue-suited, engineer members with the character of a socialist conspiracy, and between February and April they caused to be arrested and imprisoned or deported several leading figures of the Clydeside left, including Gallacher, Muir, Kirkwood, Maclean and Maxton. The rest of the shop stewards took the hint; so did the ASE. The Red Clyde was, effectively at an end.

The campaign to enforce dilution coincided with the early stages of the government's conscription policy. Arguably this was the more bitterly contested issue in Scotland, as it brought dissenting religion as well as politics into play. The ILP was particularly militant on this issue. Almost seventy per cent of conscientious objection cases involved ILPers but, according to John Paton, Scots ILPers, a more subversive, less principled bunch, usually avoided the martyrdom of prison. The previously high rate of volunteering seems however, to have led both to a particular vindictiveness by the tribunals before which Scottish COs appeared, and to a greater sense of war-weariness once really huge casualty lists came in from the Somme (July-November 1916) and subsequent battles. Perhaps the government was fortunate to break both the shop stewards and the anti-conscriptionists before the going got very rough; this may have, to some extent, accounted for the failure to participate in the disturbances which rocked the munitions areas in May 1917. On the other hand, once the shop stewards were brought back from exile (in Edinburgh and elsewhere) they proved model production managers. The *Glasgow Herald*, earlier strongly critical, was by December 1917 welcoming shop steward participation:

> They may portend syndicalism or they may not, but they certainly mean that the actual workers will be in closer touch with the machinery of their unions, and also with their employers, and familiarity is more likely to breed friendship than enmity.

In 1916 Glasgow workers sang at demonstrations a doggerel song written by Jimmie Maxton:

> Oh I'm Henry Dubb, and I won't go to war
> Because I don't know what they're all fighting for
> To hell with the Kaiser, to hell with the Tsar,
> To hell with Lord Derby, and also GR.
> I work in munitions; I'm a slave down at Weir's.
> If I leave my job, they give me two years.
> To hell with the sheriff, to hell with his crew;
> To hell with Lloyd George, and with Henderson too.
> I don't like the landlord. I don't want to grouse.
> But to hell both with him and his bloody old house.
> To hell with the factor. His rent I won't pay.
> Three cheers for John Wheatley! I'm striking today.[21]

The theme was discontent, not revolution. Henry Dubb was *Forward*'s workman Sancho Panza, usually put upon and gulled, but now fighting back, through political organisation rather than industrial action. The ILP, which had lost members from the beginning of the war, recovered through its exploitation of welfare issues, most notably rents. Its membership, down to three thousand in early 1917, with only 112 branches, had expanded to over nine thousand in 192 branches by September 1918. This wartime expansion was quite unique. It did not happen elsewhere in Britain; Labour party membership in World War I went down and stayed down. Thus the Scottish ILP came by 1918 to provide about a third of British membership. Much of the trend towards politics must have come about through the relative growth of the numbers of workers in reserved occupations, such as the mines, as well as through the general expansion of the unions. The need for political action must have been clinched by the report of the Royal Commission on Scottish Housing in 1918, and the appalling situation it revealed.

The Scottish Council of the Labour Party met for the first time on 21 August 1915. Almost two years of acrimonious discussion had preceded its creation, and few in the north were pleased with the advisory body which emerged. The miners and textile workers in particular wanted more autonomy. But, given the low level of constituency organisation, this weakness was inevitable. Scottish conference in 1917 demanded a much more powerful party, able to endorse its own candidates, but this was turned down by national annual conference in August 1918, in favour of the centralised scheme of Henderson and Sidney Webb. Before there could be any reaction, the war was over and the election campaign had begun.

One important sector of the labour movement had, however, shifted towards the Labour party. The war led to a considerable growth in the Co-ops, which were free of profiteering. Already, on average, 30 per cent larger than their English counterparts, they rose by a further 30 per cent between 1911 and 1918. Annoyed at Lloyd George's food control policies, which were to a great extent run by their old enemies, the wholesalers, they became much more sympathetic to independent representation, and were the source of some of the largest protest demonstrations towards the end of the war. Although Co-op candidates polled only 19,841 votes in the 1918 election, compared with 265,744 for Labour, their vote in the three seats contested was practically the same (6,614 against 6,813), and they came very close to success at Paisley.

The Reform Act of February 1918, besides enfranchising women over thirty, removed many of the registration and ratepaying qualifications which had debarred Scottish workers from voting. The electorate rose from 779,012 (at the December 1910 election) to 2,205,383, or 45 per cent of the population, practically identical with the English proportion. At the same time Labour began, nationally, to move to a position of detachment from the government, particularly after Arthur Henderson's dismissal on 12 August 1917 because of his support for peace negotiations being explored within the international labour movement (or what remained of it) at the Stockholm conference. Henderson was quick to coopt both the Trades Union Congress, whose affiliated membership had risen by 65 per cent between 1914 and 1917, and which was anxious to play a more independent political role, and the growing membership of the ILP; he, and Sidney Webb, who joined him in drafting the Labour Party constitution, were also determined that the 'bottom' of the party should lie in the unions and not among the active membership. The result was a party administrative structure which accommodated the various categories of members — women, constituency parties (which, for the first time, had individual membership), and unions and socialist societies (including the ILP) — but had all of these elected by the annual conference, in which the block votes of the unions predominated.[22]

Socialists in Scotland, where the ILP tripled in size between 1916 and 1918, resented this centralisation, but union support enabled the party to contest thirty-nine seats, compared with only five in 1910, in the general election of 14 December 1918. Announced within a week of the armistice, this was, in Pelling's words, 'a virtual plebiscite for or against Lloyd George, as the architect of victory', and the predominantly Unionist coalition was well prepared to fight it: the 'coupon' of government endorsement being presented to 34 Unionists, twenty-eight Liberals and three right-wing Labour candidates. This enabled a relatively small plurality of votes — 52.3 per cent — to be converted into the capture of over 75 per cent of Scottish seats. The Unionists were the main beneficiaries, their seats rising from 13 in 1914 to 28. Their total vote, however, rose by only 48 per cent on 1910, although the electorate had increased by nearly 200 per cent: the Liberal votes, if counted together (which few on either side would care to do) had risen 25 per cent. Labour's vote went up tenfold, from 24,633 in 1910 to 265,744.

Divided by the number of seats contested, Labour's improvement was much more modest — around 2 per cent. But it held Dundee and West Fife, and took Central Edinburgh, South Ayrshire, Glasgow Govan and Hamilton. F.H. Rose, a somewhat bellicose maverick in North Aberdeen, made the total up to seven when he took the Labour whip. Labour had done particularly well in the coalfields and now lay second in constituencies. The Liberals' organisation collapsed, and when Labour started to make sweeping gains in the November 1919 municipal elections, they took refuge increasingly in right-wing coalitions. Asquith's success in Paisley in February 1920 could only slow this tendency, not reverse it.

The result of the December 1918 election placed Labour in a strategic dilemma. Its percentage of the poll was promising but it had only fifty-seven MPs in the Commons — still only 'pressure group' strength. The old course of accommodation, favoured by several right-wing trade unionists, had little potential given the huge Coalition majority. At the same time trade union growth, demobilisation problems, and the prospect of economic disruption encouraged those who favoured direct action. The Triple Alliance of miners, railwaymen and dockers was still in being — until 'Black Friday', 14 April 1921 — but attempts at militant left organisations were divided by the increasing interference by the Third International, the 'Comintern'. The Communist Party of Great Britain, which it set up in the spring of 1920, had a leadership substantially recruited from Scotland, mainly from the zealots of the SLP and BSP. This hit the revolutionary left harder than the ILP, whose leaders were able to pursue a middle way — developing a mass grass-roots organisation and links with the unions while still persevering with parliamentarianism.[23] The Forty Hours strike of January-February 1919 gave a powerful inoculation against direct action, and although a year later the Scottish Division of the ILP carried 138-288 a resolution urging the ILP to adhere to the Comintern, the ideological surrender demanded by the latter was completely unacceptable. The paths of the ILP and the CPGB soon diverged, although Labour remained plagued by affiliation problems over Communist-led local parties and trades councils.

Labour gained 22.9 per cent of the votes cast in 1918 and 32.2 per cent of those cast in the next general election of November 1922. But the number of seats captured shot up to twenty-nine, half of which were in an area — Glasgow and its western environs — which had in 1918 returned only one Labour MP. The anti-imperialist writer E D Morel, in company with the prohibitionist Scrymgeour, beat Winston Churchill in Dundee, and Labour, mainly fielding miners' agents, made a clean sweep of the eleven coalfield constituencies. But progress elsewhere was minimal. After success in 1918, no more seats were taken in Edinburgh or Aberdeen.

The breakthrough in the mining areas was inevitable. Labour had held West Fife since 1910, (Willie Adamson, its MP, briefly led the parliamentary party between 1918 and 1920, so badly that his replacement by the dull and coalition-minded J.R. Clynes was considered a marked improvement); it added South Ayr and

Hamilton in 1918, and then captured Kirkcaldy and Bothwell at by-elections. With the return of ex-servicemen to the pits and the failure of the Lloyd George coalition to do anything about the crisis-ridden industry, even after the radical Sankey report of 1919, a shift to the left could scarcely be stopped. The explanation of the swing on Clydeside, however, is much more complex.

The victory of November 1922 was seen by many Glasgow socialists as the reward for their wartime struggles, and several — notably Kirkwood, Maxton and Muir — were veterans of the resistance to the Munitions Acts and conscription. Yet it was surely more the result of the post-war economic and political situation that a substantial Unionist and Coalition Liberal majority (59.2 per cent of the Glasgow poll in 1918) was destroyed. The tenacious myth of 'the red flag in George Square' during the February 1919 Forty Hours strike as the prelude to a Glasgow Soviet revolution has surely been disbelieved long since by everyone but the desperately romantic or paranoid (which at the time, of course, included M15 and the Scottish Secretary), yet there was a hyphen between the war and the advance of Labour. This took the shape of post-war inflation, the attempts of the unions to catch up with it through aggressive industrial action and the resistance of employers who, however much they merited being branded as war profiteers, were concerned at the spiralling costs of re-equipment after wartime depreciation. As early as the end of 1919 the *Glasgow Herald* was writing of the past year

> Instead of a year in which a fresh and definite start was made, 1919 has been a year of uncertainty and gradual transition.

By mid-1920 it was all too aware of which way the transition was leading. International shipping was falling catastrophically — down by two-thirds in the course of the year and dragging after it shipyard, steelworks and collieries. Unemployment mounted rapidly, reaching sixteen per cent by the end of the year and 25 per cent in 1921, and the outlook for the future, reflected in shipbuilding orders, was scarcely reassuring.

In November 1920 Glasgow held a municipal general election after the boundaries of the city were extended. Labour won over a third of the seats. Mounting unemployment played its part here, but also events in Ireland, where the 'War of Independence' was moving into a particularly bloody, reprisal-ridden phase. About 15 per cent of the Glasgow electorate was Catholic Irish, and these events made it complete its transition to supporting Labour, already evident in 1918. Concessions had to be made. Publicans played a leading part in organising the Irish vote and could not be expected to look favourably on Labour's post-war enthusiasm for prohibition.

Prohibition was tactfully squashed. The desire for Catholic schools within the state system recognised by the Education (Scotland) Act of 1918 was also supported by Labour representatives on the new Local Education authorities. Such factors would inevitably have led to some sort of alliance, but its effectiveness owed much to the fact that Labour had a superb strategist available in the person of John Wheatley.

In his ample person Wheatley linked the religious cause with that of housing. Not only did he continue to agitate for increased subsidies, as the government's scheme — the Addison Act — faltered, first through municipal pork barrelling and then through government cuts, but he helped revive the rents issue. After the war, factors had raised rents to cope with inflation. The Scottish Labour Housing Association, a Communist left-Labour body, fought them in the courts and in 1922 won an appeal to the Court of Session which ruled that rent increases since 1915 had been illegal. As the *Scotsman* angrily commented:

> the technical right of the tenant to recall money which has been illegally taken from him has been worked upon by base appeals and has been used to the utmost to stimulate the virus of Socialism in the community.

The depression was already sapping Labour's sinews. Membership in the ten biggest unions in Scotland fell 35 per cent between 1920 and 1922; membership of the Scottish Division of the ILP fell by 25 per cent. 'Destitution, hunger and unemployment are not aids to the Labour cause,' remarked Patrick Dollan after disappointing muncipal election results in November 1921. Next year Ben Shaw, Labour's Scottish organiser, thought a gain of 16 seats would be an outstanding result; he underestimated the potential for conflict between Tories and Liberals. Nine of Labour's twenty-nine seats were won on a minority vote.

The MPs who set off south from St Enoch station that November night, after an impressive service of dedication in St Andrew's Halls, were scarcely archetypal proletarians. If anything, they were socially more variegated than the MPs they would be joining at Westminster: businessmen, teachers, skilled workers, journalists. The other Labour MPs, the solid base of miners's agents, could not exactly be described as 'manual working class'. Although they had begun work in the pits, when they started working full-time for the union they moved up in social class — a four-roomed house, sometimes a son or daughter at the 'uni', Jennie Lee being an example.[24] Such would be found, inevitably, on the right of the party, frequently glowering with incomprehension at the high-minded recruits from the old Liberal families. The Clydesiders bridged the two groups although from time to time they might attack the ex-Liberal intellectuals' preoccupation with foreign affairs, they shared much of it, as they represented an exporting area which depended on the old Liberal principles of international amity and free trade.

The success of November 1922 represented an endorsement of the ILP's 'middle way'. So, when the new MPs came to elect their leader, MacDonald rather than Clynes appealed to the Scots.[25] Subsequent events were to show just how steep and thorny the middle way was.

3

Hope Deferred:
Labour in Scotland in the 1920s

IAN S. WOOD

The emotional scenes which accompanied Glasgow's ten Labour MPs on their departure for Westminster after the 1922 General Election have often been described,[1] and still loomed large in memoirs of the period written years later. 'It was a memorable, terrifying experience', Emanuel Shinwell wrote of his struggle to reach the waiting train at St Enoch station. The crowd all around him, with its almost frightening passion and expectation, seemed to him to be full of 'eyes which had once again the gleam of hope where despair had too long held sway.'[2] John Wheatley, newly elected for Shettleston where a bare ten years before his Catholic co-religionists had burned him in effigy and threatened his home, was also profoundly influenced by what he saw that night and later claimed that it had convinced him that people were ready for 'a bold Socialist lead.'[3]

Bidding for the votes of an electorate dramatically enlarged by the 1918 Representation of the People Act, Labour had fought the election with crusading passion, something perhaps minimised in recent work preoccupied with organisational factors in the party's growth.[4] This dominated many accounts of the contest in Scotland where 'the official programme was largely ignored and the election fought on a series of leaflets and manifestoes drafted mainly by John Wheatley',[5] and other accounts refer to the rotund and bespectacled Shettleston member as the 'field marshal in the fight.'[6]

Wheatley's oratory and tireless organisational flair were certainly key factors in the campaign but only in so far as they motivated and gave a central direction to the intense local activism that so many victorious Labour candidates in 1922 felt bound to acknowledge. Of the volunteer women workers who had contributed to his own victory in West Stirlingshire, Tom Johnston wrote in *Forward*: 'They hustled the indifferent to the booths: they lent shawls and held babies: they carried the sick and dying to the polls on mattresses — and they won. May black shame fall upon the individual or the party, who, having the trust of these women, ever betrays it.' In Shettleston, Wheatley himself had already put in ten years work as a councillor with a specialist knowledge of local housing problems. His support for the 1915 rent strike and his championship of the families of serving soldiers evicted by predatory house factors had helped to turn him into a local hero by the war's end, even though he had opposed the war from the outset. He missed election narrowly in 1918 and in 1922 local party workers re-doubled their efforts. Wheatley's tribute to them after the poll, recorded in *Forward* was coupled with the reminder that 'at our meetings we talked local politics, advocating the claims of the Far East of Glasgow rather than the Near East of Europe.'

1922 was not only an affirmation of faith in Scotland in what Labour could achieve, but also a celebration of what seemed to be a real breakthrough. Labour won 29 of the Scottish seats, ten of them in Glasgow, and took 32 per cent of the total vote cast. In Edinburgh, perhaps predictably, Labour's impact was slower in coming than in the west. Much of Labour's 1922 campaign in the Capital was devoted to holding the Central constituency already captured in 1918, but the Labour vote in the city was still under ten per cent of the total cast. Nonetheless, Edinburgh's Conservatives sensed the tumbril's rattle with every Labour vote. Labour's 32.5 per cent of the Scottish vote in 1922 proved better than the party's performance south of the border, a pattern to be maintained in every subsequent election until 1935. A year later, contesting 49 seats, Labour won almost half of Scotland's allocation in Westminster, and took a majority of the total vote cast in Glasgow. Although the anti-Communist hysteria of 1924 cost Labour seats, it made little impression on the actual vote with Labour's share in Scotland climbing past the 40 per cent mark, a growth maintained in 1929 and only reversed by the cataclysm brought down upon the movement by MacDonald's formation of the National Government in 1931.

Speakers on Labour platforms in Scotland seldom missed a chance of stressing what the movement in England owed to Scotland, and to Wales. In 1923 a fraternal delegate from the National Executive, speaking to the Scottish Council of the party in a debate upon self-government, enlarged upon the need for 'the Celtic fringe to save England from the folly of its own Conservatism', and in 1929 the Scottish party in conference congratulated itself in winning a more solid vote for Labour than had been achieved in any other part of the United Kingdom.

What appears to have shifted the balance of voting power quite decisively to Labour's advantage in Scotland was the extension of the franchise. Prior to the 1918 Act, both the franchise and the actual distribution of seats acted as a much firmer brake on real change in Scotland than was the case in England. Labour's Scottish gains were apparent precisely in those seats where a working-class electorate had grown most rapidly. Important though electoral reform was, it cannot widely be viewed in isolation from overall trends like the break-up of the historic Liberal ascendancy and the related process by which the working class, or at any rate a vital element within it, turned away from the Liberals in the belief that they were 'no longer the party of the working classes, but that in some perceived if undefinable way, the Labour Party was.'[7]

Perhaps one of the most decisive factors working to Labour's advantage in 1922 and in subsequent elections in Scotland was the transfer to it of so much of the Irish Catholic vote. The political organisation of those of Irish birth or descent in Scotland had for long been geared entirely to the winning of Irish Home Rule by constitutional agitation largely in alliance with the Liberals. The events of 1916 and the post-war insurrection in Ireland left the United Irish League, until 1914 a vigorous body in Scotland, in a political cul-de-sac, those of its members still identifying themselves solely with the Irish cause going over to Sinn Fein or the Irish Self-Determination League. Others accepting the partition of 1920 and the treaty of 1921 as at least a partial measure of Irish self-government, saw the old League's raison d'etre to have gone, and many of them went over either to their local ILP branches or to the new divisional Labour parties created by Labour's 1918 constitution, a course of action John Wheatley had been urging upon them ever since he himself had ceased to be active in the League and founded the Catholic Socialist Society in 1907. T P O'Connor, the United Irish League's veteran president and the only Irish nationalist ever to win a seat in mainland Britain, associated himself in 1919 with a directive to all League branches which were still active, urging the importance of the League remaining in being 'independent, separate, self-governing but an ally of the British Labour Party.' It was indeed as an ally of Labour that the League's Paisley branch campaigned in a celebrated by-election of 1920 that allowed H.H. Asquith to return to the Commons. Asquith resented and denounced what he saw as the Irish defection to Labour.[8]

O'Connor with failing strength gave his backing to attempts to revive an Irish organisation in Britain for the General Election of 1922. Indeed, he took the chair at a London conference claiming to represent Irish voters, but little more was agreed to than the revival of the old United Irish League structure at constituency level at a time when Sinn Fein and Labour were drawing off its life-blood. The 1922 General Election in Scotland seemed to provide proof of where Irish and Catholic allegiance had come to rest, as *The Times* stated: 'The Roman Catholic vote on the Clyde is a primary factor in every election. It represents about 20 per cent of the electorate. In the old days of Home Rule it voted faithfully by direction and came to form the backbone of the Liberal Party. There was no official direction this time though Mr T P O'Connor made a tentative effort to win back his lost empire, but there is little doubt that unofficial direction was equally effective for the vote went solidly Labour.'[9]

Some of the evidence upon which this analysis was based came from John Wheatley who was freely quoted in *The Times* article:

> There is nothing in British Socialism that is directed against the church. The two can live separately. One result has been that since we came into the movement Socialist attacks on the Church have practically ceased and all round there has been a marked diminution of the old sectarian feeling.[10]

Wheatley may well have been right in thinking that sectarianism within the Labour movement was on the wane, with the assimilation of the Irish vote, but implacable antagonism to him as an Irish Catholic from some of his opponents pursued him almost to the grave.

The importance of this shift in Catholic-Irish allegiance was accentuated by electoral reform, for the Catholic vote turned out to be especially concentrated where the overall increase in the working-class electorate was greatest. In 23 Scottish seats after the 1918 Act, Catholics constituted 20 per cent or more of the total electorate. This proved to be a factor bearing substantially upon Scottish Labour MPs' support for the special status of Catholic schools, and specifically for the Catholic Relief Bills of 1925 and 1926. These bills were intended to amend the 1829 Catholic Emancipation Act so that clergy in full vestments might parade publicly on occasions like those prompted by acts of worship at the Carfin grotto outside Motherwell, a shrine to St Bernadette of Lourdes laid out after the war, largely with the donations and labour of Catholic miners. The Catholic vote then represented a permanent accession of strength for Labour in Scotland and research has simply served to quantify this fact.[11] On the other hand, Labour had to face often bitter attack for its political relationship to an Irish community which was in the 1920s and later, the target of xenophobic hostility from public figures, sections of the press, and consistently from the Presbyterian churches whose annual assemblies were occasions of predictable kailyard racism whenever the position of the Catholic Irish in Scotland was debated.[12]

Local activism and organisation had been vital in making Labour a movement capable of a national impact, but the need to keep its presence an effective one in local government politics was a major preoccupation in the post-war years. In Glasgow particularly, an increasingly strong Labour and ILP presence in the council chamber and committee rooms of one of Britain's most extensively governed cities had given men like Wheatley and Patrick Dollan the chance to develop and sharpen essential skills both in debate and in administration. This they had succeeded in combining with a capacity for dramatic confrontation with the city's commercial and professional establishment, represented on the council by moderate or ratepayers, councillors which ought perhaps to have served notice on Westminster what a Glasgow presence might mean there. The Clydesiders' taste for challenges to Parliamentary protocol, usually well-rehearsed, and the penalties these incurred, cemented their relationship with the electorate which had returned them, but their apprenticeship in calculated irreverence had been served in Glasgow City chambers.

Dollan, though he stood more than once for Parliament, was content to build a real and ultimately formidable power-base for himself in Glasgow council politics. Indeed, he emerged as some sort of prophet of the future decentralised Socialist society in which major powers would rest with democratic and self-sufficient municipalities. Wheatley, in his time as a councillor, had shared a similar vision, speaking and writing of Glasgow's golden future as a landscaped, healthy, prosperous municipality with its own home and foreign trading departments, and ships with the city's arms trading from the Clyde with other Socialist cities around the world. This kind of optimism was in tune with much of what was being written on the city's potential as a human environment in the 1920s. The work of Patrick Geddes on the dynamics of urban growth was beginning to find an audience and the publication of Corbusier's *Radiant City* was not far away.

Practical politics forced upon Wheatley the more mundane task of defending such autonomy as local authorities already had, notably in his support as Health Minister in 1924 for the embattled Poplar Poor Law Guardians, then in opposition to Conservative legislation intended to allow central government to replace recalcitrant poor law authorities with its own nominees. More serious for Labour in Scotland was the comprehensive Conservative legislation of 1929 which gave every appearance of shifting control of major services like education to county councils where Labour's prospects of representation, let alone control would be greatly reduced. Labour conducted a determined campaign against the 1929 Act, and once it was passed, pressed the case for councillors to be paid under a reconstituted system which would make heavy additional demands upon their time.

The main platform from which representations on this or any other substantive matter of policy could be made was the Scottish Council of the Party, created in 1915 as the Scottish Advisory Council. Just how much autonomy this body ought to have over the endorsement of parliamentary candidates, affiliation of local bodies, and representation at British Labour conferences had been a matter in dispute from the moment of the 1918 party constitution adoption. Under that constitution the Scottish Council emerged as a body with an autonomy that was more nominal than real where Labour's overall British organisation and policy-making were concerned. Unease over this was a product in part of the party's continuing commitment to self-government for Scotland within the UK. The paradox caused by the party in Scotland being for home rule but not having anything resembling it within the labour movement at large was a factor in the several votes at conferences of the Scottish Council, for example in 1924, when a big majority of delegates supported separate Scottish representation on Labour's National Executive, something still not accepted.

The issue of the Scottish party's autonomy arose again over the question of enforcing annual conference and National Executive rulings on the exclusion of Communists from membership of the new divisional or constituency parties created in 1918. A trade union delegate to the Scottish Council's 1927 conference claimed this was a matter of principle as well as merely the technical matter of its enforcement, which they should be free to debate. A platform speaker, J Rhys Davies MP, replied, putting the National Executive's view that the Scottish Council's remit was one of 'dealing with Scottish aspects of public, legislative and administrative affairs'. He quoted conference standing orders as being designed 'to meet special Scottish requirements within the lines laid down from time to time by the British national conference of the party. These shall deal only with Scottish political affairs, trade union and other purely economic matters being avoided'. The conference must have felt obliged to accept this very limited definition of its functions for there was no recorded challenge to the Rhys Davies statement.

If Labour in Scotland was so inhibited as it appears to have been in making good in this period its case for a distinctive role within a

British movement there was paradoxically no similar timidity where its support for Scottish self-government was concerned. A major book surveyed the changing nature of Labour's relationship to the Home Rule movement in this century but, in the light of events in the seventies, it is worth re-stating the essential facts of Labour's initially strong commitment to Home Rule in the 1920s.[13] This commitment has to be seen as the sum of that of the movement's affiliated parts, like the Scottish trade unions and the ILP. It is in this sense that Labour conference votes in Scotland on the matter need to be understood between 1922 and 1930, even although tension between Labour and the Scottish Home Rule Association grew and culminated in the recession from that body of a new nationalist party prepared to put its election candidates in the field against Labour.[14]

'Had Scotland,' declared the chairman of the SCLP conference in 1923, 'been in the enjoyment of Home Rule it is certain that a Labour government would now be in power north of the Tweed, and this thought should stimulate to greater effort the large and growing number of Scotsmen who are bent upon having a Parliament in Edinburgh to manage Scottish domestic affairs'. It was precisely this apparent common cause between Labour and the Home Rule movement that confirmed the Scottish establishment in its deep-seated fear of any alteration of the basis of the 1707 constitutional settlement. *The Scotsman* expressed the hope that the 1922 election results would be a salutary warning to all still flirting with the idea of a Scottish legislature, since such a body would be 'dominated by extreme industrial elements representing only a very small part of the total area of Scotland.' Fears that a Labour government would give the matter priority were soon to prove unfounded though the Home Rule movement had high hopes of Labour. R.E. Muirhead, that tireless campaigner, welcomed Labour's formation of a government in 1924 because of what he believed to be the depth of Ramsay MacDonald's commitment to Scottish self-government.

The Home Rule campaign of the 1920s had a style and momentum which gave vivid colour to the Scottish political scene, but Labour's affiliated organisations honoured the national cause in their own way. In June 1923 David Kirkwood MP, a man who had contributed not a little in his time to the legend of 'Red Clyde', was the main speaker at a Bannockburn rally organised by the ILP's Stirlingshire federation. After Kirkwood and other speakers had been enthusiastically received, the thousands present sang the 'Internationale' and 'A man's a man for a' that'. In August the Home Rule Association organised one of its biggest ever demonstrations in Glasgow; according to a *Scotsman* estimate, 30,000 people attended a march in which ten Scottish MPs also took part. Three years later, the Association marked the anniversary of William Wallace's execution with a lavish pageant at Elderslie. *Forward* devoted an entire page to this event, including speeches by James Brown and Rosslyn Mitchell, Labour MPs for Ayrshire and Paisley respectively. Mitchell declared that his experience of Westminster, which he had entered in 1924, had already convinced him it would be better to be badly governed by Scots than well governed by Englishmen. Home Rule resolutions were again carried and the two Labour MPs remained present to join the William Morris choir in singing what *Forward*'s reporter called the 'Scots national anthem' (probably 'Scots wha' hae').

Failure by two Labour governments in the 1920s to treat their Home Rule commitments with any urgency has clearly had major long-term consequences. In the short run it served to hand the initiative to an increasingly populist nationalism capable of harbouring and giving voice to some of the uglier prejudices of Scottish society. Among these was the anti-Irish bigotry already referred to, and exemplified by Andrew Dewar Gibb, Regius Professor of Law at Glasgow University and a recruit to nationalism from the Conservatives. His lengthy political life was substantially taken up with a malignant and sectarian racialism which lay at the very centre of his many calls for 'the proper disposal and treatment of the deplorable Irish colony in Scotland.'[15] An architect of the unified national movement of the 1930s, Dr John MacCormick, it should here be added, worked hard to distance nationalism as far as possible from the baleful influence of this kind of xenophobia.[16] For Labour in Scotland the Home Rule commitment remained something lurking in the shadows and would more recently be resurrected under the guise of the ill-fated devolution legislation of the 1970s. Only since then, as later contributors show, has Labour seriously re-assessed its strategy.

One reason why Labour in Scotland could not ignore Home Rule was the apparent strength of the ILP's support for it, and in much of Scotland in the 1920s, especially in the areas of Labour's most rapid electoral advances, the ILP to many people was Labour. Labour's relationship to the ILP was not, however, a matter easily resolved by the adoption of the 1918 party constitution. Indeed the ILP's reservations about that constitution and the kind of party likely to grow out of it had prompted it to debate actual disaffiliation. The way tensions involved in Labour's partnership with the ILP were contained as best they could be until 1932 has been the subject of some major research,[17] but these cannot be said to have taken on a peculiarly Scottish dimension since the issues involved were ones of principle relating to the future of a political labour movement in Britain as a whole. Yet the predominance within this debate of men like Maxton and Wheatley was a reflection of just how strong the ILP was in Scotland and of what Labour owed to its unique blend of organisational activism and proselytising zeal.

In the 1922 General Election forty of Labour's forty-three candidates in Scotland were ILP members and many were actually sponsored by the ILP. Membership, as events were soon to show, could mean as much or as little as anyone wanted it to mean, as any comparison of Ramsay MacDonald's career with those of his compatriots from Clydeside might suggest. ILP sponsorship of election candidates had, however, clearly practical advantages in terms of the availability of cash and canvassers which it could mean. In 1924, for example, Maxton held Bridgeton at a campaign cost of little more than £100, less than a fifth of his opponents' outlay. Wheatley's victory that year a little further east in Shettleston, despite a virulent onslaught on both his Irish connections and his business reputation, cost him less than a fifth of what his opponent spent trying to unseat him.

The ILP reached its peak in 1925 in Scotland where it could claim 307 branches out of a total of 1,028 in the British Isles. 75 new Scottish branches were founded in the year prior to the ILP's April 1925 annual conference. This growth was in part a product of Clifford Allen's flair as national chairman for fund-raising and organisation, but the preponderance of Scottish branches remains striking and was regularly admitted at Labour conferences in Scotland. In 1923 a Railway Clerks' delegate speaking to Scottish Labour's annual gathering credited the previous year's election gains largely to the ILP:

> The victories were mainly due to the ILP which had under-taken the spadework in the divisions and also provided the funds for most of the elections. Indeed, had it not been for the ILP, most of the branches would not have been contested.

Herbert Morrison acknowledged Labour's debt in Scotland to the ILP in very similar terms in 1929, in a speech on how best to raise recruitment to the divisional Labour parties. There were still many fewer of these in Scotland than ILP branches, but Morrison was careful to stress that in no sense should there be a competitive relationship. In fact a variety of problems had arisen over election contests in which divisional parties had adopted ILP members as candidates only to find that ILP branches in the constituency to be fought claimed overall control of how funds they supplied might be

used in the campaign. The 1926 Scottish Labour conference felt
obliged to point out that ILP branches had no more rights than
trade unions where affiliates to divisional parties were concerned:
'as the choice of the candidate infallibly rests with the divisional
party it must equally have the general control over election activities,
including election finance.'

When in 1927 Labour proposed the creation of a Scottish
propaganda committee it clearly had uppermost in its mind the
contribution which the ILP could make, though heavy emphasis was
laid on how 'the whole was greater than any part of the movement'
and the need for the ILP to act against members who would speak
only at meetings which the ILP itself had organised. The ILP
continued to nurse grievances over the under-representation it felt it
was sometimes accorded in the management of the divisional parties
and Dollan raised this matter in a general debate in 1930 on Labour
organisation and recruitment in Scotland. Other speakers on this
occasion, with ILP disaffiliation from Labour less than two years
away, pressed for a clear demarcation of functions within the party
in which divisional parties would act primarily as electoral machines
while ILP branches would sustain the task of Socialist education.

The dramatic and now well-documented deterioration in Labour's
relationship to the ILP was a product of much more than the sort
of constituency-level tensions just referred to. Essentially of course
there was an unresolved problem over Labour's whole ideological
stance and political strategy and the ILP's relationship to the
movement as a whole and the Parliamentary party in particular. The
fact that some of the Clydeside ILP group were centrally involved
in this conflict does not necessarily, it must be realised, typify the
view of the Scottish ILP as a whole. This is a fact still in danger of
being overshadowed by the appetite of Maxton, Wheatley, Stephen,
Kirkwood and Buchanan for confrontational drama at Westminster
when in opposition and for the baiting of Labour ministers deemed
to be infirm of Socialist purpose, like the hapless J.H. Thomas in the
1929-31 government. Yet close to the climax of the ILP's struggle
for power within the Labour party splits had opened within the
Scottish ILP group of MPs. The Clydesiders' guerilla amendments
to strengthen Margaret Bondfield's 1929 Unemployment Insurance
legislation antagonised Shinwell and Tom Johnston to the point
where they sought to challenge Maxton's and Wheatley's claim to
have any mandate for their tactics either from Labour or the ILP.

A Labour leadership already in travail after only a few months
in office could draw some comfort both from this and the openly
aired disagreements between the *Glasgow Eastern Standard* owned

by Wheatley and *Forward* which Tom Johnston still edited. John
Paton, with his experience as a full-time divisional organiser for
the ILP in Scotland, was never under the misapprehension that
the left stance of the rump of the original Clydeside group echoed
the view of the Scottish ILP as a whole. After the ILP's National
Administrative Council, its major executive body, had refused to
re-nominate Ramsay MacDonald as Labour party treasurer. Paton
recalled the distribution of opinion in Scotland, 'Although it was the
home territory of Maxton and the Clydeside MPs who were backing
him, the prophets were without honour in their own country. The
great majority of the Scottish Labour MPs who were all members of
the ILP were strongly opposed to us, and their influence, combined
with the powerful help given them by Tom Johnston's weekly
Forward presented us for a time with a difficult problem.'[18]

By this time, Dollan too had emerged as a supporter of
MacDonald, despite his own strong ILP base. In the inquest
on the 1924 Labour government he had challenged Labour in
Scotland either to endorse MacDonald's leadership or to initiate
the necessary procedures to attempt his dismissal. The 1925 Scottish
Labour conference appeared to accept both Dollan's assessment of
what MacDonald had achieved in office and in increasing the total
Labour vote even in face of the 'Red Scare' hysteria of the 1924
election campaign. Only Maxton, present as an ILP delegate, was
prepared to challenge Dollan's view and to sound a warning about
the dangers for the movement of an uncritical relationship with the
leadership.

When Labour took office again in 1929, Wheatley had come to
appear to MacDonald as his most formidable threat from within
the ILP.[19] Although Wheatley had declined to serve again under
MacDonald, he could still trade on his outstanding success as a
radical and competent Health Minister in 1924. In addition to
this, his polemical skills both in Parliament and in the press
retained a large audience for his views within the movement as
a whole. He has been credited with authorship of the abortive
Cook-Maxton manifesto of 1928 challenging the Labour leadership
to wage 'an unceasing war against poverty and working class
servitude.' Yet Wheatley saw little except a political cul-de-sac
opening up before the ILP in isolation from Labour. Disillusioned
though he may have been about Labour's performance in office
and in opposition during a decade of capitalist crisis, Wheatley,
in the final months of his life threw his weight against any moves
that would give Labour a pretext for the final expulsion of the
ILP.

Its attitude to the question of Communist attempts in this period to achieve affiliation to the Labour Party could be cited as another measure of the Scottish ILP's essentially centrist stance which contributed so much to Maxton's isolation after the final split in 1932. In the heady days following upon the emergence of the Soviet Russian state, the ILP in Scotland and elsewhere had been receptive to membership of the new Communist-controlled Third International and to co-operation with Communists at local level. By 1925, however, Dollan could hold the ILP's Scottish Divisional Council firm to the policy of denying Communists any rights of affiliation, even though Maxton had urged the case for this upon delegates. This outcome has been cited as evidence that 'the organiser had a stronger hold in Scotland than the orator',[20] and there was a similar outcome when the ILP debated the matter in 1927. Bids such as these for affiliation to the broad labour movement in Britain were of course in full conformity with the declared aims of the Third International in a period where Lenin saw revolutionary prospects outside Russia temporarily on the ebb. The failure of these attempts did not, in itself, prevent individual Labour parties, notably in Scotland, from co-operation with Communists. This could mean not merely accepting them as individual party members, until a close vote condemned this at Labour's 1924 annual conference but in some cases Communists being adopted as Parliamentary candidates.

The Greenock constituency proved an intractable one in this respect. There a militant local Trades and Labour Council, which for all practical purposes was the divisional Labour Party, defied Labour's Scottish council and the National Executive by running a local Communist as its parliamentary candidate on three occasions between 1922 and 1924. Disaffiliation of the Trades and Labour council and the creation by the Scottish Council of a reconstituted divisional party was the eventual outcome after a split vote between the Communist and an 'official' Labour candidate enabled the Liberals to hold the seat in 1924.

In Motherwell a similar situation arose when bodies affiliated to the local Trades and Labour council secured the nomination of a somewhat maverick Communist, J Walton Newbold. Standing in defiance of both Labour's Scottish Council and the NEC he won the seat, though holding it barely for a year before losing it to a candidate of the local Orange Lodges. The 1924 Labour conference decision excluding Communists from individual Labour Party membership was one factor among others persuading Newbold to abandon his candidature, but both episodes seemed to suggest the over-riding need for Communists to work through local

Labour bodies and to point also to the growing power of Labour's central organisations, whether in Glasgow or London, to terminate unacceptable candidatures.

Kelvingrove in Glasgow proved to be another intractable constituency for a Labour leadership anxious to enforce agreed conference and National Executive policy on Communist members. In 1923 Aitken Ferguson, a Communist, almost won the seat against Liberal and Conservative opponents, and in a by-election the next year was endorsed by the divisional Labour Party, campaigning as 'a Communist and a Trade Unionist, standing as the official candidate of the Labour Party.' Official Labour endorsement was quickly withdrawn though several Labour MPs spoke in Ferguson's support anyhow. *Forward* was caustic about Ferguson's campaign, reporting one encounter he had in a tenement court with a group of uncomprehending women to whom he proclaimed himself 'a member of the Third International.' In spite of one or two maladroit false starts like this, Ferguson's campaign was a vigorous one and he improved on his own previous vote though the Conservatives held the seat. Needless to say, the most immediate result was a strong reiteration of Labour's existing anathemas on local party endorsement of known Communists with special admonition for the errant Kelvingrove party.

This was not the end of local defiance of party policy and not long afterwards Ramsay MacDonald allowed himself to be drawn deeply into what his biographer calls 'a somewhat foolhardy fray on his part into the depths of Glasgow municipal politics.'[21] The Springburn divisional party involved itself in 1925 in a local council by-election in one of its wards, Cowlairs, appearing to support a Communist against a well-tried local ILP man who had long-standing claims on MacDonald's friendship. The outcome was a seat lost through a split vote and the disaffiliation of the Springburn party. MacDonald acted in character by going to the aid of an old friend and recorded in *Forward* the view that 'Glasgow is a fearful bogey to the outside world and I am not sure sometimes but that our movement there is more concerned to keep up that hair-raising reputation than is good for it.'

The following year, a further five divisional parties were all identified as cases of unacceptable Communist influence: Kelvingrove (again), Gorbals, Bridgeton, Bothwell and Coatbridge. Clearly conference prohibitions were insufficient to put an end to a degree of willingness by local Labour activists to work with Communists. This had been apparent at the 1924 Scottish Council conference when 44 delegates voted for a resolution in favour of

Communist affiliation against 57 who carried an amendment simply asking the NEC to reconsider the whole issue. A larger majority carried a further amendment giving tactical backing to party policy by declaring that Communist parties be allowed to affiliate on the same basis as all bodies which accepted the party constitution.

Stalin's emerging ascendancy in Russia marked a formal end to the strategy of infiltration of and affiliation to the parties of the non-Communist left. Labour and parties like it were transformed from bodies which Communists should seek to work with into the 'social Fascist' enemy. Yet a full year after this disastrous shift of direction by Moscow and the Third International or 'Comintern', routine re-affirmation of Labour policy towards Communists seemed to be deemed necessary in Scotland, especially for the guidance of divisional parties still willing to have Communist speakers at occasional meetings.

Labour fear of the damage resulting from real or supposed Communist connections were exaggerated since, despite the loss of some key marginal seats, the party's vote had gone up in the 1924 General Election when the crudest allegations of Communist infiltration had dominated the campaign. Communist activists of the inter-war period still recall, on the other hand, the way the sectarian rigidity of their party's policy may not have confused and alienated as many Labour voters as it won over.[22] On practical local issues, in a militant area like the Fife coalfield, Labour and Communist co-operation was clearly at times improvised independently of the Labour leadership or that of the Third International,[23] though Communist strength there became sufficient by 1935 to unseat the increasingly unpopular establishment Labour member for West Fife, William Adamson, twice Secretary of State for Scotland and a determined opponent of the reform movement among those Fife miners who wanted more accountable and democratic procedures in the County union of which Adamson was the General Secretary.

The period under consideration was then one marking Labour's real arrival in Scotland as a political force. But such a time can also be one of self-examination for a movement built up on dedication and self-sacrifice when it finds its cause being espoused in unexpected quarters. One of these was the Scottish legal profession whose ranks had been unable in 1924 to yield up a single advocate of Labour sympathies qualified to fill the office of Lord Advocate. Following that a noted Scottish KC, Craigie Aitchison, who in 1923 had stood for Parliament as a Liberal and delivered some fiercely anti-Socialist diatribes, announced that he was joining Labour. This he did, in time to be adopted for a Durham constituency, less than a year after

his previous contest as a Liberal. Failing there, Aitchison then let
his name go before the Glasgow Central constituency party. They
adopted him as their candidate, swayed, it seems by a combination of
forensic skills, personal wealth, the promise of more legal talent that
he could bring over to Labour, and last but not least, the discovery or
re-discovery by the candidate of a Chartist grandfather to add weight
to his other credentials.

The Glasgow Trades and Labour council, however, were less
than enamoured with the Central Division's choice and sceptical
of whether the prospective candidate had really found his road
to Damascus. Their view was echoed by the Scottish Council's
Executive who set out their objections in some detail and for the
attention of the press, as *Forward* reported: 'Now, when the work,
tears and lives of people who have gone give us a chance to take
control of our conditions, we are informed that "legal efficiency" is
indispensable both in the field of legislation and administration, and
offers come thick and fast upon us from people who are willing to
ease the financial burdens entailed in an election, provided they are
selected as candidates. We feel that in many instances it would be
far better for local organisations to refuse such offers and carry on as
those before did, allowing the inspiration of independence that has
carried us so far to finish the job: Mr. Aitchison is far too closely
related to opportunities which an advancing party may contain, and
it is not for such that we work.'

'Mr Aitchison's' conversion, whether Pauline or not, had convinced a divisional party who had followed the correct procedures
in adopting him and he just failed to capture the seat in 1929,
quickly moving on to a safe Labour seat in Kilmarnock vacated
by its occupant's death later that same year. Aitchison, by then
Labour's Lord Advocate, won the by-election, held the seat in 1931
by virtue of his support for MacDonald's National Government, and
less than two years after that, left Parliament and Labour to become
Lord Justice Clerk.

Any dilemma in finding a Lord Advocate had at least been
resolved for Labour in 1929 by Aitchison's availability. Five years
before, MacDonald had been obliged to appoint Hugh MacMillan
who had actually been a prospective Conservative candidate before
the war and who, only a year before had been offered the position
of Solicitor-General for Scotland in the Bonar Law government. The
memoirs he later wrote are emphatic about his amicable relations in
office with MacDonald. This amity was clearly reassuring to him at
the time but rather less so to those who hoped for even a few radical
initiatives from a minority Labour government.[24]

There is a revealing passage in the same memoirs about the author's dealings in 1924 with Labour's Secretary of State for Scotland, William Adamson, ex-miner and MP for West Fife, mentioned here already for his uncompromising opposition to the reform movement in his own union. Writing of his first meeting with Adamson at Dover House in London, MacMillan recalled how a pleasant and undemanding relationship between them was quickly established:

> Almost his (ie Adamson's) first remark to me was: 'You'll help us, won't you? You must remember I'm only a miner'; and then he added, with a twinkle in his eye, 'You'll be surprised to find what a Tory I am.'

Fife miners battling for accountability in their own union and for some real challenges to the coal companies over wages and conditions would not have been surprised.

Another ex-miner who had entered Parliament in Labour's post-war breakthrough was James Brown from Annbank in Ayrshire. Locally known as a Church of Scotland elder and total abstinence advocate, he personified a douce Calvinism which helped to earn him his appointment in 1924 as Lord High Commissioner to the General Assembly, not a body conspicuous at that time for its sympathy with Labour or for any radical measures to attack the brutal poverty and injustice which so scarred urban and rural existence for many in early twentieth century Scotland. Brown and his wife plunged into the role required of them with apparent relish and to a chorus of praise from Labour's enemies. The *Scotsman* drew large conclusions from this kailyard triumph, declaring that: 'it may even be hoped that the experience may have done something to abate or remove that hostility and animosity of the classes of which we have heard so much but which in Scotland does not appear to go so deep or so far as is sometimes assumed. It may be hoped also that it will have done something to impress upon the unruly elements in society that in ordered ceremony and historic forms there is a spiritual value which the iconoclast in his haste would wantonly destroy.'[25]

Similar effusions greeted Brown's second appointment as Lord High Commissioner in 1929 and serve perhaps to underline the fact that the militant and emotional Socialism of Clydeside had its counterpart in men like Brown, Adamson, and perhaps also Willie Graham. He was a prim and, it would seem, almost humourless journalist who held Central Edinburgh for Labour between 1918 and 1931, a glutton for blue books and committee work. In the two Labour governments he was Financial Secretary to the Treasury and President of the Board of Trade. He died comparatively young

after losing his seat in the landslide rout of Labour following upon
the creation of the National government. The product of a still not
quite extinct Scottish Calvinism which conceives of life as some kind
of personal and moral assault course to be tamed by those with
sufficient reserves of rectitude for the task, he carried always with
him the childhood memory of a grim old grandmother with whom
he had lodged in order to attend school in Peebles, and her regular
admonitions to him and his brother about whistling in the morning:
'stop that noise, ye'll be greetin' afore nicht.'[26]

Men like these, able enough though they were, could never have
given Labour in Scotland what it needed most at that time and what
it is still best remembered for — passion. One man who would have
supplied it in abundance from outside the political labour movement,
or within it, as he had been briefly when he stood for the Gorbals
constituency in 1918, was MacLean. Had he lived longer Labour
might have found itself, especially in the west of Scotland, judged
against his austere standards and found wanting by those who had
experienced his power as an orator and lecturer. Yet MacLean's
charisma had a meteor-like quality to it, seeming to have spent
itself before his early death. He ended his life politically isolated as
Labour made its first forward movement along the 'parliamentary
road' to Socialism with all its pitfalls and ambivalences. Yet the
measure of the man lay less in what he may have achieved, which
was perhaps less than Maxton or Wheatley, but in the legend that has
subsequently grown around his name and the courageous strivings
of his short lifetime.

The unique and extinct political culture of the skilled working
class which gave MacLean his following and provided soil in which
to nurture the legend of the Red Clydeside caught the imagination
of contemporary commentators, arriving in Glasgow's shipyards and
closes after the war as some of them did like explorers penetrating the
African interior. Some of them felt even a certain awe after making
contact with the nucleus of a movement apparently growing from
strength to strength, and could write memorably of Clyde workers:

> these shipbuilders, artists in the geometry of iron, whose
> machines and whose ships carry the empire of the seas; whom
> Kipling himself celebrated as the innermost strength of that
> empire, men educated in a thorough, logical, desperately
> limited Scottish way, who have added to their Socialism not
> the self-complacent innovations of Lenin but the not less
> dangerous fire of fierce democratic connections ingrained in
> their nation and passed down unaltered from generations of
> bleak Covenanting ancestors.[27]

Ian S. Wood   47

The celebrated Clydeside 'class of 1922' entered Parliament not
as revolutionaries like MacLean which most of them were not, but
rather as agitators in a struggle for justice which seemed to them
to warrant often calculated violations of Parliamentary decorum and
increasingly intransigent opposition to the Labour leadership itself.

Maxton exists perhaps most vividly among his political peer-group
in our imagination because of a warmth and humour which real
anger at injustice and cruel poverty never took from him. His
cadaverous appearance and famously long hair ('what about the
unemployed barbers, Jimmy?' people sometimes called out at his
meetings) was strangely at odds with the fastidious dress and
appearance of John Wheatley who has sometimes been portrayed
as an ice-cold, calculating intriguer and an enigma in contrast to
Maxton's unfeigned openness and good fellowship.[28] Comparisons
like these are less than fair to Wheatley who was almost certainly
the ablest of the Clydeside group and whom Maxton regarded as
his mentor, remaining close to him until his death early in 1930.

As Health Minister in 1924 Wheatley was widely admitted to
have performed superbly, seeing through Cabinet and Parliament
complex and comprehensive legislation on housing, the matter
closest to his practical concerns for the previous ten years. The
1924 Act was a real monument to the Irish pit-boy from Baillieston
from whom the memory of what deficient coal company housing
meant for women and for family-life had never been eroded by
time or by personal success. Wheatley's stature can be measured
in other ways too, dating to his first clashes with his parish priest
over Socialism, espousal of which took him out of the United Irish
League and into the ILP and the Catholic Socialist Society.[29] He
retained an appetite for new ideas and was prepared to campaign
for them with a tireless vigour that typified Clydeside Socialism in
the 1920s. Perhaps his was not an original intellect, but he was
a populariser of skill and clarity, helping to spread among ILP
and Labour audiences a grasp of under-consumptionist economics
which, originated by J.A. Hobson and refined by Keynes, came to
seem an urgent alternative to the deflationary orthodoxies which a
Labour Chancellor of the Exchequer like Philip Snowden seemed
merely to echo.

At times too, he could sound very like an enthusiast for the
Soviet Russian state, urging his audiences to keep an open mind
on what still seemed a great Socialist experiment, and deriding
the scare-mongering onslaughts on the new Russia of Labour's
opponents and their allies in the press. In 1926 Wheatley was an
unhesitating champion of the miners, having been one himself for

eleven years, and once the TUC Council called off strike action in their support he kept faith with them campaigning constantly in their support and donating generously to their funds during the six-month lock-out.[30]

Wheatley's death in 1930 came as a second Labour government drifted into uncharted waters where it proved ill-equipped to navigate. The collapse of that government in 1931 was a failure both of nerve and of intellect, the price for which Scotland had to pay a heavy share. In the election debacle of that year, Wheatley's seat, with a new member, survived the rout, as did Maxton's, but 1931 must have seemed to activists up and down Scotland a moment of almost terminal disaster when the high hopes and achievements of a decade had turned to ashes.

4

Scottish Labour in the Depression: The 1930s

IAN DONNACHIE

The French often described the Depression of the thirties as 'La Misère' — a word which somehow catches better than our own language can the essence of general despair felt during much of the decade. Clearly any assessment of Scottish Labour politics during the 1930s must be viewed against the background of both domestic economic recession (and partial recovery) and major international developments like the rise of Fascism, the Spanish Civil War, Appeasement, and the outbreak of the Second World War. British politics after the fall of the second Labour government was essentially dominated by modified but still old-fashioned Conservatism in the guise of National Government. This, by definition, determined the nature of policy on unemployment and economic reconstruction in Scotland and other distressed areas. But amid the gloom there were many positive developments, not all of which bore immediate fruit certainly, but which indicate that received notions about the Scottish economy in the thirties need at least some modification. The same is perhaps true of Labour's record in Scotland, for there was an impressive recovery in the General Election of 1935, some notable by-election successes, and a sustained achievement throughout in local government and seen in the capture of Glasgow in 1933.[1]

International events aside, the major domestic issue throughout the thirties was the economy. Scotland certainly suffered more severely in the depression than the UK as a whole — partly due to over-commitment to a narrow range of traditional industries, and partly through slower growth when recovery came later in the decade. The world slump of 1929-1931, which coincided with the period of office of the second Labour government, brought an alarming rise in unemployment and a widening gap within the UK as a whole. While there was a notable rise in the insured labour force in

Scotland during the thirties the actual number in employment only reached its 1929 level as late as 1935; in other words, recovery was longer delayed and only came about in 1936, rather than during 1934 for the UK in general. Differences in industrial structure were also reflected in lower productivity and persistently lower earnings, so the social consequences of the depression were more deeply felt in Scotland than elsewhere, with the possible exceptions of South Wales and Tyneside, which shared similar problems. More positively, the thirties saw a modest growth of 'new' industries, which by 1935 represented about 11 per cent of net output. Even this development left over 30 per cent of the labour force in Scotland's traditional trades of coal-mining, iron and steel, shipbuilding, heavy engineering, and textiles. The upturn when it came was based largely on improved exports and re-armament, though even in 1939 unemployment — at 13.5 per cent — exceeded the 1929 level.[2]

Against this background, still sadly all too familiar in the 1980s, Scotland in the thirties presented pockets of deep poverty, severe overcrowding, disease and poor diet. The picture that emerges from the many inquiries and statistical surveys of the period could hardly be one for self-satisfaction on the part of any government, even for Scotland as a whole, far less districts hit hard by unemployment. Sir John Boyd Orr, then Director of the Rowett Institute, Aberdeen, estimated in 1934 that twenty per cent of the population lived 'at the economic level of the dole' which placed them, in his words, 'near or below the threshold of adequate nutrition.' Another survey thought this an underestimate, especially in areas of high unemployment, where anything up to 75 per cent of those out of work were 'well below the minimum considered necessary' by the BMA.[3] Scotland had one of the worst infant mortality rates of any industrialised country, certainly far worse than anywhere south of the Border. Not only this, Scotland was one of the worst-housed areas in the UK: 1 in 4 Scottish houses were overcrowded, as against only 1 in 26 in England and Wales. Overall in 1931, 44 per cent of the population lived in houses with one or two rooms, though in Glasgow the figure rose to 55 per cent, and in Dundee 56 per cent. Although something was achieved by slum clearance and council housing programmes under Wheatley's act during the thirties — housing remained Scotland's major problem by the outbreak of the Second World War.

In terms of Scottish political and constitutional change the thirties was a period of notable malaise. The electorate recorded a modest upturn in line with population growth, from 2.9 million in 1931 to 3.1 million in 1935, and around the same at the close of the decade. The Scottish electorate was almost equally divided between the burghs and the counties (1.4 to 1.5 million respectively in 1931), with a further 47,000 in the Universities. The Combined Universities returned three members with the elections (exclusive of by-elections) conducted by Proportional Representation, often amid lively campaigns which involved undergraduates as well as the graduates actually eligible to vote. There were no major redistributions or boundary changes. Five by-elections occurred during the life of the Labour government, 1929 to 1931, ten between 1931 and 35, and eleven during the years 1936 to the outbreak of war.[4]

In 1930, following the General Election of 1929, Scottish Labour held 37 of the 74 seats at Westminister: by sheer coincidence Labour was in a minority of 37 to the combined Tory and Liberal opposition. Scottish Labour's strength lay once more in the industrial heartland of west Central Scotland, although there were several important rural-mining seats on the margins. The Glasgow stronghold alone was represented by ten seats, while Edinburgh returned three, and Aberdeen and Dundee one each. Affiliations — other than to the Labour Party itself — were still of considerable significance, for no fewer than fourteen MPs were ILPers, while eleven had union affiliations. The Miner's Federation supported five MPs in South Ayrshire, West Fife, Bothwell, Hamilton, and South Midlothian, while two members described themselves as Independent Labour, and one maintained the long-established link with the Co-operative Party. So one half to two-thirds of Scottish Labour MPs were probably on the left of the party in terms of ideology and practical politics.

Apart from MacDonald, major Scottish figures in the second Labour Government were few and far between: William Adamson, a lifelong Macdonald supporter, was Secretary of State for Scotland; Tom Johnston received belated recognition as Under Secretary for Scotland (later becoming Lord Privy Seal); Graham got the Board of Trade; while Shinwell started as Financial Secretary at the War Office (an unlikely situation), ending up at the Mines Office as Parliamentary Secretary. Wheatley, of course, had already quit the Front Bench so was given no post, despite his earlier success as Minister of Health in the first Labour government. Discounting Johnston then, no men of the old Scottish Labour Left were accorded recognition by MacDonald, despite the debt he owed some since his election to the party leadership in 1922.

One among several areas hit by acute recession, Scotland badly needed fresh policies. So what of the record of the short-lived Labour government in Scotland between 1929 and 1931? During 2 years and three months Labour achieved a great deal in the circumstances, particularly in the alleviation of unemployment, the development of agriculture, and social welfare. New employment opportunities were provided through work programmes under the Unemployment Grants Committee, Home Development, Roads Schemes and other miscellaneous schemes, Scotland receiving its proportionate share of £183 million allocated by June 1931. Under the Coal Mines Act of 1930 fresh attempts were made to reorganise the industry, for earlier efforts to organise the production and sale of coal had completely broken down. In Scottish agriculture there were notable improvements, including assistance for agricultural drainage (£60,000 during 1931-32), arterial land drainage schemes, financing of agricultural research and education, and an Agricultural Credit scheme. Land Settlement was accelerated with expenditure of £607,000 in two years, and 43.5 thousand acres of land acquired by outright state purchase for land settlement. The fishing industry was assisted in various ways: exports to Russia were boosted after the restoration of relations with the Soviet government; finance of £250,000 was provided for harbours, piers, etc; and a sub-committee of the Economic Advisory Council on the problems of the fishing industry established.[5]

As regards social welfare, the Wheatley Act subsidy was restored and the new Housing Act of 1930 provided grants for slum clearances. The Act required local authorities to submit a statement of their housing needs and details of a three year programme to meet these. Statements received by July 1931 showed that Scotland needed 77,640 houses of which 52,792 were proposed under all the Housing Acts over a three year period. Up to that date, however, only 2,780 houses had been approved for erection under the 1930 Act. The government also passed a measure granting additional assistance for building new houses in rural areas, Scotland's share being 4,500. Limitations on the scale of Poor Law Relief were abolished, which resulted in a raising of allowances in Glasgow. Additionally, the system of offering the Poor House as a test for able-bodied men out of work for a long period was cancelled, with outdoor relief paid directly — or employment offered, if available. What was described as 'the largest dietetic experiment in history' was tried in Lanarkshire, where 10,000 children of 5-12 years were each provided with three quarters of a pint of milk daily for four months. The results showed (presumably to no one's surprise) that 'the addition of milk to the diet was reflected in a definite increase in the rate of growth, both of height and weight'. From our standpoint this might seem like a trivial experiment, but in the context of the times it was a notable success. Finally, improvements were made in medical services in the Highlands and Islands and in the extension of the Widows' Pension Scheme.[6]

With the benefit of hindsight much of this programme might seem like too little too late, yet given the constraints within which the second Labour government was forced to operate, the improvements added up to more than might have been expected. Whether the implementation of more radical policies — such as those advocated by the ILP, by Lloyd George, and by Sir Oswald Mosley in his famous 'Memorandum' would have dramatically improved Scotland's economic prospects in the early thirties is another question.

The Glasgow Shettleston by-election, along with those at Fulham West and Nottingham Central, was an early portent of reverses still to come in a persistent and strong anti-government swing throughout 1930-31. The vacancy was caused, of course, by the lamented death of John Wheatley, who had held the seat continuously since the great Clydeside victories of 1922. After consultation with the Scottish Executive Committee and the Shettleston Divisional Committee, the nomination fell to John McGovern, a prominent ILPer. On the recommendation of the SEC the NEC endorsed his candidature (despite the earlier decision to postpone endorsement of other ILPer nominations). The by-election itself, on 26 June, registered a nine per cent swing against the government and the result was a close one for McGovern due to the intervention of both a Scottish Nationalist, McNicol, and the veteran Communist, Saklatvala. Wheatley's majority of 6,274 in 1929 was cut to 396, but with McGovern's return to the House of Commons the ILP gained a staunch fighter in the Maxton mould. He soon showed his true colours, for the SEC afterwards complained that irregularities had occurred at the selection meeting and that McGovern was 'not a fit and proper person to represent Labour in Parliament' — a paradoxical judgement given the quality of many of the Scottish Labour MPs during the thirties.

Labour's unpopularity was subsequently registered at the East Renfrew by-election in a seat the party had come close to winning in 1929. Nor did the circumstances reflect well on the unity of the Left for there was no Labour candidate in the field, and Baillie Tom Irwin of the ILP was selected. But the NEC disqualified him and refused to endorse him, though the early issue of the writ meant that no other candidate could be found. The field was left clear for the ILP again, but the intervention of Oliver Brown, the Scottish

Nationalist, pushed the conservative majority to over 7,400, when previously it was only 1,500.

During 1931 there was further evidence from two Scottish industrial seats of the increasingly high swings against Labour. The veteran James Stewart's death caused the St Rollox contest, the Labour and Co-op candidate being Councillor W Leonard. The seat was held, but with a greatly reduced majority and an anti-government swing of 9.6 per cent — again partly a reflection of the Scottish Nationalist presence. A fortnight later on 21 May, Baillie David Hardie, Keir Hardie's half brother, only just managed to retain Rutherglen in a straight fight with the Conservatives. Hardie had been selected by the ILP and had received NEC endorsement only after signing a written undertaking 'that he was not committed and would not commit himself to conditions other than those of the Labour Party'. These four results could give little comfort to Scottish Labour,for the lessons of the by-elections were clear long before MacDonald defected to head the National Government.

The General Election of 1931 was an unmitigated disaster for Labour in Scotland, for despite gaining a third of the popular vote only seven candidates were elected, while National Government candidates almost swept the board with 64 MPs returned to Westminster. No fewer than 26 seats were lost to the Conservatives, 2 to the Liberals, and one each to National Liberal and National Labour. The Unionists thus found themselves holding 48 of the 74 Scottish seats — a dramatic advance on the 20 held in 1929, and almost a return to the situation that existed before 1918. Many key figures disappeared (temporarily in most cases) from the national scene, including in Glasgow, Rev. Campbell Stephen, John S. Clarke, George Hardie and Tom Henderson; Benn in Aberdeen, Tom Johnston in Stirling and Clackmannan; Brown in South Ayrshire; Willie Adamson in West Fife; Rev. James Barr in Motherwell; Shinwell in Linlithgow; L. MacNeill Weir in Clackmannan and East Stirling; and Jennie Lee in North Lanark, scene of the famous by-election victory in 1929.

Important though the personalities were, a geographical analysis of Scottish Labour's defeat has perhaps more relevance to our discussion of electoral politics in the thirties. In the constituencies where Labour fell, for example, some interesting conclusions emerge. Perhaps the most striking fact is how disastrous Labour's defeat was in its traditional strongholds with the loss of five seats in Glasgow, six in industrial Lanarkshire, as well as mining constituencies like South Ayrshire, West Fife, Linlithgow and Stirling. The complex party system and affiliations make analysis of swings somewhat tendentious (mainly because of the disposition of parties that made up the National Government), but if the overall polls of 1929 and 1931 are examined with this in mind, the anti-Labour swing in 1931 was 4.5 per cent if the Unionist and Liberal votes of 1929 are included. The swing from Labour to Tory, discounting the Liberal votes, was still 3.5 per cent: there were much higher anti-Labour swings in Springburn and in Stirling and Falkirk burghs, though in the latter case the intervention of a Protestant League candidate in 1929 probably exaggerated the result. Elsewhere, in those constituencies subsequently regained in 1935, the anti-Labour swing averaged around 2.5 per cent.[7]

Several minor parties had at least some influence on the bad results for Labour in Scotland. The Scottish National Party fielded five candidates and got 21,000 votes, just under one per cent of the poll. The party fought Edinburgh East (9.4 per cent); Inverness (14.9 per cent), where John MacCormick was candidate; Renfrew West (10.9 per cent); and Glasgow St Rollox (13.2 per cent), with two lost deposits and little initial success. On the left, the Communist Party did better, with 35,000 votes, or over 1.6 per cent of the poll. Eight candidates took the field, including Helen Crawford in Aberdeen North; in Gorbals, the ubiquitous Harry McShane; in Greenock, Aitken Ferguson, in West Fife, where Willie Gallacher's 6,829 votes helped defeat Adamson and return a Unionist advocate; McCourt in the staunch miners' district of Bothwell; and Stewart in Dundee, where the party got 10,264 in the two-seat contest.

Another interesting footnote to the debacle of 1931 was the presence of Mosley's New Party, then still advocating Keynesian-type solutions to economic reconstruction which we might be forced to admit with the benefit of hindsight, were far more imaginative than anything Labour had to offer. The party fought five seats in Coatbridge, Shettleston, Cathcart, West Renfrew and, in the agricultural south-west, Galloway, where the Liberal member, Dudgeon had defected to Mosley's group. But even Dr Robert Forgan, one of Mosley's leading supporters, who had been elected as Labour member for the West Renfrew seat in 1929, fared miserably with only four per cent of the poll. The Scottish Nationalist candidate, R.E. Muirhead, the Bridge of Weir tanner and a founder of the old National Party of Scotland, returned a far more impressive performance on that occasion.[8]

The overwhelming conclusion from the General Election of 1931 is that Labour was defeated not by its own failure or the failure of its policies — but by the unity of the opposition. 'By exploiting patriotic sentiments, by panic mongering, by calumny and misrepresentation', said an NEC report, 'the so-called "National" Government secured a further lease of power.' Labour took the view that the new government's protectionist policy, its humiliation of the unemployed, the curtailing of social services, its attitude to the Irish Free State and India, its lukewarm advocacy of disarmament, were proofs of the essentially Tory character of the government. 'Instead of dealing with the emergency which was its primary duty, it has attempted to fasten more or less permanently on the country, the policy of the Tory Party.'

Despite local difficulties caused by the ILP disaffiliation by 1932 there was a feeling of greater optimism and determination in the party, strengthened as it was in its conviction that

> only along the constructive lines of Socialist policy and action, can the economic, social and political problems of our time be solved: Our ideals must be clear, our aims must be understood, our plans must be definite.

A Labour government, equipped with adequate power, would turn its immediate attentions to the reorganisation of banking and finance as a public service, to the transference of the land to the nation, and to the development under public auspices of the power and transport services. 'It is imperative', delegates to the Annual Conference in 1932 were told, 'that the party work out its general programme of national economic and social planning, in order that the various parts may be seen in proper perspective, and so that the essential unity of the programme may be emphasised.'

That year there were already indications of Labour's electoral recovery in Scotland. At the Dunbartonshire contest on 17 March Labour achieved a swing of 9.6 per cent and the candidate, Tom Johnston, 'put up a splendid fight under difficult conditions.' But for the intervention of a Scottish Nationalist and a Communist he might well have secured victory; as it was, the Unionist majority was cut from over 12,000 at the General Election to 3,045. In some ways this was a personal disaster for Johnston, who might well have emerged as Labour leader. Another strong Labour poll was recorded at Montrose Burghs on 28 June when Tom Kennedy did even better, for the National Liberal majority was a mere 933. A Scottish Nationalist presence again harmed Labour's chances of victory.

The only contest of any interest in 1933 was East Fife, though with so many candidates standing the result was inevitably difficult to analyse. This was an old Liberal stronghold, so much so that the former MP, Sir J.Duncan Millar, had actually been returned unopposed in the 1931 election. Joseph Westwood, a former Under

Secretary at the Scottish Office, increased the Labour vote — and this with little local organisation and faced with a whole coterie of opponents, notably Eric Linklater for the Scottish Nationalists, and J.L. Anderson of the Agricultural Party (an off-shoot of Beaverbrook's Empire Crusade), who came third.

Although there was no real test of opinion in 1934, there were no fewer than five by-elections the following year. Labour had little hope of capturing any of the seats, but nevertheless polls indicated some recovery. Yet in both Aberdeen South and Edinburgh West, Labour's vote was well below the level achieved in 1929 — a situation which caused concern to party officials like Arthur Woodburn, Secretary of the Labour Party in Scotland. The result at Dumfries in September was more encouraging, for Downie, the Labour and Co-op candidate, got over 10,500 votes and 40 per cent of the poll.

Scottish Labour went on to achieve considerable success at the General Election of 1935, though it hardly restored the party to its strength of 1929. In Scotland Labour got nearly 864,000 votes or 36.8 per cent of the poll, although the joint votes of Labour, the ILP and the Communists in Scotland represented 42.4 per cent of the poll, compared with a total anti-Government share in the UK as a whole of 38.7 per cent. This gave Scottish Labour 20 seats in the new parliament — with four ILPers and the Communist, Gallacher, bringing the Left's total to 25 members. Urban seats recaptured included Aberdeen North, Dunfermline Burghs, Edinburgh East, three in Glasgow, Kirkcaldy, Stirling and Falkirk Burghs, and in the counties, South Ayrshire, two in Lanarkshire, Linlithgow (Shinwell's old seat), and the two Stirling and Clackmannan seats. Moreover, Labour made a significant gain from the Liberals in the Western Isles, a seat the party had not fought in 1931, where Malcolm Macmillan was returned for the first time. Those returned elsewhere included Pethwick-Lawrence (Edinburgh East), Henderson (Glasgow, Tradeston), Hardie (Springburn), Kennedy (Kirkcaldy), Westwood (Stirling and Falkirk), Brown (South Ayr), Rev J Barr (Coatbridge), MacNeill Weir (Clackmannan and East Stirling).[9]

The ILP fielded eleven candidates, got five per cent of the poll and were triumphant in their Glasgow strongholds of Bridgeton, Camlachie, Gorbals, and Shettleston, securing the return of Maxton, Campbell Stephen, Buchanan, and McGovern. The only other real challenge was in North Lanark, where the ILP had a dynamic candidate in Jennie Lee, who had held the seat from 1929 to 1931. She attracted 17,267 votes to Gilbert McAllister's 6,763 and the

Unionists' 22,301 — so senseless vote-splitting cost the Left victory on that occasion.

Elsewhere there were few surprises, saving perhaps Willie Gallacher's personal triumph for the Communist Party in West Fife, though even this could have been predicted given the long Left-wing tradition in this mining district — and the apparent unpopularity of the ageing Adamson. Gallacher had previously fought the seat in 1929 and 1931 and in this instance polled remarkably well, with 37 per cent of the total and 13,642 votes.

Between the General Election of 1935 and the outbreak of war, by-election results in Scotland registered some revival for Labour with the capture of Dunbarton and Greenock the best tests of anti-government feeling. In February 1936 there were two disgraceful sops to MacDonaldism on the part of the Baldwin administration with the return of the ageing 'Ramsay Mac' for the Scottish Universities, (Professor A Dewar Gibb, the Scottish Nationalist, came second on that occasion), and of Malcolm Macdonald for Ross and Cromarty (as 'National' Labour), a peerage having been rather conveniently arranged for the sitting National Liberal, Sir J Ian Macpherson. But the following month brought a notable Labour gain at Dunbarton, where Tom Cassells upset a Tory majority of 4,000, being elected by 984 votes over Major Duffes, his opponent. The Greenock by-election of 26 November saw the return of Robert Gibson, a Fabian and advocate (later Lord Gibson, Chairman of the Scottish Land Courts), who in a straight fight with the National Liberal secured 53 per cent of the poll and a majority of 2,604.

In the two by-elections of 1937 there was no change. Labour could be expected to make little headway in a seat like Glasgow, Hillhead, where Gilbert McAllister was candidate, and the by-election saw the return of a Unionist as expected with a large majority. The Scottish Nationalist flag on that occasion was again carried by 'King' John MacCormick, but he put up a less than favourable performance. At Springburn on 7 September, on a low turnout, George Hardie's widow easily retained the seat for Labour with a majority of nearly 6,000. The only contest of any note the following year must have been tinged with bitterness for some of the old Labour guard in Scotland, for it followed the death of Ramsay MacDonald, and saw his replacement as a member for the Universities by a staunch supporter of the National Government, Sir John Anderson.

Municipal and county elections might well occupy a full chapter but sadly there is only space here for a cursory mention of Labour's achievement during the thirties. Despite Labour's great success at Parliamentary elections in Glasgow, the big breakthrough in municipal politics in the city was delayed until 1933. At the November elections the party registered a net gain of 15 seats and the previous Moderate majority of 21 was converted to a Socialist majority of nine. In the next two years their majority was increased to 28, and although this fluctuated during the rest of the thirties, Labour remained firmly in control.[10] Indeed such was Labour's success in local government elections elsewhere that by 1936 the party controlled no fewer than 19 burgh councils in Scotland, including Glasgow, Clydebank, Falkirk, Greenock, Hamilton, Motherwell and Wishaw, Port Glasgow, Cumnock and Cowdenbeath with the same number of seats as the opposition in Airdrie, Bo'ness, Dundee and Rutherglen.

Housing was one of the major issues for Labour-controlled authorities during the thirties: Patrick Dollan maintained of Glasgow in 1936 that it was not just one of the city's problems, 'It is our *chief* problem.' 'But,' he continued, 'the solution is complicated by this curse of politics'.[11] Yet Labour achieved what it could in slum clearance (much of it by direct labour after 1936), and managed to build nearly 20,000 house in Glasgow between 1934 and the outbreak of war.[12]

Apart from a new professionalism there were few dramatic developments in Scottish Party organisation during the thirties. In 1936 the SEC was made up of seven trade union representatives, four from Trades Councils and Divisional Labour Parties, four from the Women's Sections, two from the Scottish Socialist Party (a Scottish counterpart of the Socialist League), and one each from the Scottish Fabian Society and the Social-Democratic Federation. There were two District Organisers to take care of day-to-day business and act as propagandists, in the old ILP tradition. Inevitably finance was always a problem, both at national and local level: an important decision for Scottish Labour was the establishment in January 1933 of a central By-election Insurance fund, whereby needy constituencies faced with by-elections could be subsidised up to £375.[13]

As might be expected, membership was concentrated in areas of traditional Labour support, making a total in 1930 of over 9,200. This, of course, discounts the large trade union membership, which is almost impossible to quantify given the complex overlap between Scottish and UK representation. Certainly, after the election defeat of 1931 there was a big individual membership drive with successful Mass Conferences held that autumn in Glasgow, Edinburgh, Dundee and Hamilton. The Seventeenth Annual Conference of the Labour Party held in Glasgow in May 1932, while discussing important national issues like the Means Test and Scottish housing, devoted most of its time to party administration, membership, procedures for the selection of Parliamentary Candidates, and party literature — so there was acute awareness everywhere of the need to improve party organisation. Further propaganda work was undertaken as part of the 'Call to Action' campaign of 1932-33, with an educational conference in Aberdeen, where the subjects covered were the socialisation of industry, the economic situation, banking, finance and agriculture. This was followed by organisation conferences for local Labour Parties, Ward Committees and branches of the League of Youth which provided training in electoral machinery, the development of individual membership, the conduct of propaganda and educational work. Individual membership in the UK as a whole rose by forty per cent before 1939, though in Scotland it was perhaps less than a third.

But in this as in much else it seems that relations with the British Labour Party, then increasingly dominated by a new 'intellectual' wave, were superficially amicable though often uneasy. The Scots were essentially men and women of the Left, some as uncompromising in their rejection of gradualism as they had been in the heady days of Red Clydeside. There can be no denying that the great controversies generated over the ILP's relationship with the Labour Party and the ultimate disaffiliation in July 1932 had a dramatic and detrimental effect both on relations with the British Labour Party and on some aspects of local organisation in Scotland. Certainly some felt that the NEC's interference in Scottish party affairs, and especially the selection of candidates, was a violation of local rights. Others on the Scottish Left saw the humiliation of 1931 as a vindication of their belief that the crisis of capitalism was at hand, yet it seems to have been left to the Communists to organise the unemployed. In some places official Labour and trade union leadership apparently failed to take a bold lead though the Vale of Leven and Fife were obvious exceptions.[14]

While much more space than is available here would be needed to chart the course of the final rift with the ILP, we ought to look briefly at its impact on Scottish Labour. The origins of the disaffiliation lay, as is well known, in the ILP's swing to the left and its increasing rejection of gradualism — specifically the performance of the second Labour government on the issue of unemployment. What started out as spirited opposition to government policy degenerated through an impassioned argument about PLP Standing Orders to become a major disagreement about policies and leadership that split the ILP from top to bottom and sent it on the road to ultimate destruction.

It is interesting to note that one of the first resolutions calling for actual disaffiliation was outvoted at the Annual Conference of the Scottish Division of the ILP in January 1931, with Dollan the strongest supporter of staying in the Labour Party — and Maxton and other leading dissidents by no means entirely committed to disaffiliation.

The events of the summer, the resignation of the Labour government, and MacDonald's emergence as leader of the National government — confirmed with an overwhelming majority in the October General Election — served to delay matters further. But in November the issue was aired again at another Scottish ILP conference. Although the ILPers in parliament — by then whittled down to five — had begun acting as a separate group from the beginning of the session, their leader, Maxton, was still speaking against 'immediate' disaffiliation. His attitude, and that of Brockway and the other (largely London-based) disaffiliationists toward the Labour Party seems somewhat perverse given the speed with which events had moved since the demise of the Labour government. Certainly there were major disagreements over policy between the Labour Party and the left-ward biased ILP, for at a Special Conference at Bradford in July 1932 the disaffiliationists won the day and the ILP left the Labour Party. The impact was immediate and dramatic: between July and November the ILP lost 203 out of 653 branches, 128 in Scotland alone. There were also major defections in municipal politics. For example 40 out of 44 ILP councillors in Glasgow left the party — a disaster in one of its last remaining strongholds.

Dollan, who had supported unconditional affiliation on the grounds that outside the Labour Party the ILP would rapidly dwindle into a sectarian minority, was instrumental in persuading some breakaway Scottish branches to form themselves into the Scottish Socialist Party. Like the Crippsian Socialist League this affiliated to the Labour Party — but it had a short and unhappy history. Relations with the Scottish ILP were bad from the start, and were apparently more dominated by petty squabbles about branch premises and funds, rather than concerned with the great campaigns of the day, like the Popular Front or the Unity Campaign with the Communists.

More and more ILP supporters ultimately returned to the Labour Party fold, leaving Maxton and his associates, like McGovern, increasingly isolated. No doubt this helped strengthen Labour Party membership and local branches in difficult times, but the whole sorry episode did little for the unity of the Scottish Left at a point when relationships between all Socialist parties and movements needed to be stronger than ever before.[15]

Although Scottish Labour was thin on personalities in the thirties, a handful of giants — mostly of the old guard — stamped their mark on the party. The legacy of one, John Wheatley (b. 1869), who died in May 1930, lived on both in the minds of his contemporaries and practically in the revived subsidies of the Housing Act. According to Johnston, writing much later, Wheatley had drifted away from most of his old government colleagues after the General Election of 1924, and as a result lost much influence in the party. He had become more and more identified with the revolutionary socialist views of the Maxtonites, and although highly critical of the second Labour government his activities were much impaired by indifferent health. But this could hardly detract from his achievements in propaganda, journalism, local and national politics in a lifetime devoted to practical socialism.[16]

Another of the pioneers was William Adamson (1863-1936) who started out life as a miner and subsequently became General Secretary of Fife, Kinross and Clackmannan Miners Association. He first contested West Fife in 1910, a seat he held until the election debacle of 1931. Chairman of the Parliamentary Labour Party 1917, he became Secretary of State for Scotland under MacDonald, January-November 1924 and again during 1929-31. Defeated in the General Election of 1931 he returned to the fray in 1935 only to be beaten by Willie Gallacher — sadly, perhaps Adamson's greatest claim to fame.[17]

A third Labour minister, Tom Johnston (1881-1965) had a more notable career as a politician and journalist. He was founder and for 27 years editor of *Forward*, the great Labour weekly, and at the time one of the few newspapers that could be relied upon to report the activities of the Left without bias. At first he had been active in local government in his native Kirkintilloch, initiating many municipal schemes. He entered Parliament as the member for West Stirlingshire 1922-24, contested the Dundee by-election 1924, holding the seat till 1929, returning to West Stirling 1929-31 and again 1935-45. He was Parliamentary Under Secretary for Scotland 1929-31, Lord Privy Seal (again 1931), and ultimately Secretary of State for Scotland under Churchill, 1941-45. His numerous publications included *Our Noble Families*, an indictment of the Scottish landed gentry, and the pioneering *History of the Working Classes in Scotand*. His later public life included spells as Chairman of the North of Scotland Hydro Electric Board, and of the Scottish Tourist Board.

One of the newer men with a reputation to make was Arthur Woodburn (1890-1978), who in earlier life had a technical and financial background in the engineering trade. He was associated with the Labour College from 1919, though his first venture in Parliamentary politics came only in 1929, when he contested South Edinburgh — followed by Leith in 1931. Woodburn was Scottish Secretary of the Labour Party from 1932 to 1939, when he entered the Commons as MP for Clackmannan and East Stirling, a seat he held until 1970. During the war he was Parliamentary Private Secretary to Tom Johnston, Parliamentary Secretary at the Ministry of Supply 1945-47, and himself Secretary of State for Scotland 1947-50.

But the outstanding personality of the period was the redoubtable James Maxton (1885-1946) leader of the ILP from 1926-31, again during 1934-39, and the major deviationist of the Scottish Left. Maxton's activities in the thirties would require a separate chapter, so what follows is much compressed. He and his fellows were highly critical of the second Labour government, which in his opinion was not leading the country to Socialism and therefore had no right to claim his 'continuing and abiding loyalty'. His stand on Bondfield's Anomalies Bill, which was designed to disqualify casual workers and married women from receiving unemployment benefit, brought a storm of protest both from the Labour Party and from over a hundred ILP MPs. Ultimately it led to ILP disaffiliation in 1932 and, as we have seen, created many problems for Scottish Labour long after the dust had settled. Gradualism became more and more of an anathema to Maxton, and he and his ILP colleagues kept up a well orchestrated campaign against the National Government's socio-economic policies, especially the Means Test. He actively supported the Hunger Marchers and was instrumental in getting the Commons to debate unemployment in 1934. Significantly when the marchers presented themselves at Downing Street, MacDonald refused to see them. Maxton's later interests reflected the growing international tension over the Italian invasion of Abyssinia in 1935, the outbreak of the Spanish Civil War in 1936, and the Munich crisis in 1938. On these as on other issues there was no questioning his integrity — a quality others clearly lacked in those challenging and difficult days.[18]

The worsening international scene is perhaps best considered in the wider context of British Labour Party history, but on the domestic front unemployment remained the dominant issue. At the Edinburgh Conference of October 1936 the party appointed a Distressed Areas Commission, consisting of Hugh Dalton MP,

George Dallas, Mrs B Ayrton Gould, with G Grant Mckenzie as secretary; while for the Scottish investigation they were joined by Duncan Graham MP and James Walker MP. A preliminary conference was held in Glasgow in December 1936 and valuable written evidence received afterwards, followed by a tour of investigation in February 1937. It found over 20 per cent (or 67,735) of insured workers in the Scottish Special Areas unemployed — twice as high as the 10.9 per cent for England as a whole. In March that year Ernest Brown, Minister of Labour, admitted that 9 of 42 Special Area districts in Scotland had over 30 per cent unemployment during January-December 1936, 13 had 20-30 per cent, and only 20 less than 20 per cent. Glasgow, outside the Special Area, had nearly a fifth of insured workers on the dole. Against this grim background the Commission suggested some sensible and far-reaching proposals, some of which later found favour in the post-war years. Scotland should be seen as a single planning unit, and Glasgow, parts of Stirlingshire and West Lothian included in the Special Areas, with a Minister of Cabinet rank given wide powers and substantial funds to plan Scotland's reconstruction. An improved communications infrastructure was called for, including bridges over the Forth and Tay, and electrification of the railways. New industries would be established on trading estates, but at the same time small businesses encouraged. Tourism — or what was then described as 'holiday traffic' ought to be developed on a planned basis. Land settlement should be further encouraged, while assisted transfer (especially of young people) to the Midlands and elsewhere south of the Border should cease. Finally, local authority social services should be overhauled to cope with new conditions and provide a modern service to those in need. The conclusion that emerged was prophetic and might well have been re-read to advantage by post-war Labour governments:

> If the Distressed Areas problem had been tackled with the same energy and on the same scale as rearmament, unemployment in Central Scotland would not be twice as high as in England. . .(The) foundations of Scottish industry will continue to decay unless drastic action is taken by the State to deal with fundamentals.[19]

Discussion of Labour politics in the 1930s until recently has been dominated by the failure of the second Labour government, MacDonald's defection in the 1931 crisis, and by the overwhelming defeat which followed at the polls in the General Election that year. In all of this Scotland was a microcosm of the UK experience, but enough has been said here (and elsewhere) about the by-elections during 1929-1931 to convince us that Labour's defeat was apparently inevitable sooner than later. Yet we must recognise that defeat did not follow from lack of policies designed to improve matters. On the contrary there were plenty useful policies that might have helped Scotland, though Labour was either in no position to implement them or had to water down those which were acceptable to the Opposition parties. The defeat of 1931 was at first sight devastating, yet Labour ultimately recovered in Scotland — as elsewhere — thanks largely to a new dynamism in party organisation nationally and locally. Certainly as the clouds of war cleared before 1945 Scottish Labour emerged with a more precise programme of measures designed to put its socialist beliefs into practice and at least get to grips with the problems Scotland had faced in the dark days of the Depression.

5

The Recovery of Scottish Labour, 1939–51

CHRISTOPHER HARVIE

As the 1930s drew to a close, Scottish Labour's fortunes were mixed. The prospect of a general election in 1940 was not regarded with much enthusiasm.[1] The 1935 election results, plus a couple of by-election successes and the readmission of one of the ILP MPs still gave the party only 25 out of 74 seats, well short of its 1929 level of 37. Its municipal advance had been held in check since 1936; individual membership was stuck at under 30,000 and trade union affiliates, around 150,000, were less than half the numbers in the member unions of the STUC. It was difficult to foresee the party's situation a decade later. In 1951 Labour polled its highest-ever Scottish vote, over 1.12 million (47.9 per cent) compared with 874,000 (36.8 per cent in 1935). It claimed 60,000 individual members which (even making allowance for those parties 'on the minimum' of a hypothetical 240 members) was an increase of over 50 per cent on 1939, and with the restoration of 'contracting-in' in 1947 its union affiliates grew by more than 200 per cent to over 470,000. In 1951 it held on to 35 Scottish seats and monopolised the left in the North, having defeated the last Communist and readmitted the last ILP MPs. It had also defeated the 'consensus nationalism' of the Scottish Covenant movement because of its successful advocacy of administrative devolution. Successive Labour Secretaries of State urged that this policy gained Scotland not only special treatment in the cabinet, but a role in deciding the greater destinies of Britain and her commonwealth.[2]

In October 1951 the winning streak ran out. Labour had lost power — in Glasgow as well as in Westminster. This setback did not inspire recovery and the party slid further in 1955, when the Unionist camp actually secured a majority of Scottish votes as well as seats. Even at the zenith, between 1945 and 1947, there were auguries of decline. Two of the great men of Scottish socialism,

Jimmie Maxton and William Elger of the STUC, died; Tom Johnston moved out of politics. The socialist groups which had once bloomed in *Forward*'s columns — the Scottish Socialist Art Circle, Bailie Kerr and his Socialist Choristers — were withering to a rather depressing core of Women's Sections and a fissile Labour League of Youth. Victory did little to improve the quality of Scottish MPs. In 1946 John Taylor, Secretary to the Scottish Council (SCLP), had discovered fourteen presentable MPs, only three of whom came from Glasgow. Throughout this period the 'Second City' — once the forward position of the parliamentary Left — remained an organisational quagmire. In February 1948 Labour lost Camlachie, held since 1935 by Campbell Stephen. William Marshall (who was to succeed Taylor in 1951) reported to the NEC's Elections Sub-Committee that, at most, only 54 workers had helped in the campaign, and only 30 had turned up on polling day.

Such problems were aggravated by the national leadership's apparent distaste for matters Scottish. In the 1920s Scots MPs had played leading parts in the Parliamentary Labour Party (PLP) and there were always at least two or three on its executive. The catastrophe of 1931-2 weakened this, though Anglo-Scots such as George Dallas, Mrs Jenny Adamson and Emanuel Shinwell were still important on the NEC. Among party officials William Gillies, Secretary to the International Committee, was Scottish, and J S Middleton, the party secretary, had strong Scots connections. After 1945, when they departed, Scotland tended to be pushed to the sidelines. According to Arthur Woodburn, Scottish Secretary, 1932-39 and Secretary of State, 1947-50, Clement Attlee knew much less about Scotland than Winston Churchill who had been MP for Dundee from 1910 to 1922.[3] This did not prevent Attlee tartly criticising Scottish Labour's performance, at its celebratory conference in 1945:

> Scotland had not made anything like the progress in gaining seats as had London and certain parts of England. . . In that great increase in the numbers of the Labour Party in the House of Commons from 191 to 394 — an increase of 203 — Scotland has contributed the odd three. It is surely up to you to find out the reason.[4]

The NEC was similarly sceptical about requests for more attention to Scottish policy, devolution in particular, while Attlee's dismissal of two of his Secretaries of State, Joseph Westwood and Woodburn, showed him at his most brusque and ruthless. His answer to Westwood's 'Why?' became legendary: 'Cos you don't measure up to the job. That's why. Thanks for coming. Secretary will show you out.'[5]

What were the reasons for this predicament — which endured until the 1970s? The problem is that modern political history has tended either to generalise about 'British' class structure and political homogeneity, or it has accepted political movements like nationalism, on their own, sometimes highly imaginative terms. And Scottish Labour, only intermittently distinctive in nationalist terms, showed organisational and policy-making behaviour rather remote from the 'British homogeneity' norms of Butler, McKenzie and Blondel. This did not express itself as the enthusiasm of left-wing legend; Scottish Labour was distinctive in being weak. In the 1940s it caught up with the south, but inadequate organisation, sub-standard MPs and misgivings over policy remained. If Robert McKenzie saw the British parties in 1955 essentially as supporters' clubs, whose 'primary function' is 'to sustain competing teams of potential leaders in the House of Commons in order that the electorate as a whole may choose between them'[6] then, in several important ways the Scottish Labour story does not conform.

The experience of the depression was fundamental to Labour's 1945 victory. But it was in the prosperous south rather than in the stricken north that this was transformed into political action. London and its surroundings, which bounced back from 1929-32 slump most energetically, also showed the strongest growth in party membership. In Scotland, with higher and more prolonged unemployment, membership went down and stayed down, although under the wise guidance of Wlliam Elger, the STUC actually held its membership better than the British TUC, and was gaining recognition in the various cross-party and quasi-official planning groups which the National government and its Scottish commissioner encouraged.

By comparison, the SCLP was neither prestigious nor influential. Its privilege of having its minutes tabled at meetings of the NEC (although they were rarely, if ever, discussed) ended in 1942, when the party's other Regional Councils were set up. These, according to Robert McKenzie, played 'an insignificant part in the life of the party'.[7] Transport House paid for Labour's Scottish operations, including the salaries of the Secretary, Scottish organiser and women's organiser. It made grants for by-elections and particular organisational problems; in all, in the war period Scotland met less than 10 per cent of its costs.

The SCLP was little more than, in Taylor's words, 'a piece of internal machinery providing the movement with advice on

Scottish affairs, and the movement in Scotland with a coordinating authority to review, advise and cooperate (sic) the membership and organisation'. At most it could express Scottish opinion and try to deal with troublesome situations before they got the length of London. Scottish membership was, by constituency, the lowest of any British region. The average English constituency party had 754 members, its Scottish counterpart 410.

The constituency situation was chaotic anyway — constituency Labour Parties as membership organisations being a new and somewhat nominal phenomenon. William Ross, for example, only joined the Labour party when adopted as PPC for Ayr Burgh in 1936. This vagueness led to continual conflicts in most of the bigger towns, where the Trades councils were still directly connected with the party. The bitter fighting with the ILP which had marked the 1935 election had been open; now, with the Communists preaching the Popular Front, Labour feared permeation through the Trades Councils. Accordingly in 1938 it reached agreement with the STUC to reform their operation: 'Trades and Labour Councils cease to meet as combined bodies. . . . instead Trades Councils and Labour Parties (or Industrial and Political Sections) function separately, each being completely and finally responsible for its own business.'

This left problems in Dundee (whose two-member constituency provided the largest Labour Party in Scotland, and a hotbed of left extremism) and Glasgow. In Dundee a combination of Communist pressure, extended through the Linen Workers' Union, and the need for 'good men with cash' (the party having been in debt since 1929) secured the selection of the Indian left-winger Krishna Menon in June 1939.[8] The NEC disqualified him in May 1940 for sharing platforms with proscribed speakers. In Glasgow things were far worse, and organisational breakdown seemed complete. Even in 1939 only 3 out of 15 parties were above the minimum, and by 1941, with the expulsion of Pollok and membership decline, only one. The NEC had to disaffiliate the Glasgow Burgh Labour Party in December. A memo by Taylor was scathing: only seven CLPs could be said to function; a further five had spasms of activity; in three there was no organisation at all: 'There is an absence of Party spirit and team work in most of the CLPs and the general attitude of querulous criticism of every party action is encouraged by the lead given by the Burgh party which invariably plays to its gallery of disgruntled individuals with a grudge against life. People of balanced mind and outlook have thus been frozen out or have left in disgust.'[9] Taylor attributed the problem to the majority on the corporation of ex-members of the 'pacifist' SSP, and morale lowered by recent corruption cases. Undoubtedly Glasgow was particularly hard hit by the ILP split and its aftermath, but even Edinburgh had four out of its six parties 'on the minimum' and probably fewer members than Aberdeen, a northern bastion of Socialism since the 1890s, with 1,700 members in its two parties in 1939.

Were such deficiencies in party organisation made good by MPs? When Arthur Woodburn announced his intention of standing for the Commons in August 1939, Labour's National Agent, C.G. Shephard, tried to deter him: 'In all probability the House will meet infrequently if war breaks out, and you may find yourself an MP without scope or responsibility.'[10] In fact, daily sessions fell only from 155 to 120 per annum, but the contribution of Scottish Labour MPs was scarcely impressive — about 3.8 per cent of interventions in a House one-half thinned by departures for government service and the forces. Only one MP became a minister before Johnston's move to the Scottish Office in February 1941, and he was the London-based carpet-bagger, George Garro-Jones (Aberdeen North). Attlee thought the senior Scottish MP, Frederick Pethick-Lawrence 'too old' for a post; he became titular leader of the opposition between November 1941 and February 1942. Johnston had withdrawn from the front bench in May 1939 to become Scottish regional commissioner for civil defence. A year later he wrote to the NEC enquiring whether or not he should retain his seat; its affirmative answer was to have important consequences.

Such political and administrative problems complicated Labour's first reactions to the war. The Nazi-Soviet Pact drew the teeth of earlier Crippsite and Popular Front pressure on the party; Woodburn was able to tell the SCLP executive in December 1939: 'In the Trades and Labour Councils of Edinburgh, Glasgow, Aberdeen and Dundee there was a consistent tendency to follow blindly the changes of Russian policy. Generally speaking, however, this opinion had considerably declined in the movement itself.'

Residual pacifism was still strong. In December 17 Labour MPs appealed for a negotiated peace; 9 of them were Scots. Most were identified with the Scottish Peace Congress, founded in 1938 as an impeccable expression of Liberal high-mindedness, quite separate from popular front activity (the Communists then being anti-fascist). After the outbreak of war, however, they started to manipulate it; in December 1939 its secretary, a Labour Party member, resigned, and in October 1940 it was banned by the NEC. More embarrassing were by-elections. At Clackmannan, on 13 October 1939, Arthur Woodburn, a pacifist in World War

I, was opposed by an independent socialist and pacifist Andrew
Stewart, with the support of the ILP, some Labour members,
including MPs, and Emrys Hughes, the editor of *Forward*. In
April 1940 the party at Glasgow Pollok defied the electoral truce
and put up a candidate against the Unionists; for its action, it
was disaffiliated. *Forward*'s attitude to both elections rankled with
the Labour organisation. Woodburn, hitherto a regular columnist,
accused it of 'steadily becoming a definitely anti-Labour paper'. The
new monthly *Edinburgh Clarion* (founded November 1939) was also
pacifist in outlook. Yet Labour could turn nowhere else: not a single
Scottish daily was remotely sympathetic.

The Unionists partly disbanded their organisation on the
announcement of the electoral truce, but Labour observed only
the electoral truce and kept its organisation in being.[11] Its Scottish
establishment amounted to three officials, and about the same
number of full-time agents in the more prosperous constituency
parties, against about fifty Unionist agents. (Even in 1946 Labour
had only six agents in Scotland, compared with 24 in London).
Moreover, it was very accident-prone. After Woodburn's departure
the NEC appointed John Taylor, previously in East Anglia; in 1941,
when the women's organiser, Agnes Lauder, died, it forced the
SCLP (which preferred a younger woman), to accept Mary Auld
(sic). In 1943, after forcibly reforming the Glasgow Labour Party,
it appointed Ian Dean as secretary with a grant. But in August of
that year Taylor fell seriously ill, and in September Dean died.
J.T. Anson, agent at Consett, was appointed Acting Scottish
secretary, but until Taylor returned in October 1944, he was
short-staffed. Members and collectors left for the forces, and there
were no annual municipal elections, which had always drawn in the
faithful. This decline seems to have hit Scotland more acutely than
the rest of Britain. As Taylor told the NEC in January 1942, it was as
much as the party could do to keep its general organisation in being.

This situation made Tom Johnston's move to the Scottish Office,
on 8 February 1941, crucial. Ironically, it seems to have stemmed
from the failure of Attlee and Greenwood to make much of their
overall responsibility for home policy. The unions were pressing for
a reform of health insurance, and Churchill wanted Johnston to take
over health. On a trip north in January 1941 he was very impressed
by Johnston's work for civil defence,[12] and decided that Ernest
Brown should move to health and Johnston take over the Scottish
Office. In his *Memories* Johnston wrote that he confronted Churchill
with a slate of demands, on which his acceptance depended: 'I would
be given a chance to inaugurate some large-scale reforms under the

umbrella of a Council of State, and which reforms, if we emerged intact at the end of the war, might mean Scotia resurgent.'[13]

Johnston was a good journalist, and may have exaggerated the extent of his initiative. But, according to Paul Addison, Churchill, as Lloyd George's successor in Munitions in World War I, remembered the Clyde troubles, and was sensitive to anti-war feelings in the industrial areas which the Communists were trying to exploit. The man who had written the foreword to Davie Kirkwood's *My Life of Revolt* (1934), and who held an annual party for Maxton and his associates at Downing Street throughout the war, realised the importance of getting the Scots left on his side.[14] At any rate, Labour would be kept happy with another cabinet post, and Scotland (like domestic policy in general) would be kept out of the way.

Johnston's 'Council of State' consisted of all living ex-Secretaries. Inaugurated on 29 September 1941, it met, usually alternately in Edinburgh and London, sixteen times between then and January 1945. The remit of the Council was initially to deal with post-war problems (thus contradicting Johnston's claim that he would be able to 'inaugurate large-scale reforms'), but at its third meeting, on 8 December 1941, Walter Elliot raised as a matter of urgency the consequences of wartime industrial 'concentration' for Scotland, with the closure of industries and the narrowing of the country's industrial base. As a result Johnston set up, at a public meeting on 2 February 1942, the Scottish Council on Industry, in which the Scottish National Development Council, the Convention of Royal Burghs and the STUC acted together to attract wartime industry to Scotland. By the end of 1942 the amount of Scottish factory space used for manufacture (as opposed to storage) had risen from 9 per cent in 1941 to 42.6 per cent. By 1943 action had been agreed on a comprehensive scheme of Highland hydro-electric power, an issue which, before the war, had proved insoluble. Some 32 sub-committees had been set up into post-war problems as varied as hill-sheep farming and the teaching of citizenship in schools; planning powers in Scotland had been devolved to the Secretary of State, and the Emergency Medical Service hospitals were being used as the basis of an important extension of social welfare.

When he set up the Council of State, ILP MPs warned that Johnston would become the prisoner of his Liberal and Unionist predecessors. The Council's appointments to its various sub-committees certainly reflected the fairly conservative structure of Scottish pre-war politics, but the tendency of Scottish government reflected a collectivist tide, and as the Council effectively lapsed in 1944, Johnston was virtually on stage alone to take the plaudits.

Not surprisingly, the Labour Party chose him to make its second broadcast, on 8 June, in the 1945 election campaign. Yet in asserting his muscle in government negotiations, Johnston plainly derived little of it from Labour's position in Scotland. As Herbert Morrison later recorded: 'He would impress on the Committee that there was a strong nationalist movement in Scotland and it could be a potential danger if it grew through lack of attention to Scottish interests.'[15]

Was this 'nationalist threat' fact or myth? Certainly, throughout the war, SNP candidates and others with home rule on their programme polled respectably, and ultimately gained two seats, Motherwell and the Scottish Universities, in the closing weeks of the war. Moreover, there was a steady undercurrent of discontent at the way the war was affecting Scotland, not at all confined to political nationalism, as a supply debate on Scottish industry in May 1942 disclosed, with a Unionist MP commending Johnston for 'putting the interests of Scotland first.'

Labour's support for home rule peaked quite early. In 1939 it had the backing of over half the Scottish Labour MPs, while members of the London Scots' Self-Government Committee moved north, and formed the Labour Scottish Self-Government Campaign. This group was represented on the Executive by A B MacKay, the secretary of the Scottish Banker's Association, and in 1939 it instructed him to prepare a 'Scottish economic survey'. This may have been a counter-measure to the 'cross-party' Scottish Convention arranged by John MacCormick and the SNP for 27 September, which despite the support of the Rev James Barr MP, aroused Labour hostility, particularly in Glasgow. In response to a motion passed at the 1940 Scottish conference in September and without consulting the NEC, MacKay's inquiry became a Committee on Post-War Policy in Scotland. Presumably stimulated by the activities of Johnston's Council of State, this anticipated by over six months the NEC's creation of thirteen sub-committees on post-war affairs. The *Plan for Post-War Scotland*, published in August 1941, was quite different from Dalton's scheme if 1937, and from Labour's subsequent policies. Scotland was to be self-governing, initially under a parliament of Scottish (Westminster) MPs meeting in Edinburgh. Although heavy industries were to be state-controlled by a Ministry of Production and Industry in London, utilities such as electricity, gas, water and the fire services were to be controlled by regional boards. The Scottish parliament would be directly responsible for housing and education.

The *Plan* was Scottish Labour's first and only attempt at independent policy-making, for which it was censured by the

NEC. Unfortunately, as socialist devolutionists recognised, it was also riddled with contradictions. How was the Secretary of State to govern if a majority of Scottish MPs were not of his party? Where were the demarcation lines of industrial control to be drawn between Scotland and Whitehall? To whom were the regional utility boards to be responsible, given the omission of local government reform from the measures contemplated? Such inadequacies made it fairly easy for the NEC to censure the SCLP — 'such an initiative should not have been undertaken without the knowledge of the NEC' — and absolve itself at its most centralist, from the need to take Scottish self-government seriously. Apart from the isolated and unpopular Shinwell, who had travelled far from his early home rule beliefs, there was no Scot on the Central Reconstruction Sub-Committee. Although the SCLP upheld the *Plan* at a special conference on 6 December, and a toned-down version was adopted by the Scottish Reconstruction Sub-Committee in February 1942, Shinwell still managed to keep it away from the party's formal policy. The 1942 conference was told that the *Plan* 'has not been able to make the progress it had hoped to make'. Shortly afterwards — possibly because of this — MacKay resigned, and the plan drifted into a limbo in which it was shortly to be joined by Shinwell's committee.

There are various other reasons for the decline in Labour's support for home rule. The absence of constituency activity meant that pressure could not be sustained while Johnston's 'government by consultation' policies seemed possibly a more secure option to a party which still had only a minority of Scottish seats. The complex business of achieving home rule seemed less attractive when compared with the 'reconstruction' potential of the machinery of war-time government. This may have underlain the Labour Scots' Self-Government Campaign's transformation into the Scottish Reconstruction Committee in 1943. Further, several leading Labour home-rulers were not the easiest of comrades to work with, and its leading Parliamentary advocate, John Davidson, MP for Maryhill and former chairman of Glasgow Burgh Labour party, seems simply to have gone to pieces. He left parliament in 1945 and vanished from sight.[16] Above all, Russia's resistance and 'planning' gripped the imagination of the Left. Virtually the antithesis of local self-government, enthusiasm for Russia not only affected Labour's ways of thinking, but revitalised what remained of party organisation, in Aid to Russia committees.[17] The Glasgow committee, organised jointly by the Labour Party, the Trades Council and the Cooperatives, raised over £13,000 by the end of 1944, and the Scottish Labour movement as a whole £85,000 by the end of the war. Even the Hawick Labour party collected £600. Paradoxically, this campaign, in which Trades Council Communists played a prominent part, ran in tandem with strong opposition to Communist Party affiliation. In fact, supporting Russia was a way of emphasising Labour's rejection of Communism, and fairly effective. Although Communist party membership increased during the war, no Scottish Labour parties supported its affiliation, and the CP's performance in the 1945 election, outside West Fife, was very poor.

Labour had, however, increasing problems with the electoral truce. Addison and Calder have highlighted the success of English independents and third-party candidates at by-elections, but Scottish by-elections were measurably more volatile. 53 per cent of UK seats falling vacant were contested, and eight per cent of these changed hands. In Scotland eighty per cent were contested and eighteen per cent changed hands. Admittedly, when expressed in numbers, this boils down to two seats, but Johnston was sensitive to the shift in opinion. In a conversation with Lord Reith in July 1943, he emphasised 'the great danger of Scottish nationalism coming up', and political nationalism, indeed, staged a revival which caught up with Labour just at the end of the war. In mid-1942 the SNP split, John MacCormick leaving to pursue his consensus aims in Scottish Union, later Scottish Convention. While this was to attain significance post-war, the SNP (continuing) proved a lively opponent, taking over the third-party role performed by Common Wealth in England. However, one of CW's earliest successes was a near-victory for Tom Wintringham in North Midlothian on 11 February 1943, when, according to Paul Addison, 'the local Labour parties were the backbone of his organisation'.[18] Tory lukewarmness on the Beveridge Report, which had come out on 1 December 1942, and a particularly hidebound Edinburgh lawyer Tory candidate, were too much for most local socialists. Home Rule figured on Wintringham's platform, and Common Wealth's Scottish representative was David Cleghorn Thomson, former prospective Labour candidate for West Renfrew and an active promoter of the 'Scots renaissance'.

A year later on 17 February 1944, Douglas Young, who had been a member of the Labour party until 1942 as well as a member of the SNP, polled 41.3 per cent against Labour at Kirkcaldy. This emphasised not only the appeal of nationalism, stoked by the steady irritant of civilian, and especially female conscription, but further disorganisation within the Labour party. A local miner, Councillor Tom Hubbard, had been adopted as a result, it was alleged, of a combination of Communist and Unionist machinations. The Communists favoured him because he had supported CP affiliation to the Labour Party; the Unionists because he would prove a weak opponent once they were given the chance to contest. But although the NEC suspended the selection and reopened the list, Hubbard still won 34-33 against J.J. Robertson, the LPSC's favoured candidate. Only in October 1944, the month Taylor returned to duty, did Labour start to prepare for a general election.

Just before the coalition broke up, Labour received a bonus with the decision of the ILP to contest only the three seats which it still held in Glasgow. It had planned to fight another twelve (seven Unionist and five Labour-held) but withdrew in order to assist its attempt to reaffiliate to Labour. But Scotland also provided two jolts. On 12 April Dr Robert MacIntyre won Motherwell for the SNP, and on the following day the distinguished nutritionist Sir John Boyd Orr won a Scottish Universities seat as a nationalist-inclined independent, with 71 per cent of the vote. *Forward* attributed the Motherwell upset to Tory anger over an attack by Bevin on Churchill, on 7 April rather than nationalism *per se*, but MacIntyre's career as a conscientious objector, and the fact that his father was a minister well known for his pacifist and radical views probably counted for more. Norman Mackenzie in the *New Statesman* saw it as the release of 'pent-up Scots irritations', triggered in particular by the refusal of the government to commit itself to Forth and Tay Road Bridges, and the threat that Prestwick Airport, hitherto the busiest in Britain, would be down-graded. The NEC told Harold Laski to enquire into Scottish Nationalism, a subject in which he was once something of an expert, through an essay on 'The Political Theory of the Disruption' in which he urged 'the essential federalism of society',[19] and, as an immediate step convened a meeting of Scots Labour MPs. As a result, a pledge to consider measures of Scottish home rule was included, not in the manifesto but in notes for speakers in Scotland, 23 out of 37 successful Labour candidates declared themselves in favour of self-government and Attlee himself gave general endorsement to the idea.

What was significant was the extent to which collectivism had penetrated Scottish society during the war. The Kirk was not just typical but politically important — it reached twenty-five per cent of the population compared with the Church of England's seven per cent — and its commission 'on the present crisis' broke with a tradition of somewhat xenophobic utterances on social questions. Its 1943 report *God's Will for Church and Nation* was as radical as Archbishop Temple's demarches. When the most articulate of Scottish Unionists, Walter Elliot, campaigned on the theme of 'a partnership between the State and industry, and a partnership in the international sphere between America, Britain and Russia' this was sure evidence of the way the tide was turning. Thanks to Johnston, Labour was able to point to a success in carrying out such a programme, acclaimed on all sides, even by Churchill when he visited Glasgow. At the very least, this was probably sufficient to compensate for the bias in the press.

Counting votes took three weeks, because of the need to bring troops' voting papers (approximately ten per cent of the electorate) back from abroad, and results were not declared until 26 July. The 'stupefied surprise' of the *Glasgow Herald* at Labour's sweeping gains in the UK typified the response of the Scottish press, and overshadowed Labour's modest Scottish advance. The country had shifted 'not drastically, but a little to the left'. The swing from 1935 was the lowest of any British region, 9.8 per cent overall, against 12 per cent for the UK, 17.5 per cent for London and even 11.4 per cent for Wales, which had polled strongly left in 1935. In all, Labour's representation increased from 22 seats to 37, the same total as in 1929, and in terms of votes cast, from 36.8 per cent in 1935 to 47.6 per cent. But the result could have been worse, and there was a bonus in November when Labour gained two hundred seats in the local elections. Hopes of a 'clean sweep' at the next general election were not utterly fanciful.

Labour retained power for six and a half years, and the local election results give a rough guide to the government's popularity. This was pretty sustained, despite the complexity of its legislative programme, the esoteric nature of its pressing overseas commitments — Indian independence, Palestine, the creation of NATO, the Korean War — and the recurrent financial crises which dogged it.

In November 1946, after a year which had seen the nationalisation of coal, aviation and the Bank of England, Labour took a further 57 seats. This reflected the smooth running of the demobilisation programme, the apparent success of Dalton's Direction of Industry Act (actually carried by the caretaker Unionist ministry of May-July 1945) and above all the boost which the export drive gave to the industries of an exporting area. The reason for the drive was, however, less inspiring: the cutting-off of lease-lend in 1945 and the need to conform to the conditions of the American loan which replaced it. In 1947 this was bringing the government's economic strategy into increasing disarray, along with the effects of the winter of 1946-47, which imposed intolerable strains on run-down mines and transport facilities. Unionist resistance to nationalisation — railways, road transport and electricity were taken over in 1947 — had also become much fiercer. Labour registered these setbacks in November with a loss of 57 seats.

Government cohesion fell to its lowest point in the autumn of 1947, with Stafford Cripps' attempt to oust Attlee, which the latter trumped by making Cripps economic overlord. This led, somewhat belatedly, to a tight and logical system of economic planning, the true 'age of austerity'. Perhaps mercifully, Labour was spared local contests in 1948 as, following boundary changes, a 'general' election was scheduled for May 1949. By then the inauguration of the National Health Service by the government's most charismatic minister, Aneurin Bevan, boosted support. Labour won back fifteen seats. Thereafter devaluation, rearmament and Korea took their toll of a tired and ageing government. Labour lost eleven seats in 1950, seven in 1951. Yet the vote in October of that year was to be its highest-ever in Scotland. Throughout the six and a half years Labour technically did not lose a single by-election, but Camlachie, an ILP seat in 1945, went Unionist in 1948 — largely because of 6.4 per cent ILP vote for Annie Maxton, sister of James.

During the war Labour's strength had lain in Johnston's role at the Scottish Office. After the war this became Labour's weakest Scottish link, and exposed the party to nationalist criticism which further restricted its room for manoeuvre. For the first few months of the new government, the figure of Johnston still stalked the corridors of St Andrew's House, although a scheme he had floated early in 1945, that he continue as Secretary of State in the Lords, was decisively rejected by the Labour MPs. His secretary and former PPS, Westwood, insisted that he would carry on Johnston's work. Generally regarded as pedestrian, Woodburn credited him with 'a mind like a needle', but he was struck down by illness after only a few meetings of the new cabinet, in October 1945, and did not attend again until late January 1946. As this was when the government strategy was hammered out, and its centralising tendencies grew more pronounced, he was never able to make good this absence. Thereafter Westwood had to fight continual rearguard actions against centralised control of the nationalised industries; he kept the Hydro Board under his control, but his attempts to gain a Scottish division of each executive of the Transport Commission and the nationalisation of Scottish coastal steamers, were checked by the hostility of Alfred Barnes, the Minister of Transport, who strongly deprecated any provisions in the Bill which would require him to treat Scotland as a single self-contained area.

How much was this due to Labour's ethos of centralisation, how much to a certain hostility to Scotland? George Pottinger has alluded to a Whitehall feeling that, under Johnston, the Scottish Office had been allowed to 'get away with too much' and a backlash was now evident'.[20] Yet so disorganised were Labour's nationalisation blueprints that sheer horror at further complexity seems the main reason.[21] At any rate, Westwood's protestations died away; by July 1947 he actually rejected an initiative of the Minister of Town and County Planning, Lewis Silkin, to establish a Scottish Committee of the Central Land Board. Restiveness among Scottish Labour MPs grew, and on 7 October Attlee sacked him.   Westwood's successor was Arthur Woodburn, promoted from Under Secretary at the Ministry of Supply. With his stronger grass-roots links (his wife was also a prominent Labour bailie in Edinburgh) Woodburn was aware of increasing party discontent at over-centralisation, as a motion had been passed at the Scottish Council's Dundee Conference on 24-26 October 'restating the demand for an enquiry, (into devolution) with some censure for the delay.' There were also stirrings further to the right. John MacCormick's long-planned Scottish National Assembly had met in Edinburgh on 22 March and appointed a 'balanced' committee to draw up a scheme of home rule. Labour remained aloof but there was some sympathy from the Co-operatives and Unions, and also, rather alarmingly, from the Communists.[22] As Woodburn informed the Cabinet in December 1947, 'nationalistic' discontent in Scotland ran well beyond the 'picturesque and articulate but (in support) negligible' SNP,[23] and the more important Convention, to embrace a substantial group whose criticisms, yet to be cohesively articulated, centred on Scotland's suffering at the hands of remote government. In part, it was a repetition of Johnston's 'après moi, les Nats' approach; it was to be repeated by Woodburn's successor Hector McNeil — a means whereby the Secretary of State staked his claim to Cabinet attention. It also turned out to have immediate relevance with by-elections pending at Paisley and Camlachie. In late 1947 MacCormick started selling home rule to the right (with which his contacts had earlier been poor), through informal discussions between the Scottish Liberal Party, the National Liberals and the Unionists. In December, Oliver Baldwin succeeded his father and caused a by-election at Paisley, a seat with a strong Liberal tradition. MacCormick was adopted for it as a 'National' candidate on a home rule platform but with Unionist support.

In retrospect this had disastrous consequences for his inter-party schemes. Several prominent Liberal and left-wing home rulers resigned, and the breach with Labour became total. But the threat was still considerable, and underlay the rapid transformation of Woodburn's Cabinet Paper, approved on 11 December, into the

White Paper on Scottish Affairs of 29 January 1948. The White Paper proposed giving powers to the Scottish Grand Committee to consider at Second reading all Scottish Bills, and, for the first time, estimates. There was to be a Scottish Economic Conference, meeting 'possibly at intervals of two or three months' which would bring together St Andrew's House and the heads of the nationalised industries in Scotland [24]; an enquiry into Scotland's financial relations with England 'should be explored'.[25] The White Paper appeared on the day of the Camlachie election, which Labour lost. It was not greeted with much enthusiasm: 'All I can say about Mr. Woodburn's White Paper is that it gives me a pain in the neck', the playwright James Bridie was reported as saying.[26] But it seems to have rallied Labour against MacCormick's campaign. At Paisley on 18 February he polled 20,000 votes but lost by 6,500.

The White Paper could be implemented merely by changes in standing orders. These were carried on 28 April 1948. Despite some grumbling from old home rulers, Labour accepted them, and at the Scottish Conference in October further discussion of home rule was prorogued to give the new measures a 'fair trial'. Labour now showed itself bluntly hostile to Scottish Convention, whose second Assembly in December 1948, with only 300 delegates, was something of an anti-climax. Press support for it fell off, enabling Woodburn to write, rather complacently, to Hector McNeil in November 1949: 'When it became clear that there was no possibility of splitting our party, and that we had been consolidated on a clear position, they realised that any divisions accomplished by Scottish home rule agitation would be among the other parties.' He had already been contra-dicted. MacCormick had launched a Covenant in support of home rule on 29 October. Two days after writing to McNeil, Woodburn made a violent attack on MacCormick, interpreting a mild rhetorical flourish of the latter's as incitement to sabotage. This speech would soon cost him his job. MacCormick's Covenant movement, on the other hand, went from strength to strength during the winter, and by May 1950 it had been signed by 1,250,000 — more than a third of the population over the age of eighteen.

The 1950 election was held, rather precipitately, by Attlee as his administration lost momentum and was increasingly assaulted by the Left over the issue of German rearmament. The campaign began on 3 February and polling day was 23 February. It was very muted on both sides, enlivened only by a very large flock of Liberal candidates, who looked increasingly bedraggled as it wore on. Labour fought on its record, set out in *Forward Scotland* in 1949, and particularly on the Health Service; the Unionists on over-taxation, the 'Dollar

Gap', and hostility to nationalisation, an issue which scarcely caught fire. But housing proved a telling challenge, especially in the hands of Walter Elliot, fighting Glasgow Kelvingrove, who pointed out Labour's very limited post-war achievements.

The results were poor, despite a growth in the Labour poll to 1,262,086 from 1,144,410 in 1945. Edinburgh North and Glasgow Kelvingrove were lost, although Camlachie and West Fife were regained, the latter from William Gallacher. Labour's percentage was 46.2 per cent (UK 46.1 per cent) compared with 48.7 per cent for the Unionists and their allies. Woodburn was an immediate casualty of the election. Attlee plainly thought that he had been badly rattled by the Convention challenge and in his reshuffle asked him to move sideways to Fuel and Power. He refused to budge and resigned instead. Attlee must, however, have had his replacement by McNeil in mind *before* the election. Otherwise, why was McNeil interested enough in nationalism to write to Woodburn about it in November 1949? McNeil was an ex-Beaverbrook journalist, and most unusually came to St Andrew's House from the Foreign Office, having made his reputation as Bevin's representative at the United Nations, where he took a strongly pro-American line. Westwood and Woodburn had a background of support for home rule, McNeil had no interest at all in it, and little enough in any of the schemes of administrative devolution Woodburn had devised to obviate it. In a debate requested by the new Liberal MP for Orkney and Shetland, Jo Grimond, he conceded an enquiry into Scotland's financial relationships with England, but the Cabinet minutes confirm that this was as far as he was prepared to go. Later that year he effectively disbanded Woodburn's cherished Scottish Economic Conference which had never been a great success. McNeil seemed marked out for promotion in view of his undoubted success in attracting new industries, where government policies had failed. But his time in office was short. Originally a Bevin man, he had transferred his allegiance to Morrison and might have had promotion if Labour had not been defeated in 1951.

Weakened by illness, deaths and growing dissension, Attlee's government struggled on for a second term of twenty months with an overall majority of only five, eventually going to the country on 25 October 1951. This was the occasion on which, nationally, Labour achieved its highest-ever share of the popular vote — 48.8 per cent — yet lost a crucial twenty seats, including Berwick and Rutherglen in Scotland. Its Scottish vote was less impressive: 1,330,235 or 47.9 per cent, but this could be attributed to a marginally higher third-party vote (3.5 per cent) which otherwise collapsed from 10.4

per cent to 3.2 per cent. 1951-55 was to be the apogee of two-party politics in Britain, and (somewhat deceptively) in Scotland, but for the moment the advantage lay with the Unionists.

By the 1951 election one troublesome factor had vanished — the Scottish Convention. McNeil's tactics of benign neglect had worked, at least up to a point, but the real failure was MacCormick's. The Covenant topped two million signatures early in 1950, the National Assembly of that year had 1,000 delegates. But MacCormick never followed this up, becoming embroiled in the drama of lifting the Stone of Scone from Westminster Abbey. The Unionists offered a Minister of State resident in Scotland and a Royal Commission on Scottish Affairs; Labour maintained its root-and-branch opposition; the Liberals, who were closest to Covenant's ideas, gave up. Delegates to the 1951 Assembly dropped to two hundred; by October its influence was negligible. Nationalist politics were due for a decade of hibernation.

Labour had certainly recovered in the 1940s, but the advance was not, as in left-wing mythology, due to strong grass-roots socialist organisation and convictions. Organisation was weak until *after* the victory of 1945; ideology remained vague throughout. Yet Scottish Labour was not the creature of the parliamentary leadership. It persisted with its own preoccupations — self-government, Highland policy, housing — when Downing Street and Transport House would have preferred other priorities, such as cleaning up political organisation in Glasgow. It returned MPs who were authentically Scottish — although far from stimulating — instead of accommodating ambitious carpet-baggers. The key factor in this was surely the Scottish Office, and the fact that Labour controlled it for all but one year of the decade. Johnston's period in power legitimated both collectivist social policies and the Labour hierarchies in local government. It also meant that Labour did rather better in 1945 than it deserved to do. Thereafter St Andrew's House, rather than Westminster, became the terminus for many Scottish political issues. Administrative devolution had been seen to work; small wonder that it became after the war Labour's panacea, supplanting self-government on one side and a preoccupation with Westminster on the other.

In 1951 Labour organisation began to fail. Television came to Scotland a year later and political parties, like drama groups and church organisations, began to lose membership. The election meeting became marginal; and the socialist press rapidly decayed. *Forward*, which had produced ten 'election special editions' and many other broadsheets in 1951, was all but dead by 1959. Even in

1951 the Women's Sections were faltering and the Leagues of Youth had halved in number. The quality of MPs stayed low; indeed, after the effective withdrawal of McNeil from politics in 1952 Scottish Labour was all but leaderless. It was a somewhat melancholy end to a period which had been energetic and fruitful compared with the one which preceded it. A National Health Service had been set up which owed much to Scottish enthusiasm and Scottish precedents; infant mortality had already fallen by fifty per cent. Agricultural subsidies had revived the countryside and hydro-electricity and forestry — the Highlands. Jobs in manufacturing industry had risen almost threefold on 1935. These advances were defended, justifiably, by the Labour Party. The problem was that this stance precluded more imaginative thought about the exercise of control and choice in a socialised economy. Devolutionist pressure and the Unionist revival were both responses to this; by assaulting devolution, the weaker alternative, Labour merely strengthened its more malignant rival.

'Wheatley – The Sower'. *From* The New Leader, *6 June 1924*

J. Keir Hardie in later life. *By permission of the Labour Party Library*

James Maxton. *By permission of John Murray Publishers Ltd*

MACBETH—Mr. Ramsay MacDonald (Prime Minister).
LADY MACBETH—Mr. Maxton : " *Infirm of purpose ! Give me the daggers.*"
[Within two months of its taking office, Mr. Maxton attacked the Labour
Government.]
By permission of the Proprietors of Punch.

6

The Labour Party in Scotland, 1951–1964

MICHAEL KEATING

It is difficult to assess the state of the Labour Party in 1951 from the standpoint of the 1980s. Certainly, hindsight gives some advantages but it carries its own perils. Labour's crisis of confidence of recent years, the deep divisions in the party and the inexorable contraction of its electoral base can make the problems of thirty years ago appear minor in comparison. A balanced assessment of British Labour's state in 1951 shows a party with both strengths and weaknesses. It had lost office at the General Election but had achieved its highest ever vote and, indeed, across the country as a whole, had out-polled the Conservatives. A record of solid achievement had been established and, while much remained to be done, the loss of office did not come as a traumatic shock. Membership was high and the alliance of parliamentary party, consitituency parties and trades unions remained firm. There had been splits and ideological divisions in 1945-1951 but these had mainly concerned defence and foreign policy and, in general, did not bring into question the very nature of the party itself.

Following the loss of office, however, a series of divisions emerged to bring the party to the point of crisis several times during its long spell in opposition. The 'Bevanite' split, developing since the resignations of Bevan, Wilson and Freeman in 1950, deepened in 1952 when a rebellion by 57 left-wingers against the official Opposition line on defence led to the reimposition of the Standing Orders of the Parliamentary Labour Party. This shifted the battle ground to the party in the country and at the annual conference of 1952 Bevanites took six of the seven constituency seats on the NEC, displacing Morrison and Dalton in the process. However, in contrast to some more recent battles in the party, these struggles saw the right still dominant both in the trade union section and in the PLP. In 1952 Bevan was able to secure only 82 votes to 194 for Morrison in a contest for the Deputy Leadership and Bevan himself was the only member of his group to gain election to the Parliamentary Committee. By 1954, the leadership was winning the battle at conference too, with votes for Gaitskell as a party Treasurer and in favour of the official line on German rearmament. A PLP vote, by 113-104, to accept German rearmament led to Bevan's resignation from the Parliamentary Committee. This was followed by a Bevanite abstention on an official Opposition motion on defence and the withdrawal of the Whip from Bevan himself. Only narrowly, Bevan then avoided expulsion from the party itself.

In 1955 Gaitskell was elected party Leader, defeating Bevan and Morrison while the balance in the Conference began to move to the left with the succession of Frank Cousins to the TGWU leadership and the election of Bevan to the party Treasureship in 1956. While these developments foreshadowed deep divisions later on, for the next few years the party enjoyed relative peace. Opposition to the Suez adventure produced a front of unity on foreign affairs and by 1957 Bevan, now Shadow Foreign Secretary and from 1959 Deputy Leader, had come to accept the leadership line on nuclear weapons, declaring in a famous phrase that no British Foreign Secretary could go 'naked into the conference chamber'.

Following the 1959 election defeat, however, divisions re-emerged. Gaitskell, convinced that, to regain power, Labour needed to shed its 'old-fashioned' and working class image, launched a campaign to drop clause IV of the party constitution, calling for the common ownership of the means of production, distribution and exchange. He was forced to retreat but soon faced another crisis, when the 1960 Conference under the influence of the Campaign for Nuclear Disarmament, narrowly endorsed the unilateral renunciation of nuclear weapons. However, Gaitskell was still supported by the NEC, the TUC General Council and most of the big unions and was able to beat off a challenge for the Leadership by Harold Wilson by a comfortable margin in the PLP. The following year, the conference defeat was reversed by a large majority.

In 1960 Bevan had died and in 1963 Gaitskell's death resulted in the succession of Wilson to the leadership. As we shall see, Wilson's leadership differed from Gaitskell's in style more than in substance, but it did succeed in uniting the party to a greater extent than for many years, in the run-up to the 1964 General Election. In particular, Wilson's analysis of the crisis of the party and the need to adapt to a changed world had a lot in common with Gaitskell's. Three election defeats in succession had raised the question of whether

Labour could ever regain office, given what became fashionably known as the 'embourgeoisement' of the working class. This theory held that the spread of affluence and increasing social and economic equality were drawing the working class into middle class life-styles and rendering old class divisions redundant. A party, such as Labour, which based its support upon the working class, would thus suffer a steadily shrinking electoral base. Anthony Crosland[1] was the leading ideologue of the 'revisionist' response to this, arguing that Labour must shed its class image and its emphasis on nationalisation and emphasise instead social equality, economic growth and a pragmatic partnership of public and private sectors. Later evidence from Butler and Stokes[2] suggested that the embourgeoisement theorists were largely wrong at the time — though they were perhaps to be proved right ten or fifteen years later. Crosland's and Gaitskell's arguments at the time were widely rejected because they challenged some of the basic principles upon which the party was founded. Wilson, on the other hand, was able to recast the party's message in the language of modernisation and technology. At the 1963 Conference he promised a new Britain forged in 'the white heat of the technological revolution'.

The approach had been foreshadowed in the 1962 policy document *Signposts for the Sixties*. This started: 'We live in a scientific revolution. In the sixteen years since the war ended, man's knowledge and his power over nature — to create or to destroy — have grown more than in the previous century. In such an epoch of revolutionary change, those who identify laissez-faire with liberty are enemies, however unwitting of democracy. The enlargement of freedom which we all desire cannot be achieved by opposing State intervention, but only by ensuring that national resources are wisely allocated and community services humanely planned. Indeed, the three main ways of achieving this must be: first, to harness the forces released by science in the service of the community. Secondly, to plan and supervise the balanced growth of the economy; and, thirdly, to ensure that the ever-increasing wealth created by modern techniques of production is fairly shared.'

In 1964 Wilson pursued the theme: 'In two decades, the scientists have made more progress than in the past two thousand years. They have made it possible for man to reach out to the stars and to bring abundance from the earth. They have made it possible to end the dark ages of poverty and want, to take mankind forward to a future which our fathers would not have dreamed possible. Yet Britain lags behind, lacking the will or the plan which can bring this future within the reach of all.'[3]

There is probably less that is distinctive about Scottish Labour in this period than at any other in its history. The 1930s and 1940s had seen an almost complete integration of the party in Scotland into the British party, in terms of policies and priorities as in terms of organisation.[4] This was determined by three principal factors. The first was the experience of the Depression and the decline of the Scottish economy, both indicating centralised remedies based on statist planning. While post-war reconstruction and rearmament provided a short-term boost to Scotland's heavy industries, by 1954 the trend of relative decline was again visible. The growth years of 1954-60 saw UK industrial output expand by 23 per cent but for Scotland the figure was a mere 9 per cent.[5] This led the party — and, indeed, the Conservatives — to a renewed interest in regional policy and in economic planning from the centre.

Secondly, there was the predominant focus, especially after 1945, on gaining and retaining power at Westminster. 1945 had shown that Labour could gain an overall majority and put through reforming measures, but only by a united effort. Concentration on Westminster politics left little room for Scottish or other diversions and prescribed a clear career route for ambitious politicians; and the structure of Scottish government provided few opportunities for political leadership or advancement other than through Westminster.

Thirdly, there was the organisational weakness of the party in Scotland. This had been a factor making for assimilation as early as 1915.[6] In 1932, the party's organisation had been dealt a further blow with the disaffiliation of the ILP which, in Scotland, had been responsible for most constituency organisation. The building up of constituency Labour Parties often from scratch had absorbed a great deal of Arthur Woodburn's time and energy as Secretary of the party's Scottish Council for the remainder of the 1930s. By the 1950s, matters had improved but Scotland's share of individual party membership in our period never exceeded eight per cent and for most of the time hovered around 6.5 per cent-7.5 per cent, figures well short of Scotland's share of population or of Labour MPs. Of course, true membership figures are more difficult to establish, given the basis of constituency affiliation to the party but the low Scottish membership does indicate a relatively large number of constituencies failing to pay affiliation fees and also a large number with a lower than average membership.

Assimilationist trends were reinforced by electoral movements in the fifties and sixties. Between 1945 and 1955, the Labour-Conservative electoral balance in Scotland almost mirrored that of England, with just a slight Conservative bias in Scotland.[7]

Yet, given the class composition of Scotland, with its working class preponderance, Labour should have had a natural 8 per cent lead there. In 1955 the Conservatives polled a bare overall majority of Scottish votes but in 1959, Scotland swung to Labour and, while the Tories remained slightly ahead in votes, in terms of parliamentary seats Labour gained the overall majority which it was to hold for at least the next twenty years. In by-elections at Woodside and Rutherglen in 1962 and 1964 it made further gains and by the 1964 General Election was doing better, relatively, in Scotland than could be explained purely by reference to social class.

Many causal explanations have been advanced for the swing to Labour in Scotland in 1959, mostly connected with the economic downturn. In appraising these, it is well to bear in mind Miller's comment that 'Scotland did swing to Labour while England moved further towards the Conservatives but that only represented a drift back towards the norm. . . the Conservatives lost most of the special Scottish advantage they had enjoyed since 1945 but they lost no more than that.[8]

One factor which would be consistent with the findings of Butler and Stokes[9] is the decline of the religious factor which had led many working class Protestants to vote Conservative. Labour had traditionally enjoyed the support of many middle-class Catholics but the numerical preponderance of the working class made this less significant than working class Orange Conservativism. Budge and Urwin[10] found ample evidence for religious voting, particularly among working class Protestants, into the 1950s and 1960s. The 1959 Coatbridge and Airdrie contest is a good example. Labour put up a Catholic candidate James Dempsey, while the Tories put up Mrs C.S. Morton, sister of Alan Morton, 'the wee blue devil', Rangers' star of inter-war years. Against the trend in Scotland, as a whole, Labour's safe majority fell to 795. Impressionistic evidence from the author's own experience in 1974 bears this out. Having been warned to take care when canvassing a solid working class part of Glasgow where 'their sashes choke them', I encountered a striking example of shifting attitudes. A working man came to his door to reveal that, though a lifelong Conservative, he was now going to vote Labour. The reason? Labour had promised a referendum on the Common Market 'the biggest Catholic racket yet invented'! In 1963, a 'Protestant Ratepayer' candidate scored enough votes in Dennistoun to cost the Progressives (ie Conservatives) the seat and the following year the same candidate ran second (albeit a poor second) to Labour in Dalmarnock.

The Conservative decline in Glasgow was dramatic, a drop in General Election votes from 272,155 in 1951 to 183,558 in 1964. From holding seven seats to Labour's eight in 1951, they were left in 1964 with only two, and one of those looking very precarious. So great has been the shift in behaviour that it comes as something of a shock to remember that as recently as the 1950s such seats as Govan and Glasgow Central were held by the Conservatives. A large part of the change in Glasgow of course, can be explained by the movement of population, especially the middle class, out of the city. While the Conservative vote fell, Labour's remained steady. Yet the decanting of population did not lead, as in many English cities, to Conservative gains in the hinterland. On the contrary, our period saw Labour advances in Dunbartonshire, Lanarkshire and Renfrewshire. So it appeared that population movement and social mobility were not breaking down the class structure as was happening in parts of England. In this situation, Butler and Stokes' finding[11] 'that the relationship between class and voting was becoming *more generalised* as other factors diminished in importance', was particularly significant — and without the Butler and Stokes caveat that this relationship was, in most places, becoming *weaker* and *less binding*.

Scotland was still very much a class society and not only in the cities. While traditions of deferential voting made Labour advances difficult in many rural areas, it did have a solid basis of support in the coalfields and in some parts of the Highlands and Borders. So it was probably less of an exclusively urban party than it was later to become. This rising trend of Labour support and the resilience of class divisions made the 'revisionist' argument less attractive in Scotland. There was not the same perceived need as in the more prosperous parts of England to recast the party's image or to build bridges to the middle classes. This, in turn, had a deep influence on the development of the party's organisation, image and policies.

Assimilation was further encouraged by the role of the trade unions. During the 1950s these, with some exceptions like the Miners and the few remaining Scottish unions, tended to be run in a highly centralised manner. This was partly a reflection of the growing concentration of industry and thus of the employers with which they had to deal but it was also a matter of leadership style under the predominantly right-wing general secretaries of the time. Although the Scottish Trades Union Congress was an old-established institution, its influence varied considerably according to the times. Under the Labour government it had established a consultative role which it sought to develop further in the consensus years of the 1950s. On the other hand, it could only claim to be a major force in trade unionism by enlisting the support of the big (centralised) unions to which most Scottish workers belonged. There were, further, ideological difficulties. The STUC, which included representatives from trades councils and a significant shop steward element at its congress, was subject to considerable left-wing and Communist influence. Both this and its independent Scottish line created suspicions in the minds of right-wing union general secretaries and, from time to time, embittered relations.

To a degree, it must be conceded that, in the 1950s, Scotland was something of a backwater in the Labour Party. Scots could play a full part in the party, of course, and rise to high office, but this could be done only in London. Scottish conferences were not made any more lively by the rule banning debate on all but Scottish subjects, a rule often interpreted with considerable strictness at the behest of the NEC. So few of the great battles in the party were fought out in Scotland, at least until the early sixties when, as we shall see, a new generation began to emerge. In 1952 not even a visit from Nye Bevan as the fraternal delegate from the NEC produced a 'Bevanite' split at the Scottish conference. It did, however, produce complaints about the infrequency of visits from the party's 'big guns', particularly during elections. In 1957, Gaitskell visited the STUC but does not seem to have taken in the Scottish Labour conference, which was sitting at the same time.

Scotland's Labour MPs were, by and large, solid trade union loyalists. Compared with their English counterparts, they were older, more working class, more likely to have been local councillors and less likely to lose their seats.[12] They were also increasingly less likely to be non-Scots incomers. Before and just after the war, it was not uncommon to find non-Scottish candidates winning Scottish seats — John Strachey, Emrys Hughes and Willie Hamilton of the post-war recruits come to mind. From the 1950s, this became more and more unusual; and the home-bred Scots MPs became less inclined to play roles on the UK stage.[13] To this extent, there was an undercurrent against assimilation though not in favour of Home Rule or independent Scottish initiative. It was, rather, a retreat into a secondary or dependent role. The parochialism of most Scottish MPs is highlighted by the exceptions, such as George Thomson, a specialist in colonial affairs who went on to become Commonwealth Secretary in the Wilson government, or Emrys Hughes, a left-wing rebel. Scottish successes in the Parliamentary Committee (Shadow Cabinet) elections were so few that on more than one occasion Scottish backbenchers had to complain to the leadership about their lack of representation. Of 32 MPs elected to the Parliamentary Committee between 1951 and 1964, only one, Tom Fraser, was a Scot.[14] He sat on it from 1956 to 1964, for most of this time as Shadow Secretary of State for Scotland.

One major obstacle remained to the assimilationist strategy of the fifties — the party's traditional support for a policy of Home Rule for Scotland. The leadership's commitment to a British strategy is no better illustrated than by the dedication with which they set about exorcising this Home Rule ghost.

Labour had emerged from the war in favour of devolution but with no definite commitment to action. Under the Attlee government, pressure was kept up both by John MacCormicks's Convention and Covenant movements and by agitation within the party. Both the parliamentary leadership and the Scottish Executive fought consistently to contain this agitation and to avoid further commitments. At the 1951 conference in the run-up to the General Election, a compromise was reached. A mammoth, 600-word resolution contained something for all points of view. The nationalists were attacked, the government congratulated for its efforts on behalf of Scotland and, without any commitment being made for or against devolution, a Royal Commission to examine the subject was demanded.

By 1952 with the Conservatives in power, the leadership was able to back the demand for a Royal Commission more strongly and when the Conservatives did appoint a Royal Commission on Scottish Affairs, to condemn its terms of reference. At the same time, however, the Scottish Executive and the parliamentary leadership were able to use the commission's existence to play for time. When it finally reported, in 1955, the steam had gone out of the Home Rule campaign but it was not yet dead. Despite Gaitskell's remarks at that year's Scottish Conference, that Labour had now changed its view on Home Rule because of the growth of economic planning and national wage settlements, a resolution was passed instructing the Executive to examine the economic and constitutional issues involved in the proposal for a Scottish Parliament. This the Executive saw as an opportunity finally to ditch the Home Rule policy and its report, presented at the 1957 conference dismissed the idea of a Scottish Parliament 'on compelling economic grounds'.

Home Rule was now doomed but the Party was not yet prepared to kill it off so peremptorily. The Executive's report came under strong attack from, among others, Alex Moffat of the Miners and two young parliamentary candidates, John Mackintosh and Judith Hart, and was referred back by 108 votes to 71. It soon became clear that the fruit of the Executive's reconsideration would not differ in substance from the original report especially after its spokesman dismissed a call by Tom Oswald MP for a return to the old Home Rule policy with the comment 'Although we as a party do not believe in a Scottish Parliament, we should not stop an MP from saying so. The question is to be raised at our next Conference. But it is a hardy annual and will no doubt be treated as such'.[15] The question was indeed raised at the 1958 Conference but, as the Executive report was not yet ready, it was deferred to a special conference later in the year.

This was presented with two documents, a general policy statement, *Let Scotland Prosper* and an Executive report on devolution, rejecting absolutely a Scottish Parliament. Motions to remit this back were overwhelmingly rejected and so, for the first time in its history, the Labour Party in Scotland explicitly repudiated Home Rule. It must be conceded that it had been a long time since the Scottish Executive of the Scottish or British parliamentary leaderships had taken the policy seriously but its abandonment nevertheless came as a blow to those elements in the party who still believed in it; and it left Labour exposed not only to attacks but to ridicule when, sixteen years later, it was forced to do another about-turn. However, abandonment of Home Rule was entirely consistent with the leadership's line of tying Scotland closely into the UK and using this position to argue for more material rewards. It thus laid the ground for the strategy of the sixties which we examine below.

Within Scotland, much energy was devoted to local politics. In 1952 Labour recaptured Glasgow after a brief period of Progressive control and held it, with around fifty per cent of the total vote, for the rest of our period. Control was also secured and retained in Aberdeen and Dundee but not in Edinburgh. Problems differed in Scotland's cities and so did Labour's solutions. In Aberdeen, a relative prosperity enabled Labour to build up some impressive public services, notably in education. However, Glasgow can be used to illustrate most of the facets of Labour's urban policies in the 1950s and 1960s.[16]

In Glasgow, the council faced one of the most massive problems of urban decay in Europe. Of all its problems, the most severe was that of housing. Large areas of the city were blighted by overcrowded and sub-standard housing on such a scale as almost to give rise to despair. Given the sheer magnitude of the problem, judgement on Labour's successes and failures must be cautious. Their task was not made any easier by the framework in which they had to operate. The city boundaries had been extended before the war to take in the land for the peripheral housing schemes of Easterhouse, Castlemilk, Pollok and Drumchapel but, while these protruded as fingers from the city core, the areas in between them, such as Bearsden, Milgavie, Bishopbriggs, Rutherglen and Newton Mearns, remained outside, to be developed as middle class dormitory suburbs. This both reduced the resources available to the city and increased its dependence on central government.

Within these constraints, the policy was to develop the peripheral schemes for council housing at low rents, while co-operating in a policy of 'overspill' of population to the New Towns such as Cumbernauld and East Kilbride. The low rents policy, which caused clashes with central government in Glasgow as elsewhere was seen as a practical expression of municipal socialism but the character of the new estates has been widely attacked since as more typical of socialism of the East European variety. In the rush to provide housing units, social facilities were delayed or ignored altogether while the influences of presbyterianism and of the Scottish Labour movement's temperance traditions was felt in the banning of pubs from most of the schemes. Of course, this was also a reaction to the problem of drunkenness and alcoholism in the old city but the solution was criticised as tackling the symptom, not the disease, and as bringing equal problems of alienation in its wake.

The low rents policy was widely seen in the Labour movement as a redistributive measure but, as the proportion of council housing in Glasgow reached 43 per cent in 1965[17] the scope for redistribution diminished, especially given the middle class flight to the suburbs. Nor was housing conceived as part of an overall socialist approach to the city. While rents in the schemes were low, transport from them into the city where all the facilities remained was increasingly poor and expensive. In the early sixties, while British Railways was closing city railway lines, the Corporation commissioned the grandiose *Highway Plan* of 1965. This proposed one of the most ambitious programmes of urban motorway building in Britain — for a city in which car ownership was the lowest. Several of the proposed highways were explicitly intended to facilitate private car movement from the middle-class dormitories outside the city boundaries into the city centre, passing through areas of comprehensive redevelopment on their way. The regressive effect of such proposals in redistribution terms, later so apparent, could be drowned at this time by the rhetoric of modernisation and 'redevelopment'.

So there was a great deal of conservatism in the policies and performance of municipal Labour. This, too, was masked by rhetoric, a language of political debate based upon concepts of working class solidarity and drawing on the myths of Red Clydeside. If Clydeside had ever really been Red — which is doubtful — it had largely ceased to be so by the 1950s. Labour had become the local political establishment, the path to municipal power and parliamentary careers, and as such attracted people, particularly Catholics, who might, elsewhere, have found themselves in other parties. Nor was there any effective competition from the left to keep Labour on its toes. The ILP faded in the early fifties following the movement of its MPs into the Labour Party and, while the Communists fielded a large number of municipal candidates in Glasgow in these same years, they failed to make much impact and after the 1956 Hungarian uprising lost a large part of their membership. SNP candidates, Social Credit-ers and a Modern Labour Party all appeared in the late fifties and early sixties but were no more successful. So Labour's complacency grew undisturbed until the hammer blows of 1967-8.

Elsewhere in Scotland, the picture was similar. In Fife, Communist strength was steadily reduced after the defeat of their MP Willie Gallacher in 1950 and Laurence Daly's independent Fife Socialist League proved short-lived. Pockets of Communist strength remained in the Fife coalfield and parts of Clydeside but in general the CP saw its best prospects as lying in industrial organisation and caused few problems for Labour in local or in national elections.

Labour had inherited from its radical forebears a concern for the plight of the Scottish Highlands and a tradition of opposition to landlordism and depopulation. This has never been abandoned and during the fifties and sixties repeated efforts were made to develop a Highland policy. A Highland Conference met annually up to 1957 and there was usually at least one resolution on the Highlands at Scottish conference. Yet, in devising a strategy for the Highlands, Labour faced a series of major dilemmas. The first concerned land tenure. Everyone could agree on opposition to landlordism but the electorally most attractive alternative, to promote a land-owning peasantry, would bring into being a class which would almost certainly be conservative. On the other hand, to call for land nationalisation would appear to tenants as merely substituting one landlord for another, more remote and bureaucratic, one. The second dilemma involved industrialisation. Should Labour promote industrial development in the Highlands, allowing improved living standards and creating a basis for a strong Labour vote? Or should it concentrate on maintaining traditional ways of life, reviving agriculture, fishing and crafts? Even if the former were acceptable in the Highlands, it could cause problems with Labour supporters elsewhere, as was made clear by the Scottish organiser of the Iron and Steel Confederation at the 1952 Scottish Conference, when he declared that the Highlands should not expect to receive heavy industry or subsidised transport. Instead, they should learn to help themselves.

The third dilemma concerned the means by which Labour policy was to be delivered to the Highlands. There was wide agreement on the need to establish new machinery to tackle the problems of crofters' rights, of land reform and of industrialisation. The disagreements arose on the form this should take. On democratic grounds, it should be elected or at least have a strong elective element. Yet any elected body in the Highlands would be dominated by precisely those interests which Labour was pledged to combat. So in 1953, the Highland Conference rejected the proposal of the Scottish conference that a proposed Highland Development Corporation should include elected members.

Eventually agreement was reached on a body which was to become the Highlands and Islands Development Board but with key issues of strategy left for the Board itself to resolve.[18] There was little reward. Caithness and Sutherland, which had a traditional Labour vote, was won in 1966 but elsewhere it was the Liberal Party which benefited from the anti-Tory mood. While, in rural Wales Labour was taking over as the main vehicle of radicalism, in Scotland it was increasingly identified as an urban party.

By the early 1960s, the party in Scotland had begun to liven up under the impact of a new generation, including some post-1956 refugees from the Communist Party. The major radicalising influences at this time were the Bomb and the growth of the Campaign for Nuclear Disarmament, which brought many young people into politics and specifically left-wing politics for the first time. In 1961, a motion criticising the stationing of American nuclear weapons at the Holy Loch was ruled out of order at the Scottish conference on the grounds that this was not a 'Scottish issue'. The hand of the anti-unilateralist NEC was suspected here and the ruling caused a row which rumbled on for the next year. In 1962, Gaitskell's speech at the Glasgow May Day rally was interrupted by anti-nuclear demonstrators. This led directly to the disbanding of the Glasgow Federation of Young Socialists and an inquiry into Woodside CLP, some of whose members were suspected of being involved. Later that year, Glasgow City Labour Party contemplated withdrawal from the May Day demonstration altogether because of alleged Communist influence.

CND in Scotland had an identifiable target in the local nuclear bases and, for a time, one of its most intense centres of activity was on Clydeside. It faded there, as elsewhere in the sixties and, after Labour's renunciation of unilateralism in 1962, some of its members left the party: but its effects were long lasting. It had provided a crusading moral issue for a generation impatient with cynicism and recruited into active politics people whose aspirations were not limited to securing a seat on the local council. Party membership went up in those years, as did Scotland's share of it; and the influence of radical ideas was not confined to the nuclear issue. It extended too, to industrial and community politics. The question was whether Labour in Scotland would be able to harness this idealism to its solid working class support to forge a renewed radical alignment. It was a question whose (negative) answer lies outside our period.

After 1959, the British party leadership began to appreciate the importance of Scotland for Labour's prospects of regaining power. With the election of Wilson came the new 'technological' image for the party, an image that could quite easily be given a Scottish face. Modernisation was to be achieved by harnessing technology and enterprise through planning. Indicative economic planning was an idea borrowed from France; in essence it involved concerting the activities of the various sectors of the economy in such a way as to eliminate waste and production bottlenecks and, by providing the expectation of growth, encouraging people to invest to the extent required to make that growth happen. It thus requires consensus and co-operation. These are to be secured by careful distribution of the fruits of growth. In Labour's vision, there would be enough to reward all those whose decisions had helped create it, and a surplus for distribution in accordance with social priorities. So growth was to be a non-zero-sum game. There would be no losers, only winners, whether one was referring to individuals, social classes or regions. Regional policy was an important dimension of this planning idea. In a growing economy, the encouragement of industry to move to the depressed regions would help not only those regions but also the prosperous regions, by reducing congestion, and the nation as a whole, by moderating inflationary pressures and bringing into use the whole of the national resources.

There were weaknesses in the vision from the outset. The dependence on voluntary co-operation ignored the strong authoritarian element in French planning and the centralisation of the French state. Economic growth and a climate of confidence were not so much the end product of the scheme as essential prerequisites for starting it; and the problems of managing a mixed economy in a perilous international environment were under-estimated.

Nevertheless, this idea seemed ideally suited to Labour's emerging Scottish strategy especially after the appointment of Willie Ross as Shadow Secretary of State. The strategy was assimilationist in that, with the Home Rule issue out of the way, Scotland was to be seen as an integral part of the British economic and political system. This allowed Scottish politicians to use universal criteria to complain about relatively high unemployment or a lack of industrial development in Scotland, Yet, at the same time, the special institutions of Scottish government, notably the Scottish Office, could be used to gain special advantages; and a range of domestic issues of no concern to Whitehall and Westminster could be settled on the basis of an informal system of 'home rule'.

In 1963, the Scottish Council of the party published *Signposts for Scotland*, the Scottish counterpart to *Signposts for the Sixties*. This took up the planning theme of its British counterpart and added a Scottish dimension. There were sections on housing, education, transport, the Highlands and Islands, agriculture and fishing, but the main emphasis was on economic growth. Indeed, it was recognised that 'If the new developments we want for Scotland are to be built on sound foundations, we shall need a substantial and continuous increase in our national wealth year by year'. Scotland's economic problems, it was pointed out, were worse than those of England. 'The Labour Party in Scotland believes that Scotland's special problems can be solved only if industry is diverted from the South to the North. This calls for purposeful economic planning on a United Kingdom scale.'

However, this was a plea not for special discrimination in favour of Scotland, merely for equity. 'Scotland will stand to gain more from this fairer sharing of both benefits and burdens just because of our present relatively greater needs. This is the answer to those who claim that Scotland should cut herself off from the rest of Britain and make herself economically and politically independent.' Nor was it a threat to other parts of the UK: 'We believe that the vast majority of the people of this country — in the prosperous Midlands and South as well as in Scotland and other less fortunate areas — regard a fairer sharing of improving living standards as a far more worthy and desirable objective.' So we are back with non-zero-sum politics. Science and planning can produce abundance and the only enemies are the old-fashioned Tory ruling aristocrats whose dead hand is stifling innovation and enterprise.

Such a strategy could and did work — in 1964 and 1966 Labour's Scottish vote reached record heights — but only as long as it was delivering the goods. For it contained within itself a serious contradiction between the historical trends of *assimilation* and *particularism*. Assimilation was represented by opposition to Home Rule and the demand for equity — in employment, living standards and public services — with the rest of Britain. Particularism was represented by the defence of the role of the Scottish Office, the informal measure of Home Rule and the insistence on special treatment and extra resources on the ground that Scotland is different. A shrewd observer like R H S Crossman could spot this contradiction in the 1960s: 'Willie Ross and his friends accuse the Scottish Nationalists of separatism but what Willie Ross himself actually likes is to keep Scottish business absolutely privy from English business. I am not sure this system isn't one that gets the worst of both worlds which is why I'm in favour of a Scottish Parliament.'[19]

Labour was thus appealing both to a Scottish vote and to a working class vote. It could only succeed by satisfying both or by a continued absence of serious electoral competition. Already in 1961 and 1962 the SNP had shown their potential at by-elections but it is arguable that it was not until Labour had raised the Scottish issue for its own purposes that the nationalists were able to exploit it; and that could only be done if Labour were seen to fail. That, however, was for the future. We must leave Labour in 1964 with its strategy succeeding and poised on the brink of power.

It was a more united party than for many years. It was a more youthful party, even in Scotland. It was above all, a party which, in Scotland, enjoyed a very wide measure of public support, but, still, a relatively weak organisational base. How it would use that public support and how it could retain it were to determine not only Labour's fortunes in Scotland but the future of the party itself as a mass movement and a broad coalition.

7

Scottish Labour
in Government and Opposition: 1964–79

FRANCES WOOD

Between 1964 and 1979 Labour Governments were in office for eleven years, and over the period as a whole Labour moved sharply to the left. In doing so, it was often at odds with its leaders. The late seventies witnessed a series of great, public battles over constitutional issues: the method of electing the leader; the writing of the manifesto; and the re-selection of sitting MPs. A deeply-divided party was then subjected to further splits with the desertion of a section of the social-democratic right to form the Social Democratic Party. If Labour's own members were not always constant, its voters were scarcely more so. By the seventies, Labour's traditional electoral base of the urban, working-class had been severely eroded. Growing volatility among voters and the lessening of class allegiances made the days of the post-war two party system look distinctly numbered. A shift back to two-party voting in 1979 would, with the advent of the SDP/Liberal Alliance, look to be only temporary. The continued activity of the Nationalist parties alongside the newly-formed Alliance pointed to a continuation of the pessimism and uncertain electoral behaviour which characterised the sixties and seventies. The economy also engendered much pessimism and doubt. The early sixties were the days of Harold Wilson's 'white heat of the technological revolution' when planning was the answer to economic decline and regional disparities. Incentives to development were seen as the key to increased growth and higher living standards, but by the late seventies regional economic policy was in shreds. Government's role had moved from that of encouraging the setting up of new industry to that of attempting to prevent the closure of basic industry. During Labour's government years there was a growing acceptance of the impossibility of central economic planning without the mechanisms of a siege economy and a late effort to promote more regional autonomy. As early as 1966 'outside' factors had intervened to make unworkable Labour's National Plan. The 1974-1979 Labour government was even more plagued by the intervention of things beyond its control: oil prices; IMF loan conditions; world recession. Labour's leaders were accused of a sell-out by an irate and active Party membership which used Annual Conference as a stick with which to beat its public representatives. Not since the early sixties, when Hugh Gaitskell attempted to remove Clause IV, had the Party been so rent asunder as it was by the disputes over Chancellor Denis Healey's 1976 IMF-inspired public spending cuts.

Against this backdrop of strife we must look at the Labour Party in Scotland. In many ways completely assimilated into the British Labour Party, it reflected and followed the trends discernable over the whole of Great Britain. It declined from its 1966 electoral apogee of 49.9 per cent of the vote; it moved in a generally leftwards direction and attacked its leaders for failing to get to grips with the economy and deserting the goal of full employment. It mourned the further decline of Scottish manufacturing industry and the passing of control out of Scottish, or even British, hands into those of the multi-nationals.

In contrast to the assimilationist economic trend, however, came the separatist political movement of Scottish nationalism against which Labour was forced to react. In doing so it embraced decentralism and increasingly devoted its attention to the formulation of policies which took account of the peculiarity of the Scottish situation, even if it did not fully accept the existence of Scottish nationhood. From an almost outright rejection of its long-standing 'Home Rule' commitment, in 1958, and subsequent reaffirmations of this in the sixties, Labour in Scotland did an about-turn. With anxious BLP prodding, the concept of Scottish Home Rule was re-adopted in August 1974 and enjoyed a renaissance over the following five years which culminated in the downfall of the British Labour government in the wake of its disastrous referendum on whether or not to set up a Scottish Assembly. What may originally have been adopted as a panic reaction to the electoral threat of the SNP has become of vital importance not only to Labour in Scotland but to the whole of the BLP. In a time of reactionary Conservative government a Scottish Assembly would have provided Labour with a natural platform from which to attack the Westminster Tories. Considerable dissent surrounded the adoption, by Labour in Scotland, of legislative devolution as Party policy but the advantages of a less centralised system of government are now more obvious and it seems unlikely there

will be any going back along the centralist road of the fifties and
sixties. The trend to decentralisation appears to be permanent,
whether or not it eventually comes to fruition in a Scottish
Assembly.

The Scottish GDP had begun to lag behind that of the rest
of the UK from as early as 1954 and the 1958 economic crisis
pushed unemployment over the 100,000 mark by early 1959.
The Conservatives, already committed to regional economic policy,
introduced a further Distribution of Industry Act which added new
development 'places' to the existing 'areas' of Glasgow, Dundee,
and Inverness. Scotland was also suffering from enormously high
emigration rates from its large non-industrial area. Between 1951
and 1966, 476,000 people left Scotland: 89 per cent of the natural
population increase. Unemployment in Scotland as a whole was
bad enough but in rural areas it reached staggering heights. The
Western Isles, for instance, had over thirty per cent unemployment
in 1958. The Local Employment Act of 1960 made further attempts
at refining Conservative regional policy with the introduction of
new criteria for development assistance. Employment Exchange
areas with over 4.5 per cent unemployment became Development
Districts and the previous development areas were joined by the
Highlands and Islands, except Perthshire, and around Aberdeen.
Little change, however, took place between Scottish unemployment
and the national average. If the UK average in 1964 be taken as
100, then Scottish unemployment reached an annual average of
209.5 per cent.

In addition to the gloomy economic situation, Scotland also
suffered from acute housing problems which Labour considered
'in part a reflection of the country's general lack of economic
well-being'. In *Scottish Election Special 1964* it pointed out that of
300,000 slum houses identified in 1956 only 92,000 had been cleared
by 1963. Housebuilding had seen virtually no rise since 1957 and
over-crowding was chronic.

In 1958, at the same Special Conference at which Home Rule
was rejected, the SCLP had adopted *Let Scotland Prosper* which
outlined its economic plans for Scotland. The keynote was the
planned distribution of industry: 'Scotland's problems can best be
solved by socialist planning on a United Kingdom scale'. The 1964
General Election provided Labour with a chance to campaign on
its policies of jobs and houses. Despite the warning bell rung in
some Labour members' ears by the 1962 West Lothian by-election
in which the SNP's William Wolfe came second, to Labour's Tam
Dalyell, it was a confident, ascendant Labour Party which entered

the election period hungry for power after the thirteen frustrating years of Conservative rule.

The Labour Party in Scotland which entered the fray in the 1964 General Election was very much a part of the British Labour Party. Its election material was produced in London by the NEC, albeit via one of its sub-committees containing leading Scots members. Its centralist policies reflected its origins. In 1960 the Scottish Office had instigated *An Inquiry into the Scottish Economy*. Its report of 1961 became known by the name of the Chairman, *Toothill*. It ignored heavy industry almost completely and, instead, went for new industry 'growth points', improvements in infrastructure and regional incentives. In doing so, it was in line with Labour's earlier *Let Scotland Prosper* and a fair amount of consensus arose around its central ideas. Like Toothill, Labour in Scotland firmly asserted that Scotland's prosperity was tied to that of the UK. 'There must be national planning', said William Ross MP, Labour's Shadow Secretary of State for Scotland, and promised that Labour would direct its efforts to 'expanded production, greater efficiency, and increased exports. . . the only way to get growth without inflation'. With the emphasis mainly on the economic, Labour's plans also included the creation of 40,000 jobs per year, the replacement of 500,000 sub-standard houses, the introduction of comprehensive schooling and the creation of a Highlands and Islands Development Board.

Labour enjoyed a large measure of public support in Scotland — with disproportionately high anti-Conservative swings in the General Elections of 1959 and 1964 — but could not consider itself the natural party of government in Scotland. Writing a couple of years before Labour's big electoral breakthrough, Magnus Magnusson reflected that Labour in Scotland was 'just a branch office' of the British Labour Party.[1] To a great extent this was true. In 1962 the SCLP had an independent income of only £760 and employed only five full-time agents: the Conservative and Unionist Party had 55. Transport House, in London, provided payment of all wages of full-time Labour officials and was the source of most material distributed in the Party's name. Labour's Scottish Annual Conference was restricted in its discussions to matters purely Scottish and tended to the parochial. A look at Conference Agendas of the early sixties shows an almost complete preoccupation with the three subjects of the Scottish economy, housing and education, and indicates a strict application of the embargo in discussing national or international policy. Constituency parties were moribund and Scottish MPs tended to be older, and from more working-class backgrounds, than their English counterparts. Conscious, however, of the approach of power, Labour in Scotland was making attempts to attract more young people into its ranks with the setting up of Young Socialist Branches. The youth section of the party was always, however, to prove a problem for its parent. Following the disbandment of the Glasgow Young Socialists in 1962 due to incidents at the Glasgow May Day Rally came the formation of a group which was to be the constant target for Trotskyite organisations. In the early sixties the Socialist Labour League, forerunner of today's Workers' Revolutionary Party, successfully controlled much of the YS in Scotland. Later its place was taken by the Militant, front-organisation for the Revolutionary Socialist League, which controls the LPYS in Scotland, and the UK, to this day.

Labour did well in the 1964 General Election: 43 seats were taken to the Conservatives' 24 and the Liberals' four. Over the whole of the UK Labour scraped home with 44.1 per cent of the vote and, due to the workings of the electoral system, 60.5 per cent of the seats. Even at this early date it could be seen how important to a British Labour Government was the disproportionate majority of seats the electoral system afforded the LPS. The early sixties, however, were days of complacency about Labour's position as one of the partners in the two-party system. Taking only 2.5 per cent of the vote, the SNP appeared a remote threat. Labour emerged from the election impatient to put into practice its corporatist planning ideas.

The public face of Labour in Scotland over the years 1964-1976 cannot be separated from that of William Ross, MP for Kilmarnock and Labour's Secretary of State for Scotand while Labour held office, A dour ex-schoolmaster, Ross fitted well into the image of the Scots dominie: stern, old-fashioned and a Kirk elder given to quoting the Bible in his orations. Firmly on the right of the Labour Party, Ross was also a conservative member of the Church of Scotland, reflecting its traditionalist wing's views on 'such matters as liquor licensing, Sunday observance, homosexuality, family planning and divorce.' Always a close ally of Labour leader, Harold Wilson, Ross remained a firm opponent of Scottish devolution throughout the sixties, earning the nickname 'hammer of the Nats'. He believed, rather, in 'economic discrimination in Scotland's favour' and always tried to wring the maximum amount possible out of reluctant Cabinet colleagues when Scotland's interests were at stake.[2] In this he had more than a measure of success, ensuring the location of the fast breeder reactor at Dounreay and the aluminium smelter at Invergordon, in 1966 and 1968, as well as the setting up, in 1967, of a Scottish Transport Group and the securing of aid for Upper Clyde Shipbuilders in 1968-69. There were failures too, though. Scotland lost the battle for the new Royal Mint, the Vehicle Taxation Unit of the Ministry of Transport, the HQ of the British Steel Corporation and the Land Commission. But this does not detract from the image of a man who fought hard for Scotland in Cabinet and strengthened the economic planning machinery of the Scottish Office while he held tenure, creating the Regional Development Division in 1964 and the Scottish Economic Planning Board in 1965 as well as the later Scottish Development Agency.

After the General Election victory Labour went ahead with its National Plan and results came quickly for Scotland. Ever-conscious of the need for another General Election at which the Labour majority could be increased, Labour in Scotland campaigned to publicise its government's achievements. In June 1965 the publication of *Go Ahead Scotland* hammered home the message that planning was the answer to Scotland's job hunger. With George Brown at the head of the Department of Economic Affairs and Ross in charge of the Scottish Economic Planning Council, it assured voters things were coming Scotland's way. There were new development districts, an industrial estate at Bellshill, nine advance factories and over £10 million of industrial assistance, seven per cent up on the previous nine months. In Labour's first year of office unemployment fell by over 10,000. The Scottish Special Housing Association had been set up to aid local authorities in meeting the government's target of 40,000 new public sector houses per year and education was being made comprehensive and given more teachers and new school buildings.

Another election promise was fulfilled in the autumn with the creation of the Highland and Islands Development Board. Although 'free to acquire land and manage it', it lacked the powers of compulsory purchase which many wished to see. It was not designed to undertake general land acquisition or implement the sort of far-reaching reforms needed to make the Highlands a living area rather than an idyllic, rural wasteland. The 1945-51 Labour government had fought shy of tackling the enormous privileges of those who owned most of the Scottish Highlands, and their successors in 1964 did not locate the basic problems of the Highlands in the ownership of the land, or if they did, had no wish to do anything about it. This issue was to cause much bitterness when the next Labour government moved to reform crofting land in Scotland. Still, within its remit, the HIDB did have its successes though they were small in scale. By March 1968 it had allocated £2.8m in assistance to promote social and economic development from which an estimated 2,400 jobs ensued. By the end of 1970 5,000 jobs had been created and the HIDB's lobbying for Dounreay and Invergordon rewarded.

In January 1966, in the White Paper on the Scottish Economy, Labour abandoned the Toothill strategy of specific development points and made the whole of Scotland, except Edinburgh and Leith, a development area. Unemployment that year was to reach the lowest annual average in a decade at 59,900. Two months later Labour again went to the polls with a certain amount of confidence which turned out to be well-placed. It was the high-point of Labour popularity in the sixties and seventies. Nationally, Labour took 48.1 per cent of the vote and 364 seats and in Scotland it reached 49.9 per cent of the vote and 46 seats. The Conservatives were left with a humiliating twenty seats marking an extraordinary slide down for a Party which in 1955 had held an overall majority of Scottish votes and seats. The Liberals gained a seat, making their total five, and a Nationalist vote of only 5 per cent gave no indication of the onslaught just round the corner. In the next four years the phenomenal rise in the Nationalist vote, in Wales as well as Scotland, offered a challenge to Labour's hegemony and the concession of a Royal Commission on the Constitution. It could be argued that its setting up made some form of devolutionary commitment inescapable for Labour in any future return to office. Shortly after taking office the new Labour government was faced with economic crisis. In July 1966 the introduction of deflationary measures included the devaluation of the pound sterling and strict spending cuts. From then on Labour's National Plan began to fall by the wayside, unemployment steadily rose and discontent spread among both Labour Party members and voters. By 1969 the SCLP Annual Conference was debating resolutions highly critical of the Government and the Scottish Parliamentary Labour Group's Annual Report stated, defensively 'too many supporters of the Labour Party think that because we have not done everything, we have done nothing. The record shows differently.'

The first sign of Labour's unpopularity in Scotland came at the Glasgow Pollok by-election of March 1967. The Conservatives captured the seat from Labour thanks to SNP intervention which took 28 per cent of the vote. The greatest shock of the year, however, was Winnie Ewing's victory for the SNP at Hamilton. On 2 November a Labour majority of 16,000 was overturned and an SNP vote of 46 per cent of the poll recorded. That it was a major shock to Labour is an understatement. Writing about it at the time, Richard Crossman partly blames the way the sitting MP, Tom Fraser, resigned to go to a highly-paid job. Tam Dalyell also puts emphasis on special factors.[3] But what happened in Hamilton could have happened in any number of West of Scotland seats in which Labour, through misplaced confidence about the inevitability of electoral victory, had allowed its machinery to run down. There were so few Labour Party members in Hamilton that most of the work had to be done by outsiders. This was true, too, of the SNP but that was not surprising for a party enjoying its first renaissance in twenty years. The Hamilton defeat laid bare the inadequacy of the exclusively electoral approach to politics employed by Labour in Scotland for many years.

Although to many, especially in the Labour leadership, the SNP success was 'just a flash in the pan' the occasion was used by others to press the case for Scottish devolution. John P Mackintosh, for long a supporter of devolution who had opposed its rejection in 1958, conceded that in brighter economic times Labour would have won at Hamilton. He also spoke of a 'widespread but elusive feeling that modern government is too complex, too remote' and urged the Labour Party to 'separate those who want more local democratic control from those who wish total independence' by accepting the idea of a Scottish government.[4]

As the Scottish Council's 1968 Annual Conference approached, John P Mackintosh continued to urge the adoption, by Labour, of the principle of Scottish Home Rule in the form of 'a legislative sub-parliament with its own Prime Minister', but his fervour for the cause was matched by the virulence of those who opposed it. On 12 March 1968 the appearance of what was to be an influential tract echoed the feelings of many in Scottish Labour at the time. *Don't Butcher Scotland's Future* was written by four Scots who were later to be strongly associated with the pro-devolutionary wing of the Party: Jim Sillars, Harry Ewing, John Robertson MP and Alex Eadie MP. Sillars and Robertson were even to take their later advocacy of Scottish Home Rule to the length of forming the breakaway Scottish Labour Party. In 1968, however, all that was in the future. The four strongly argued against any form of Scottish Parliament on the basis that it would split the British working-class movement.

Labour's 1968 Scottish Conference produced a flurry of pro-devolution resolutions but they were met by a vehement attack on nationalism by Ross. Conference carried a resolution which stated that 'the time is now ripe for an overhaul of the organisation of the Labour Party in Scotland' and Will Marshall, Secretary of the LPS, lectured Conference on the need to build individual Labour Party membership in an effort to beat the SNP. In an appeal to grass-roots radicalism Marshall spoke of the SNP's appeal to idealism, something sadly lacking in many Labour representatives: 'It is not enough to have MPs who are old and wise, because when they are old and wise they are no longer a Labour Government but a Conservative government', he said. A scapegoat was found for the recent SNP success — the Labour Government which had failed in its socialist duty by abandoning its National Plan and allowing unemployment to rise and spending to fall. Economic remedies were sought to combat the Nationalist threat.

The local elections of May 1968 brought further shock to Labour. A Nationalist vote of thirty per cent included a strong showing in Labour's largest fiefdom of Glasgow, where the Conservatives formed an administration with SNP support. Control was also lost in Paisley, Clydebank, Saltcoats, Renfrew and Ardrossan. Labour's long stranglehold on local government in the West of Scotland was well and truly ended. In the East, Labour also lost Aberdeen and its Fife strongholds of Inverkeithing and Buckhaven and Methil.

In the wake of the local election defeats, great urgency attached to a joint meeting between the Scottish Parliamentary Labour Group and the Labour Party Scottish Executive on 11 May 1968. The subject was Scottish Government, but there was to be no rushing into far-reaching decisions taken in the wake of the disastrous election results. Separation was completely rejected and continuing full membership of the UK Parliament backed. The EC agreed to await the Report of the Wheatley Royal Commission on Local Government in Scotland before considering any long-term moves. The short-term moves of setting up a Select Committee of Scottish Affairs and more time for Scottish debates in Westminster were supported. A working group was formed to carry out intensive study into other matters relating to administrative devolution. So at this point Labour in Scotland was not willing even to consider legislative devolution and thought administrative devolution required careful, long-term examination. The official policy was to ride out the Nationalist storm.[5]

Later in 1968 the BLP Conference debated devolution, remitting the matter to its National Executive Committee. This debate, the only one before a form of devolution was adopted in late 1974, was carefully studied by the Scottish Government working group. Future Leith MP, Ronald King-Murray, moved a resolution calling for 'elected assemblies which would. . . determine matters that are purely of concern to Scotland and Wales'. No change in Scottish or Welsh representation at Westminster was envisaged and no economic powers called for, since 'We cannot afford to fragment the British economy'. Despite what, in retrospect, appear mild and unexceptionable demands, the resolution met with much opposition, falling into two main camps: those who felt there was nothing special about the Scottish and Welsh cases and thought administrative devolution was needed to all parts of the UK; and those who, like Scots MP James Hamilton, felt nationalism could best be defeated by socialist policies and making people aware of the Labour Government's achievements. There existed, in the Party, a basic divide between those who saw the need to tackle the centralised, bureaucratic state and those who did not. There was no simple correspondence, however, between those camps and the two sides on the devolution question. Those who had no basic objection to the centralised state were split between pro and anti-devolution: the former seeing it as an electorally expedient device and the latter as an unjustifiable sell-out to Nationalist pressure. The issue cut right across the traditional left-right divide in the Labour Party in Scotland.

That same year the STUC came out in favour of an Assembly with legislative powers[6] and Trade Union support was to be of vital importance in pushing Labour into its eventual devolution commitment. The setting up of the Royal Commission on the Constitution at the end of 1968 was a bowing to pressures both internal and external. It followed, by all accounts, vigorous debate in Cabinet about how to counter the Nationalist surge. Ross had consistently opposed any devolutionary measures and 'stuck to the traditional Labour line that all would be well given the right economic policies'.[7] He was opposed in Cabinet by Crossman, whose Diaries reveal that he favoured devolution both for its own sake and to prevent further nationalist incursions into Labour's vote. But the 'antis', led by Callaghan, won. In the end, claims Tam Dalyell in his anti-devolution tract Devolution: The End of Britain?, Wilson and Callaghan set up the Royal Commission without so much as consulting the LPS, Scots Labour MPs or the Scottish Secretary of State! The Commission was a body with whom the whole, uncomfortable issue could be left until after the coming General Election. If the Nationalists did win a batch of seats, then the Commission's proposals might be considered. If, as most of the Labour Cabinet anticipated, this did not happen then the whole issue could be forgotten. As it happened, the nationalists did do badly at the 1970 General Election, but so did Labour. When Labour recovered its national position the Nationalists also broke through, dashing any hopes of burying the issues. In 1969, though, those who supported the constitutional status quo breathed a sigh of relief. There were no more massive SNP inroads into Labour's

Scottish vote for the remainder of the Parliament. At the local elections in May, the SNP were in retreat, taking only 20 seats as against the previous year's 100, but with still 22 per cent of the vote. The SNP experience in local government had proved disastrous as the sudden upsurge in support had thrust inexperienced and ill-equipped councillors into positions of power in which their inadequacies were quickly exposed. The electorate returned to the dependable, if stolid, charms of Labour councillors.

The Report of the Wheatley Commission in September 1969 was welcomed by Labour in Scotland. The two-tier system of much more powerful local authorities was roughly in line with Labour's already declared views. No thought seems to have gone into how the new local authorities might work with any future Scottish Assembly. This was consistent with the Scottish Executive of the Labour Party's submission earlier in the year to the Royal Commission on the Constitution. The report of the working group on Scottish Government formed its basis and firmly rejected devolution, on the grounds that it would split the working-class. Two local Labour Party organisations, however, incurred their Executive's wrath by submitting pro-devolution evidence to the Royal Commission on the Constitution. Both Central Edinburgh CLP and Edinburgh City Labour Party kept alive the argument for a legislative body to oversee the large amount of existing administrative devolution in the Scottish governmental system.

Further proof of failing SNP fortunes came in the dying months of the Parliament. Labour comfortably held Glasgow Gorbals in October 1969 and was similarly relieved by the result of the South Ayrshire by-election in March 1970. Occasioned by the death of left-wing rebel, Emrys Hughes, another rebel, Jim Sillars, entered Parliament on a 54 per cent vote against the SNP's 20 per cent. Labour's strongly anti-devolution candidate seemed to prove that the mouthing of socialist policies had more appeal than the recitation of anti-London ones. Labour entered the General Election on a high note in Scotland, gaining an impressive 84 seats in the municipal and county elections of May 1970. The SNP were routed in both city and country. On 18 June 1970 Labour returned to its opposition role at Westminster though its Scottish results were good. Labour retained 44 seats though no specifically Scottish election manifesto was produced.

In the last six years until 1970, the LPS had made considerable organisational improvements. It entered the seventies undoubtedly less complacent, less parochial and more active than it had entered the sixties. In 1968 its Annual Conference had voted to end the veto on debating non-Scottish matters, despite there being no rule change to this effect till 1972, and horizons widened to encompass all but international affairs. Active Party membership had increased during the years of SNP advance, but the Party was still dogged by lack of finance and, as a result, staff. Regional Office in Glasgow, continued to house only a Scottish Secretary, two assistant Regional Organisers and office staff. In the Constituencies only four election agents were full-time, which was no improvement on 1964.

Preparation for the General Election began as early as January with a special conference for candidates, election agents, key workers and press officers. There followed a programme of meetings, factory gate rallies, leaflet drops and, nearer election time, major rallies with big-name speakers. Labour was determined not to be caught out. The campaigning accent was firmly on what Labour had achieved for Scotland: the HIDB, Dounreay, Invergordon and although the unemployment figures had risen in real terms, there had been a fall in the UK from twice the national average in 1964 to one and a half times in 1970. There had also been real developments in housing, with the clearance of slums in Glasgow's city centre and the growth of the New Towns which housed many former slum dwellers. The General Election campaign gave Labour the opportunity to fight on 'bread and butter' issues rather than what a large number of members still regarded as the 'diversion' of nationalism.

Given the bad results in England, where the Labour Party polled 43.4 per cent of the vote against the Conservatives' 48.3 per cent, the main concern for Labour in Scotland over the next four years was to fight the measures of the incoming Conservative government, which had an overall majority of thirty. Scottish issues took a comparative back-seat as the focus of national attention moved to nationwide industrial and political struggles. There were only two major pieces of Scottish legislation during the life of the Parliament: the Housing Financial Provisions (Scotland) Act and the Local Government (Scotland) Act. The Housing Act proposed to regularise Scottish council house rents by raising them and introducing a system of rebates for those who could not afford to pay. The Local Government Act proposed the introduction of two-tier authorities — Districts and Regions — to replace Scotland's city, large burgh, small burgh and county councils. It was a long-overdue move which found Labour Party support for its principle even if there were differences over the details. As in 1959, Labour found itself in a majority in Scotland despite forming the national opposition, but times had changed since then with the much more uncertain party system making Labour's dominance in Scotland crucial to future Labour

rule at UK level. The need for specific Scottish policies with which
to combat the SNP was now recognised and these were formulated in
the next four years along with a strengthening of the Labour machine
in Scotland.

In May and July 1970 the Royal Commission on the Constitution
came to Scotland to take oral evidence. Labour in Scotland gave
theirs before electoral defeat and were represented by a delegation
including Secretary Marshall and Chairman, John Pollock. Evidence
was based on the Scottish Council's report *The Government of
Scotland* which had been approved at 1970 Annual Conference and
which rejected legislative devolution. Pollock expressed the fear that
an Assembly would detract from the powers of the anticipated new
local authorities and restated Labour's belief in central economic
planning. He went on to reject even the suggestion that more
democratic control over St Andrew's House might be no bad thing.
The deputation's primary concern seemed to be the upholding of
Labour's record in relation to Scotland rather than any attempt to
find acceptable constitutional improvements. In conclusion it was
stated that although the only solution to Scotland's problems was
a Labour Government at Westminster, it was prepared to tolerate
a British Conservative Government which did not have a Scottish
majority because it feared the creation of a Frankenstein's monster,
a body which it might be unable to control. Pollock mouthed the
fears of all who saw the dilemma of how to retain central control
whilst allowing local democracy as essentially insoluble. The notion
of a Scottish Assembly which could provide a focus of opposition to
a Westminster Conservative administration was not to gain currency
till much later.

Labour's commitment to the above strategy was already being
tested when the STUC gave its evidence on 20 July 1970. Although
its written evidence of October 1969 had backed a legislative
assembly, the deputation reflected the transience of STUC decisions
in backing an assembly without legislative powers. Labour's later
return to power brought another change of heart. At this time,
however, the STUC felt it wanted to respond to the pressures for
a greater say for Scots in the running of their own affairs yet feared
this would lead to the break-up of the economic unity of the UK.
The compromise favoured was a mere talking shop.

Early 1971 brought government response to the Wheatley
Commission proposals. Three years of negotiation and compromise
over details followed but the basic two-tier structure remained intact.
Ross led Labour in its campaign against the enormous Strathclyde
region, favouring four smaller authorities instead. But many on

both sides were quite happy with the reforms, and divisions did not strictly occur along party lines. In March the first Scottish Annual conference since the General Election, presided over by a new Secretary, Peter Allison, welcomed the Wheatley proposals but denounced everything else the government was doing. A vast number of resolutions on nationalisation, housing finance and the economy reflected the concern of Scottish Labour with matters British rather than the more introspective constitutional matters. Unemployment took a leap under the Conservatives, rising from 90,600 in July 1970 to 128,700 a year later. Warning signs were already emanating from Rolls-Royce and from the shipyards and Labour must have felt more on its home ground attacking Tory injustice than it did on its new territory of nationalism and devolution. Predictable success came in the local elections of May 1971 with a net gain of 116 seats and renewed control of Dundee and Glasgow. It seemed that, as in the past, when the Conservatives were in control of Westminster, Scottish Labour was seen as the natural party of opposition.

In the wake of the elections came crisis for the Upper Clyde Shipbuilders company. Labour had saved the shipping group when it last faced financial problems. Had Labour still been in office it would have been faced, like the Conservatives, with the difficult decision of whether or not to supply further first aid. The Conservatives did not, and Labour, freed of any difficult decision-making, capitalised on the resentment felt at the government's abandonment of the firm. On 23 June 30,000 marched through Glasgow behind Tony Benn, the former Labour minister, and a week later the 'work-in' began. The issue, initially at least, united not only the whole of the Labour movement north and south of the Border, but all sections of Scottish society. In October 1971 the SCLP held a recall conference on unemployment — over 130,000 by November — where Wilson addressed the assembly of almost 400 delegates and visitors and spoke in support of the UCS workers. In Parliament, Benn proposed that the government write off all UCS debts and place orders for ships which could later be sold. Labour's British Conference backed a resolution calling for the next Labour Government to nationalise ship-building and pledged full support for the workers. A year later the work-in had collapsed, and talks between the unions involved and the Marathon group took place at conference time. Agreement was reached on saving some jobs and retraining workers. The actions of the UCS workers were a direct challenge to the bureaucracy and paternalism of central economic planning and to its inability to respond to specific regional problems.

If incentives were offered to industry to set up in depressed regions, what happened when there was no longer an incentive, in terms of profit, for the industry to stay there?

Although the 'Scottish question' was, understandably, submerged during the Heath years, it did not disappear. By late 1971 the SNP's fortunes were again reviving. At the Stirling and Falkirk Burghs by-election, on 16 September, Labour's candidate, Harry Ewing, was subjected to strong Nationalist challenge with an SNP vote of 34 per cent to Labour's 46 per cent. Labour support for devolution grew but there were no resolutions on the subject until Scottish Council's 1974 Annual Conference. The entry of Britain to the EEC and the discovery of North Sea oil helped to fuel the SNP cause. The well-timed SNP campaign of 1973 around the slogan 'It's Scotland's Oil', was a brilliant initiative which took the SNP out of small-town politics and into Labour's industrial heartland by creating a focus of protest comprehensible to working-class Scots. Car stickers and lapel badges proclaimed the message and acted as a red rag to a bull where Labour was concerned, confirming for them what was seen as the essentially divisive and selfish nature of Scottish nationalism. But struggles like the one against the Industrial Relations Act cut across borders and showed the British Labour Movement united in its own defence.

Conservative attempts to reform housing finance brought prolonged struggles both north and south of the border against new legislation designed to regularise rent levels. The Housing Financial Provisions (Scotland) Act met with stern resistance from Scottish Local Authorities under Labour control. It proposed rent increases from 1 October 1972 and the introduction of a rebates system for those on low incomes. It effectively ended subsidised low rent levels in public sector houses by insisting that local authorities balance the books of their housing accounts. Non-co-operation was punishable, in the first instance, by withholding of central government housing subsidies. Labour's 1972 Scottish Conference pledged itself to a 'united fight' and involved itself in subsequent protest action. But the resisting authorities were picked off one by one. By the end of 1972, twenty Scottish local authorities were still holding out against rent increases, and being punished for it. A year later only five were left. By early January 1974 the last of the rebel Councils, Clydebank, gave in and was faced with a £20,000 fine and the implementation of rent increases much larger than if they had put them up at the government's appointed time. In a fight which had no winners, least of all the tenants in areas which held out against increases, Labour action against the Act was hampered by the unwillingness of much of the Labour leadership to be seen to support what is now termed 'extra-parliamentary action'. They fought the measure as it went through Parliament but were less willing to carry the struggle beyond Parliamentary boundaries to the extent of condoning 'illegality'. Labour's British Annual Conference in 1972 passed a resolution, against the advice of its National Executive, pledging retrospective relief from a future Labour government for Labour councillors penalised for breaking the Conservative's Housing Finance Acts, but Parliamentary pressure caused the NEC to refer the matter back to its Home Policy Sub-Committee.

A peculiarly Scottish issue causing much division at Scottish Labour's 1972 conference was Roman Catholic schooling. The 1918 Education Act took RC schools into the state sector at a time when Catholics were too poor to maintain their separate religious schooling and had genuine reason to fear for their integrity. Given that those circumstances no longer pertained, Labour in Scotland was faced with a seeming dilemma of how to reconcile support for comprehensive schooling with the existence of separate RC schools. Any move to deprive RC schools of a measure of independence was likely to alienate many Labour supporters. Treading carefully, 1971 Conference had remitted to its Executive a number of resolutions calling for an end to segregated education. The Executive conducted an enquiry and noted the 'resolute opposition' of most official Catholic bodies to any alteration of the 1918 Act and that most Labour Parties favoured the ending of the segregated schools but had no wish to see it foisted on Catholics. The conclusion was that 'increased harmony will not be achieved by the immediate desegregation of our schools' and so Labour in Scotland decided to proceed with desegregation only on the basis of a consensus which looks unlikely ever to be forthcoming. The position remains unaltered despite sporadic attempts, mainly in the East of Scotland, to force a move on the issue.

Despite the lack of concern with the matter of devolution at 1972 Conference, the Scottish Council set up its working group on devolution in January 1973 in anticipation of the Report of the Royal Commission on the Constitution. Further proof of SNP revival came in March in the Dundee East by-election where they polled 30.2 per cent against Labour's 32.7 per cent. But Glasgow Govan proved the biggest shock of the year as Margo MacDonald swept out Labour with its 16,000 majority in traditional Labour territory, the run-down inner city. A few days before, Labour had published the result of its devolution sub-committee's research — a flat rejection of the devolution case. The timing could not have been worse and, according to Dalyell, the Govan debacle marked the beginning of Wilson's conversion to devolution.[8] Labour's policy document, 'Scotland and the UK' completely rejected any assembly, proposing instead 'the gradual but continual extension of administrative devolution within the UK Parliament.'

Hot on its heels came the Kilbrandon Commission, more than two years late. Its majority backed legislative devolution to Scotland and Wales while a minority backed decentralisation for all regions of the UK and another minority favoured non-legislative devolution. All members of the Commission, however, favoured the abolition of the office of Secretary of State for Scotland and this was siezed upon by Ross and other anti-devolutionists in Scottish Labour. On the pro-devolutionist's side was the fact that Kilbrandon favoured an elected assembly of some kind for Scotland. The official Labour reaction in Scotland tended to hostility but this was not to be of great importance in British Labour's hasty moves to adoption of the substance of Kilbrandon's majority recommendation. What mattered was that Scotland was essential to any Labour government being returned. A close-run fight with the SNP could lose Labour the right to govern at UK level and from then on the anti-devolution Scottish Executive became an irritant to the British Labour leadership, at least until it changed its mind. Although many in the LPS still favoured the economic road to combatting nationalism, they were soon to be pushed towards of devolution.

When Heath took the country to the polls in February 1974 the official position of Labour in Scotland was of opposition to devolution. There was no specifically Scottish election manifesto, the first of which was to appear in October. Coming in the aftermath of the miner's strike and the three-day week, Labour's victory came as a surprise to many as was the breakthrough of the SNP, who won seven seats. Labour's vote fell to 36.6 per cent of the total and its Scottish seats to 40. It had not put a lot of preparation into fighting an election, being preoccupied with the reorganisation of local government and the industrial troubles until the false alarm of a 7 February election set the machine in motion. A special leaflet on oil was prepared and circulated in an attempt to combat the successful SNP propaganda, but the Scottish results gave little pleasure and certainly strengthened the hand of Scottish Labour's pro-devolutionists.

As soon as it entered office the new Labour Government, with its precarious minority, set the wheels of devolution in motion. The Queen's Speech promised to consider the Kilbrandon Report and bring forward proposals, but in the debate on the Queen's Speech,

Wilson went much further. In reply to an interjection from an irate Winnie Ewing, SNP MP for Moray and Nairn, a White Paper and Bill, were promised. Dalyell believes that Wilson's remark was 'off the cuff' and unplanned[9] but this seems unlikely, given signs of Wilson's conversion to devolution as early as 1973, 'when, in a speech at Edinburgh he had called for regional government in England and implied that this should be part of a general scheme of devolution'.[10] Whether or not Wilson intended that day to give his assurance, the Labour Party had not discussed devolution since its electoral victory. Labour's Parliamentary leadership was faced with selling devolution, both for Scotland and Wales, to a sceptical party.

The same day that Wilson made his promise, the Scottish Council's Executive was meeting in Glasgow where it welcomed Kilbrandon's rejection of separation, but little else, and urged that decisions affecting Scotland be taken in Scotland wherever possible. It was hardly an endorsement of the idea of legislative assemblies, but rather a restatement of the old commitment to greater administrative devolution within existing structures. That year's SCLP Annual Conference was important: resolutions on Scottish government came from both sides of the devolution divide. A resolution from the G&MWU condemning Kilbrandon was thrown out by Conference which opted instead for an Executive statement adequate to convince many that it was moving in a devolutionary direction. The advocacy of devolution by two of the authors of *Don't Butcher Scotland's Future*, Sillars and Ewing, marked an interesting about-turn. Throughout the period of the Conservative government, the two had met with Paisley MP, John Robertson, and Alex Eadie, Midlothian, to act as a pro-devolution caucus, pushing Labour towards adoption of the policy. Their group formed the basis of a breakaway from Labour — the Scottish Labour Party to be formed in late 1975 — though Eadie stopped meeting with the others in early 1974 and Ewing in October of that year. Both became loyal members of Wilson's governments, active in the fight for their devolution commitment in the BLP. The LPS emerged from the 1974 Annual Conference seemingly poised on the brink of a policy change.

In Westminster two supporters of devolution were brought into Wilson's Cabinet to produce his promised White Paper: Ted Short, Wilson's Deputy Leader, and Norman Crowther-Hunt, a member of Kilbrandon. The product of their labours *Devolution in the UK — Some Alternatives for Discussion*, called for comments. Ross took charge of the Scottish end and it must have been a strange task for the arch-enemy of the Nationalists and former opponent of devolution now to sell it to the party which he had encouraged in its intransigent stance against devolution. The bringing to heel of Labour's Scottish Executive in Scotland was fairly quickly done. Enthusiastic grass-roots support for the concept of legislative devolution was to take a little longer and its failure to permeate all sections of the Party was to cause much trouble later.

On 22 June 1974 the SCLP EC voted down all five of the Government's White Paper options: the vote was six to five, most of the EC being absent for various reasons. In retrospect it seems remarkable that such an important meeting could have been so ineptly handled as to allow for only eleven to be in attendance and six of those anti-devolutionists. With only another two present, the decision could have gone the other way and much of what came after could have been avoided. As it was, furious reaction at the decision came from Scots and English Party members alike. At a NEC meeting on 7 July, Alex Kitson, Scottish Secretary of the TGWU, and Judith Hart, MP for Lanark, were behind a resolution pledging support for the government's devolution commitment which was carried. Earlier that month the SCLP EC had agreed to hold a Special Conference on the issue, after a bit of arm-twisting from London in the form of a letter from General Secretary Ron Hayward. A sub-committee was set up to draft a paper but the next meeting of the EC chose to ignore pressures emanating from London and Scotland, confining itself to making arrangements for the Conference and refusing even to consider changing its mind.

Labour in Scotland, then, entered its Special Conference on devolution with its Scottish Executive Committee opposed to the concept, a Government pledged to legislate on it, a NEC favouring a Scottish Assembly with legislative powers and a Party membership split down the middle. 354 delegates attended this historic conference on 16 August 1974. The NEC backed devolution for the Scottish people but not in their own party, it seemed. Allan Campbell McLean, Chairman of the Inverness-shire CLP, moved the position of the Scottish Executive as outlined in the paper 'Scotland and the UK' and in doing so declared himself a devolutionist, 'but in the sense that he believed in the devolution of power from capital to labour.'[11] This principled statement of the traditional socialist case for radical economic policies to tackle the root cause of Scottish discontent was never to be totally rejected by Labour in Scotland, but it was to take second place to what could realistically be seen as something the Labour leadership could actually deliver. In the event, even that supposition was misplaced. In 1974, though, it was imperative that Labour in Scotland make a commitment to Scottish devolution and instrumental in this were the major Trades Unions. Since March 1974, the TGWU had swung behind the devolution cause, strongly influenced by Alex Kitson who had moved the NEC resolution on the Scottish Assembly. The NUM, thanks to the dominant Communist Party influence, was, like the CP, a long-term supporter of Scottish Home Rule. The Engineers, though divided on the issue, backed the devolution line at Special Conference. The Unions alone were insufficient to provide the decisive majority that defeated the Scottish Executive line. Constituency parties, whether out of genuine commitment to devolution or just a recognition of their own impotence, generally backed devolution. Of five propositions put to the meeting, the first two, which backed the return of a majority Labour Government and opposed separatism, were unanimously carried. The third put the Scottish EC line declaring an Assembly 'irrelevant to the needs and aspirations of the people of Scotland' and affirming 'the need for unity of action by the working people of the UK'. It was lost by a large majority. The fourth proposition supported the setting up of a legislative assembly 'within the context of the political and economic unity of the UK' and was carried by a large majority. Opposition to a reduction in Scots MPs at Westminster was unanimously backed. Thus Labour in Scotland was brought into line. From that moment on, the Labour Government was saddled with a commitment which, try as it might, it was never able to fulfil.

Drafting of Labour Party devolution policy was done in London by an NEC sub-committee, and the result 'Bringing Power to the People', published on 3 September. It echoed the SCLP Conference decisions and made similar proposals for Wales. Significant in the document was the new interpretation put on past SCLP Conference decisions. Many had thought Labour in Scotland had ditched devolution in 1958, now they were expected to perceive a thread running through Labour Party policy decisions leading to Scottish devolution. No wonder many were sceptical of Labour's new-found commitment to action on the matter.

Labour's next White Paper on devolution was published on 17 September, the day before the next General Election. The result justified those in Labour who claimed something must be done quickly about devolution. The SNP swept into second position in Scotland, taking 30.4 per cent of the vote, 11 seats and 35 second places. Labour's 41 seats were won on its lowest post-war vote of 36.3 per cent. Labour just achieved its desired majority and at the commencement of Parliament, it had three more seats than the rest of the parties put together. The two-party system was at it weakest post-war point with an enormous Liberal vote in England matched by the rise of the Celtic Nationalist Parties.

For the first time, Labour in Scotland campaigned around a specifically Scottish election manifesto, In many ways just a souped-up version of the British one, it illustrated the concern with which Labour now viewed its Scottish vote. The crucial issue with which to woo Scottish voters was devolution and the manifesto promised a Scottish Assembly, dealing with Scottish affairs — with control of its own expenditure. The SDA was to be in the hands of the Secretary of State but shift of control later was alluded to, a proposal which illustrated Labour's shift in belief in central economic planning to belief in greater regional autonomy. Other important commitments for Scotland were on oil and land. Oil was not to be Scotland's, that is, it was to be exploited by a British National Oil Corporation under central government control. On land, Labour's promise to move on the vexed issue of crofting land by introducing legislation to give crofters the right to buy their crofts, flew directly in the face of much grass-roots Party opinion.

Despite the massive tasks facing Labour in seeking to restructure the Scottish economy and halt rising unemployment, the issue of devolution dominated Labour in Scotland and Scottish politics in the next four years. Consensus around the government's proposals was never achieved inside the Party and the referendum campaign allowed the differences to be disastrously aired. But as Labour emerged from its narrow October victory it was set to push ahead with legislation on devolution, something it wished to get out of the way as soon as possible, since its main concern was still Britains's ailing economy.

Ted Short, head of the devolutionary Constitution Unit, faced a continued opposition from Labour Scottish Executive. In January 1975 it wrote to him 'in some dismay at the speed with which the Government appear to be moving towards greater devolution'. Worry was expressed that the Assembly would have too much power and this would herald the break-up of the UK. The 'slippery slope' argument still had a great deal deal of currency in the Party and was to be revived during the referendum campaign. The letter also warned against separate tax-raising powers and assembly control of the SDA. The Conference in March, however, with a new EC which included Jim Sillars, narrowly backed control of the SDA remaining with central government, but from then on opinion on this was to shift.

Labour had fought the election on a platform of crofting land reforms and Conference, against the advice of its EC, backed a resolution calling for the nationalisation of all Scottish land. In 1976 the Government rejected the advice of its Party in Scotland by introducing the Crofting Reform (Scotland) Act. It entitled crofters to a share in their land's development value and gave the option of ownership of crofts and land. In doing so, said its detractors, it exposed crofters to the commercial pressures to sell up to developers. Labour's Scottish working party on crofting favoured the public ownership of crofting land and the governments's proposals provoked the resignation of two of its leading members, and firm anti-devolutionists: Allan Campbell McLean, former SCLP Chairman; and Brian Wilson of the *West Highland Free Press*, the only left-of-centre newspaper in the Highlands. The government proposals were similar to those of the last Conservative government and had little effect. By the end of 1977 only 78 whole crofts and 10 part crofts along with 38 house sites had been sold. The main effect had been to encourage tourist enterprises and extra home building. The important question of the whole agrarian structure of the Highlands and the need for job development outside agriculture and crafts was ignored. The refusal of the leadership of the Labour Party to act on the Party policy of land nationalisation increased the cynicism of many members about the willingness of the Labour Party's leadership ever to implement any radical socialist measures.

Economic worries continued to provide a backdrop during 1975 to further devolution developments. The possible collapse of British Leyland in May, was averted by a massive injection of cash which saved thousands of Scottish jobs in Glasgow and Bathgate. The same year saw the launch of the SDA and the collapse of Scotland's first workers' co-op newspaper, the *Scottish Daily News*. Unemployment leapt over the 100,000 mark again, but nationalism and devolution continued to dominate political debate in Scotland.

In August 1975 the SNP captured a seat from Labour in the Lothian Region. Their candidate, Stephen Maxwell, pushed Labour into third place in the working-class seat of Slateford-Hailes, serving to remind Labour how vulnerable its urban working-class vote was becoming. A further assault came at the end of the year in the form of a breakaway party when the Scottish Labour Party, was born. Jim Sillars, MP for South Ayrshire with Labour's biggest Scottish majority, had been a late convert to the devolution cause but had sought, with others, to push Labour towards commitment to it. The EEC referendum resulting in a 'Yes' vote, had disappointed many in Labour in Scotland who then converted their own anti-EEC position into one favouring independent Scottish representation in Brussels. Sillars advanced this line as he continued to push for a more powerful Scottish Assembly. In October 1974, Sillars' old friend, Harry Ewing, was drafted into government to deal with devolution. In November 1975 the White Paper *Our Changing Democracy* came out against economic powers for the Assembly. At a press conference launch, Ross backed the plans and asserted his support for 'the political and economic unity of the United Kingdom'. This phrase was becoming the most frequently used piece of jargon employed by Labour Party spokesmen in attempts to explain Labour's devolution machinations.

For Sillars, the White Paper was the last straw. He broke with the Labour Party over the issue of Assembly control over the SDA and on 22 December 1975, unveiled his plans for the SLP, the name of the party founded by Keir Hardie in 1888. Labour Party reaction in Scotland was furious although press statements were initially cool. Sillars' dream of dual membership with the BLP was quickly shattered by threats of expulsion. On 18 January 1976 the SLP was launched. It never achieved much electoral success, peaking at fourteen per cent of the vote in a local government by-election, but it had a significant effect on the morale of Labour Party members in Scotland. Many of its 900 members came from the Labour Party, but it ultimately fell apart, partly due to the disruptive influence of the ultra-left, and partly to the authoritarian style adopted by Sillars. Besides Sillars, the breakaway attracted only one other Labour MP, John Robertson. The MP for Paisley was never one of Labour's more dynamic assets, but Labour's Scottish machine was the weaker for his loss and that of Alex Neil, its Research Officer, Bob Brown, its press adviser, and Danus Skene, an EC member. The breakaway party failed to attract the support of any leading Scottish trade unionists and from the start, membership consisted mainly of middle-class intellectuals. It aimed to take the working-class support for independence which had, by default, gone to the SNP. If it achieved anything, it added urgency to Labour's devolution policy. Its active life was short and its members returned to the Labour Party, the SNP and the Liberals.[12]

The quest for a 'left-wing' nationalism was one which naturally arose out of the way the devolution-nationalism issue had been able to cut across the usual left-right cleavages in Scottish politics. In the SNP this could be seen in the co-existence of socialists and right-wing conservatives. In Labour it was illustrated by the strange alliances which formed around various devolution fights. Before the formation of the SLP, the Annual Meeting of the Scottish Parliamentary Group in late 1975 had witnessed a straight left-right fight between Tribunite Norman Buchan and right-winger Dickson

Mabon when Buchan proposed a referendum on devolution. Sillars and Robertson backed Mabon against Buchan. This sort of incident for Sillars must have provided added incentive to set up his SLP. The Scottish Executive was appalled at the bickering among its MPs about devolution. Jim McGrandle, acting Secretary since the resignation of Peter Allison, rebuked the MPs, reminding them that the Executive was the only body which spoke for the LPS. Shortly after the launch of Sillars' party, the SCLP started a campaign to sell devolution, 'Devolution not Separation'. In a leaflet, *The Menace of Separation: Can Scotland Go it Alone?*, the SNP were attacked on mainly economic grounds. SNP economic policy was equated with laissez-faire capitalism and it was confidently predicted that 'the Scottish people want socialist policies'. This marked a step forward for Labour in Scotland, which hoped to expose the essentially conservative nature of the SNP. Given its devolution commitment it could now turn to fighting the SNP on ground other than that of independence versus unionism.

Further evidence of the effect of Sillars' party in stimulating Labour in Scotland to abandon its reservations on devolution came at 1976 Annual Conference. The EC proposed a resolution calling for revenue-raising powers for the SDA as well as the removal of the Secretary of State's veto, and Conference swung behind those demands for more extensive devolution. In two years the SCLP EC had changed from implacable opponents of devolution to pro-devolution harriers of a grudging Westminster government. An anti-devolution minority continued to exist, but some of its members shifted into the 'minimalist' devolution camp, favouring devolution of the least amount possible. Shortly after Conference, Wilson resigned as Party Leader and Ross followed him to the back benches, his place taken by Bruce Millan, a man of similarly cautious approach.

The government's next White Paper *Devolution to Scotland and Wales: A Supplementary Statement* followed the discussion between the SCLP EC and Lord President of the Council, Michael Foot, and his deputy, John Smith, MP for North Lanark. It proposed giving control of the SDA to the Assembly, removing the Secretary of State's veto and making the seats two-member. A Bill was promised for the next session. So the government had committed itself to reforms beyond its manifesto promises, showing that it had been listening to the criticism voiced, not least from within Labour itself.

1976 saw the first discussion of devolution at a BLP Conference since 1968. The government's plans were at last given the endorsement of being official Labour Party policy, but not without a fight — the English backlash had its voice. From the start there had been opposition to devolution for Scotland and Wales from the depressed regions of England. In seconding a resolution against devolution, moved by UCATT, the construction workers' union, the delegate from Blaydon Constituency Party voiced the resentment of many when he said, 'It seems to me that eleven SNP MPs sometimes have more influence than the whole of the Northern Labour Group'. In the end, the 'pros' carried the day by almost six to one, but the anger of English Labour MPs was crucial in the later fall of the Scotland and Wales Bill. Conference also urged the government to set up the Assemblies 'without any resort to a referendum or any other delaying device'. The Scottish Council was given responsibility for drawing up an Assembly programme and selecting candidates. Michael Foot gave weight to the myth of uninterrupted Labour support for devolution by invoking the ghost of Keir Hardie in his reply to Neil Kinnock's charge of 'indecent haste': 'He (Hardie) would have asked us why we had not got on with it before'.

The Government however now had other preoccupations, for as in its last term of office financial crisis confronted it. While Annual Conference met in Blackpool, Labour Chancellor, Denis Healey was negotiating IMF loans to help Britain with its balance of payments crisis. 1976 Conference condemned its Chancellor for 'selling out' to the bankers. In this atmosphere of crisis came the Scotland and Wales Bill. It was heralded by the 'Scotland is British' campaign, launched in Glasgow by Sir John Toothill, author of the report which had given so much to the SCLP's regional policy demands of the sixties. Although financed by industrialists, it gained support from a number of Scottish Labour figures who were mainly on the right and included ex-MP George Lawson, Tam Dalyell MP, and Danny Crawford of UCATT. On 6 September 1976 the government got its Bill through the Commons on its second reading, but at a price, for the principle of a referendum was conceded.

A few days before, Labour's Scottish Council had come out in favour of a referendum 'to test public opinion'. After a rough Committee stage, the Bill eventually foundered. Dalyell, largely instrumental in achieving this, will be remembered, if for nothing else, for his formulation of the 'West Lothian question' which he set out in *Devolution: The End of Britain?*: 'We would have the absurd situation in which Scottish and Welsh MPs could continue to legislate on subjects which had been devolved to the Assemblies in their own countries. They would not be responsible to their own constituents for such legislation, nor would they be answerable to the English voters who would be affected by it.' When the Bill fell

in a 'guillotine' motion, 29 Labour MPs abstained but all areas of
the country were represented so the defeat could not be attributed
to a revolt by Labour's Northern MPs.

At Labour's 1977 Scottish Conference the main issue, despite the
Bill's recent demise, was the economy. Unemployment was running
at unprecedented levels and Conference was presented with *An
Industrial Strategy for Scotland* by the EC. The regional policy of
past governments was attacked as having been 'more concerned
with reducing the level of unemployment than with tackling the
basic deep-rooted industrial inefficiencies existing in the Scottish
economy'. The new strategy involved stimulating Scotland's run-
down indigenous industry and increased state intervention both at
industry and company level as well as in the overall management of
the economy. The SDA was to be the instrument for change. In ten
years Labour in Scotland had moved from central economic planning
and the unitary state to regional autonomy in both economic and
governmental affairs. The desertion of the old policies reflected the
new, young and on the whole, left-wing make-up of much of Labour
in Scotland's leadership.

At 1977 conference fringe meetings, delegates fought out the
devolution issue. At one 'anti' meeting Dalyell, Lawson, Allan
Campbell McLean and Brian Wilson addressed an audience, some
of whom walked out when *Scotland is British* literature was handed
out. Distrust of broad-based, extra-party campaigns was manifested
in the forthcoming referendum campaign, when although there were
two major campaigns on each side, Labour insisted on having its
own. As the Scottish Council piously insisted in its 1978 Annual
Report, when 'other political parties attempted to lure the Labour
Party into all-party alliances' it was decided that 'the Labour
Party, together with the Co-operative Party and the STUC, were
unique in their commitment to devolution for its own sake, so
attempts to form all-party fronts have been resisted'. Labour Party
memories were obviously short, or perhaps Labour's self-created
myths about its uninterrupted commitment to a Scottish Assembly
were actually believed. Long-standing Communist Party and Liberal
commitments were ignored.

In June 1977 the Scottish Executive met with the Government to
press its case for separate Scottish and Welsh Bills. The meeting
followed the May 1977 local elections in which Labour lost control
of every major District authority they had held in Scotland, with the
SNP making significant gains. At the meeting there was insistence
on allowance for a referendum in any future legislation. In July
Foot told the Commons that there would, indeed, be two bills. The

new Scotland Bill was much less detailed than before and powers to over-ride legislation were curbed. Disputes over the powers of the Assembly were to be referred to the judicial committee of the Privy Council. The Assembly as proposed, however, still lacked substantial industrial or economic functions and had no revenue-raising powers of its own. Provision was there for a referendum, but to the displeasure of Labour's Scottish Council which had wanted independence to be voted on too, there was to be only one question — for or against an Assembly. Throughout the year, hard work was done to calm down English Labour unease over devolution. A meeting in July 1977 between the SCLP EC and the Northern EC of the Labour Party went well with a growing realisation being apparent among the Northerners of the importance, to the Scots, of devolution. Visits also took place to meet the executives of the North East and North West Regions. A fringe meeting to put the Scottish case was arranged for Annual conference in Blackpool. Scottish Labour's new Secretary, Helen Liddell, spoke alongside John Smith and Emrys Jones of the Welsh Council of the Labour Party. Labour in Scotland was doing everything possible to smooth the way for the government's plans. By 14 November 1977, the Bill had passed its first reading and on 22 November the Committee stage began but real trouble came in January. A Scots MP representing a London seat, George Cunningham, managed to carry an amendment insisting that only in the event of at least forty per cent of the electorate voting 'Yes' to an Assembly would the government go ahead and set one up. From then on the fight became one not just about simple majorities but about electoral turnout as well. Cunningham's amendment was backed by five Scots Labour MPs: Robin Cook, Peter Doig, Tam Dalyell, Bob Hughes, and William Hamilton, a strange alliance of right and left. Their action ultimately sealed the fate of their Party's proposals for devolution. By the time the Bill passed through its third reading on 22 February, a 'Labour Vote No' campaign had been formed.

In 1978 the tide of nationalism was turning. Although Labour in Scotland approached three Parliamentary by-elections with immense trepidation, its fears proved to be unfounded. On 13 April the Glasgow Garscadden by-election looked an ideal opportunity for the SNP to increase its Parliamentary representation. It had won all six Glasgow District Council seats in the constituency the previous year and fielded a well-known local candidate. Labour's man, Donald Dewar, was on the right of the Party and strongly pro-devolution. In the event it was a handsome victory for Labour, with a 4,500 majority over the SNP. Hot on the heels of Garscadden came

Hamilton, scene of Winnie Ewing's astounding 1967 victory. Alex Wilson, who had first lost to, then beaten Mrs Ewing, died and George Robertson, former SCLP Chairman and G&MWU full-time official, took the seat and doubled Labour's majority. In October the death of John P. Mackintosh occasioned the third convincing Labour win of the year. John Hume Robertson, a local farmer, was returned with a 3,000 majority. These results were matched by a strong Labour performance in the Regional elections where Labour added Central and Lothian to its control of Fife and Strathclyde Regions, a blow to the SNP who took only 20.9 per cent of the vote to Labour's 40 per cent. How much the government's enactment of the Scotland Bill had to do with all this is uncertain, since electoral polls at the time suggested that this relative Labour recovery was 'not peculiar to Scotland' and may have been due to its handling of the economy. Whether or not this was the case, the victories in Scotland enormously boosted the confidence of the Labour Party.

In November 1978 the government announced the date of the referendum on the proposed Scottish and Welsh Assemblies — 1 March 1979, but the run-up to it was to be a period of acute difficulty. In July it had set a five per cent pay limit which ran into opposition in October by the Labour Party Annual Conference and in December the government was forced to abandon sanctions against employers who broke the pay limits. The New Year opened with a transport strike in Scotland followed by a day of action by local authority workers whose winter-long wages campaign had earned the period the nickname 'the winter of discontent'. On 21 February 1979 the local authority manual workers settled for a similar amount. It was a disastrous period for Labour's relations with the Trade Union movement and an unfortunate backdrop against which to stage the referendum campaign.

The details of the referendum campaign have been well-documented elsewhere so what is detailed here will be confined to the Labour Party's role. Labour in Scotland officially grouped under the banner of the 'Labour Says Yes'campaign, or the Labour Movement 'Yes' Campaign as it came to be known. Campaign plans were announced at the end of November 1978 and the NEC made a grant of £50,000 to the SCLP to cover both the referendum campaign and the subsequent assembly elections. Those in the Party who opposed the government's assembly plans were given complete freedom to campaign publicly, a fatal decision in retrospect. To demand public loyalty, however, to proposals which so deeply divided the Party would have been courting disaster and would also have been against the traditions of what, after all, has never been a democratic centralist organisation. It was hoped that harmony, certainly lacking during the campaign, could be restored after the referendum. Besides Labour's official 'Yes' campaign there was the 'Labour Vote No' campaign and numerous other umbrella campaigns. The main 'Yes' umbrella, 'Yes for Scotland', was officially spurned by Labour and seen by many Party members as an SNP front. It enjoyed support from Jim Sillars who shortly after joined the SNP. Despite this, it did attract Labour support from, among others, Alex Kitson of the TGWU, whose influence in his union had done so much to bring the Labour Party in Scotland to devolution in the first place. In contrast, the 'No' umbrella was almost entirely Conservative, Labour's 'No' men grouping in their own campaign.

The Labour Movement 'Yes' Campaign was never able to compete in financial terms with its umbrella sister, but it did receive valuable Trade Union aid. Half a million broadsheets were given by the TGWU and an extensive programme of meetings and rallies planned. There was, as previously decided, no official co-operation with other parties or campaigns. The reason for this lay partly in the threats by some in the Party to campaign publicly against Labour policy if Labour joined the main 'Yes' umbrella, and so the compliance of potential opponents was bought by the exclusively Labour campaign.

In January 1979 *The Scotsman* carried a survey by Neal Ascherson of the state of Labour's campaign in the constituencies. Helen Liddell reported that she had asked all CLPs to set up official 'Yes' committees and that all but five said they would. Doubts, however, were cast on the accuracy of this assessment, for in 1979 only 36 CLPs had active campaign committees. It is true there were no CLPs which officially backed a 'No' campaign, but seven had not yet made a decision and twenty had decided not to set up official campaigns. In many cases, such as that of Central Edinburgh, this may have been to prevent further internal rifts between a party and a member who found themselves on opposite sides of the fence. But much resentment at the government's plans also still existed and was voiced by CLPs such as North Edinburgh which came close to mounting its own, official 'No' campaign and Inverness, whose Chairman, Allan McLean told *The Scotsman* 'the 'Yes' people will not get one halfpenny from us'.

The campaign did not split Labour in Scotland on traditional left-right lines: on the 'Yes' side ranged forces as disparate as the Militant Tendency, Labour Trotskyists, and Bruce Millan. Ironically, Militant had been anti-devolution until a majority of its English members had instructed the Scottish members to back the Party line. On the 'No' side Tam Dalyell joined forces with traditional Tribune leftists like Norman Buchan. The left, however, were more divided than the right on the issue: 'those who think that an Assembly is irrelevant to the transfer of power to the working-class' and 'the young cadres who assume that a self-governing Scotland can undertake experiments in socialism which would never be passed through Westminster'.[13] However, Helen Liddell made quite clear what Labour did and did not envisage the assembly achieving: 'It would be a serious mistake to think that the establishment of an Assembly will bring Scotland to the brink of the Socialist millenium. It won't. What it will do, though, is give greater control over Scottish affairs to working people and it will take us nearer to full democratic accountability of government.'[14] A further irony was the way that some of the same people on the left who had campaigned for the primacy of Party policy publicly opposed the very policy Conference had endorsed.

Besides being a great test of the Labour Party's ability to survive massive internal strain, the referendum tested the depth of its commitment to devolution and its ability to argue its case, a test which it failed. It was easy for the 'No' people to put a case against the Scottish Assembly: more government,higher taxation, possible separation, no powers to tackle the real economic problems of Scotland. The 'Yes' side had a much harder case to make. A smallish number who had always supported a form of Scottish home rule as a way of democratising, and making less remote, central government, were joined by those who saw the creation of the Assembly as the only way to disarm the SNP and restore Labour's hegemony in Scotland. The difficulty in arguing for something which, five years before, had been virulently opposed, then reluctantly accepted by many in Labour, was apparent in its campaigning.

Throughout the campaign the possibility of achieving a 40 per cent 'Yes' vote was always in doubt. Labour put out one million leaflets and 1,000 posters, held four big rallies and countless smaller meetings which boasted the Prime Minister and seven other Cabinet Ministers as speakers, but the opposition proved too competent. Since staying at home effectively counted as a 'No' vote, the odds against getting a 40 per cent 'Yes' vote were high. The result, in a 63.9 per cent poll was a 'Yes' vote of 32.9 per cent and a 'No' vote of 30.8 per cent. It was not enough. The Labour Scottish Council, meeting the week after, reaffirmed its support for devolution without any indication of how an assembly might be achieved. Bruce Millan assured Conference the Government would not ditch devolution and, in a mood of gloom and pessimism, delegates swung behind their EC. The government, in the following days, looked for ways out of its dilemma. All-party talks were rejected after government refusal to make the repeal order on the assemblies a matter of confidence. It was clear a General Election was coming and the government fell on a Tory motion of 'no confidence' on 28 March 1979. On 20 June, the new Conservative government repealed the Scotland Act.

The General Election results were, despite everything, good for Labour in Scotland. It took nearly 42 per cent of the vote and 44 seats and returned to its pre-1974 position despite a lower share of the poll. Scotland followed once more divergent course from England, by swinging to Labour. The Sillars-led Scottish Labour Party, was wiped off the map, and the SNP were cut back to two seats and 17.2 per cent of the vote. It was a dramatic turnaround from 1974 and it seems likely that the SNP's poor showing was a product of the blame attached to them over the fall of the government and the demise of the Assembly. The election marked a return to 'British' politics in Scotland. The issues which decided people on how to vote were the ones presented throughout the country by the British parties: tax cuts, public spending, the Unions, unemployment. Devolution took a comparative back seat. But the vote left things unresolved. With victory in Scotland but defeat in England, Labour in Scotland acutely realised the value of an assembly in such a situation. As Neal Ascherson wrote in *The Scotsman* of 5 May: 'An entirely maddening poll, taken on Thursday night, showed that the very people who had evaded a clear 'Yes' vote in the referendum and then deserted the SNP still thought, by a majority of more than seventy per cent, that devolution had been a 'good idea'. While this option remains, as an escape hatch from British decline or from unwelcome policies at Westminster, Scottish politics will never be stable.'

8

The Scottish T.U.C. —
Scotland's Assembly of Labour

JAMES CRAIGEN

At the inaugural conference of the Scottish Trades Union Congress at Glasgow in March 1897, Duncan McPherson of the tinplate workers' union, the congress's first president, declared that it was being set up 'because we believe that if we want anything well done, we have got to do it ourselves. . . there are many questions which affect Scotland particularly to which our English fellow trade unionists cannot be expected to devote the necessary amount of time and attention they deserve'[1]. The seventy delegates present went on to carry resolutions on the common ownership of the means of production and political representation for labour in Parliament which would not then have been acceptable to the British TUC, one good reason why it did not recognize the new Scottish congress for most of the first two decades of its existence.

Yet in no sense was this a breakaway by trade unions in Scotland from British trade unionism. Several Scottish-based unions continued without disruption to affiliate to the older Trades Union Congress founded at Manchester in 1868 and joined the new Congress as well.[2] In the late Victorian era the STUC was viewed as another example of a Scottish body emerging in tandem with an existing British institution. Scottish MPs were said to be doubtful about its prospects and thought that the Scottish Congress would prove to be an ephemeral growth.[3] Leaders of a Liberal-leaning TUC were possibly also sceptical of the motives of the politicians associated with its formation, for Keir Hardie, Robert Smillie, George Carson and others in the Independent Labour Party all had a hand in its birth.

The Webbs put trade union membership in Scotland in 1892 at 146,935.[4] The proportion of trade unionists in British-based unions was relatively low and more evident amongst the shipbuilding and engineering crafts or organised labourers in the emergent general workers' unions. The 1895 board of Trade Blue Book estimates trade union membership in Britain at 1,330,104. However, of the 1,250 registered trade societies only twenty-five organised more than 10,000 members and nearly one thousand of them had fewer than five hundred members. Constitutional changes approved by the TUC at Cardiff in September 1895 included the use of the card vote and the abolition of trades council representation at the annual Congress. Only trade unions were eligible to affiliate and their voting strength would be based on paid membership and not the number of delegates sent. Revised qualifications for delegates also excluded those not working at their trade or as paid trade union officials.[5] The disaffiliation of trades councils and other changes were reckoned to have 'clipped the wings' of the socialists.[6]

Many small unions in Scotland never affiliated to the TUC because of cost or distance. For them local trades councils as federations of branches and district unions provided more support industrially. As unions developed in size and centralised their policy-making process the role of trades councils diminished. In Scotland, trades councils such as Glasgow, Edinburgh, Aberdeen and Dundee retained an importance as local centres for industrial and political issues and on occasions sponsored candidates in municipal and parliamentary elections. Over the years many trades councils in Scotland seldom affiliated or bothered to send delegates to the TUC anyway.[7] Yet the Cardiff TUC decisions provoked talk of setting up a rival Congress. The hallmark of British trade unionism was its development independently of the political or religious divides which were commonplace on the Continent.[8] The closed-membership craft unions or open-membership general workers' unions could all affiliate to a single TUC. Despite a reduced influence on the TUC, the ILP paper *Labour Leader* warned against splitting the movement: 'If the potential unity of British Labour is to be inevitably frustrated let the blame rest on the reactionaries and not the socialists. With two Congresses in the field one would always be played against the other'.[9] After that, Aberdeen trades council called upon Scottish trades councils to discuss their disaffiliation. The conference held at Dundee on 9 November 1895 was attended by delegates from Aberdeen, Dundee, Glasgow, Edinburgh, Govan and Paisley.[10] A protest resolution was adopted and trades councils were urged to work for re-admission. There was support for a London Trades Council call for a national conference to consider the idea of a Trades Council Congress but that proposal came to nothing.

The subsequent emergence of a Scottish TUC would imply no such threat to the British TUC, for the precedent of a territorial

Congress had been set in 1894 when Irish trade unionists dissatisfied with TUC interest in their affairs founded an Irish TUC.[11] Since ILP leaders believed in 'Home Rule all round' a Scottish Congress represented no threat of a split and politically it would be more sympathetic to them than the TUC. Another meeting of Scottish trades councils in the spring of 1896 pushed these ideas further. By then many small trades thought their survival was at stake against the background of growing employer organisation and readily available non-union labour. In November 1895 over 7,000 workers were locked out on the Clyde and thousands more affected by the dispute which began over an Amalgamated Society of Engineers' wage claim. By the end of that year the Master Engineers on the Clyde and at Belfast and in the North of England had formed an Employers' Federation.[12] The dispute lasted until January 1896 when the employers' terms were accepted.

Plans to create a protective Trades Federation to assist trade unionists in dispute were another casualty at the Cardiff TUC when a report not to the liking of the better-off craft unions was rejected on a card vote. Scottish trades councils thus readily responded when Falkirk and District United Trades Council called a conference to consider the advisability of establishing a federation of trade unions for protective purposes and 'mutual aid in times of trouble'.[13] The meeting at Falkirk on 25 April 1896 was attended by delegates from Falkirk, Glasgow, Edinburgh, Aberdeen, Dundee, Govan, Paisley, Greenock, Motherwell, Dunfermline and Montrose. Significantly three organisations promoting trade unionism amongst women employees were also represented: Glasgow Council for Women's Trades, the National Council for Women's Trades, and the Women's Protective and Provident League. Apologies and messages of support from Arbroath, Hawick, Inverness, Kilmarnock and Kirkcaldy trades councils emphasise the strength of feeling.

The British TUC met in Scotland for a sixth time in 1896. This Edinburgh TUC had affiliations from 145 trade unions and the membership exceeded one million. There was no mention of trades council re-admission even by the chairman of Edinburgh Trades Council in his opening address to the 350 delegates. The Scottish Trades and Labour Federation Committee presented a six-point scheme to a meeting in Edinburgh on 11 September 1896. The chairman of the Congress told the delegates of the difficulties in drafting a scheme to suit everyone.[14] A further conference was to be held in six months time after the Federation Committee had finalised the scheme. A delegate from the Glasgow Iron and Steel Workers proposed that an annual Scottish Trades Union Congress be held.

An attempt by two Glasgow delegates to postpone the decision until a Federation got established was defeated by twenty-two votes to six.

When the first STUC met in Glasgow on 25 March 1897 for three days, apart from the presence of trades councils and an absence of card voting, its business procedures drew heavily on established TUC practices. If not a 'Parliament of Labour' as Victorians dubbed the TUC, the Scottish Congress conducted itself as Scotland's Assembly of Labour. There were 47 trade unions in affiliation with 41,090 members, but only eight trades councils considering the original fuss. Glasgow gave a civic address to the delegates in the former St Andrew's Hall on the opening day and a Civic Reception on the Friday evening attended by 700. The 74 delegates, it is recorded, 'included several ladies' and Glasgow Council of Women's Trades gave a luncheon that Friday. The Federation Committee was now styled interim Parliamentary Committee thus emulating its TUC counterpart.

The larger Scottish unions like the Miners, Ironmoulders, Iron and Steelworkers, Masons, Tinplate Workers, Bakers and Typographers were affiliated, as were several British unions such as the Railway Servants and the Musicians, and Tailors who had both Scottish and English societies. Other British unions had complained of shortage of time or the need to make some constitutional provision to be represented in future. Govan No 3 Branch of the Amalgamated Society of Engineers was affiliated, but the union itself showed no great interest in the STUC until after the First World War. Disputes over recruiting rights and membership were a regular feature in early STUC debates. Eventually amalgamation settled their feuding and not STUC attempts at conciliation.

For Scottish trade unionists, differences in the system of law and court administration from those in England and the separate traditions in education or organisation of local government, required special debate for which there was more time than at the TUC. A debate on the Fatal Accidents (Scotland) Act 1895 was introduced by Robert Smillie (Lanarkshire Miners) who wanted the same type of enquiry in Scotland into fatal accidents at work as at Coroner's Inquests in England. In another debate, John Cronin proposed the establishment of a Scottish Branch in the Labour Department at the Board of Trade which could take up the 'question of declining industries'. The STUC approved that idea, but rejected another proposal that the Parliamentary Committee should set up a Labour Information Bureau for trade unions. Cronnin, on behalf of the Parliamentary committee, replied that it was job for the Board of Trade. The STUC also debated issues which over the years had

found less favour at the TUC and supported the miners' eight-hour
bill, limitation of hours of labour, and payment of MPs. A motion on
nationalisation was also carried with only three delegates dissenting.
Labour Leader noted that eight ILP members were elected to the
new Parliamentary Committee. Only one of the twelve members
belonged to a British-based union. A Miss Irwin topped the poll with
60 votes, but at the first meeting of the Parliamentary Committee
she declined the chair because 'feeling was not quite ripe enough
for a woman to occupy such a position'. Smillie, who got 57
votes, became chairman and exerted considerable influence in
the formative years of the new body. In a separate election for
Secretary a factory inspector Andrew Ballantyne, nominated by the
National Council for Women's Trades, beat Chisholm Robertson of
the Stirlingshire Miners, but within two months he resigned because
his Civil Service employer raised objections. Miss Irwin took over
as interim Secretary of the Parliamentary Committee which was 'to
watch all legislative measures directly affecting questions of labour'
and amongst its other duties 'to initiate such legislative action as
Congress may direct'.

A printed annual report was presented to the 1898 STUC at
Aberdeen with the Parliamentary Committee confident that 'an
important future lies before it'. Scottish issues likely to result in
some success had been given priority. A meeting in Edinburgh on
27 October 1897 with the Secretary for Scotland and Lord Advocate
on the Fatal Accidents legislation apparently produced a satisfactory
outcome. Robert Smillie and Peter Ross of the Carpenters went to
London to lobby Ministers and MPs on the case for a Scottish
branch within the Board of Trade's Labour Department. The
Board President told them he was not convinced of the merits of
this; nor did the Secretary for Scotland want this special Labour
Department under his control. Lord Balfour made it plain: 'I think
the Board of Trade is a department which ought to be Imperial
in its operations'. The Home Secretary proved less accessible and
thought no useful purpose would be served by 'a separate deputation
of persons resident in Scotland', where legislation like the Mines
act, Conspiracy Laws, Factories Act, Early Closing of Shops, Seats
for Shop Assistants, or even the Smaller Dwellings (Scotland) Bill
were concerned. By November 1898 he relented and met the
STUC Chairman and Secretary. Although the 1898 TUC received
a telegram of good wishes from the TUC Parliamentary Committee,
a proposal at the 1898 Bristol TUC to establish fraternal contacts
with the 'Scotch and Irish Congresses' got roundly defeated. The
situation was summed up by one delegate who complained of 'the

diffusion of interests with a Scotch and Irish TUC' and of being
'threatened with a similar organisation for Wales' and until the end
of 1914-18 War the TUC remained distant.

The Scottish Trades Federation was still-born. The interim
Parliamentary Committee told Congress that consultations over the
scheme were continuing. Keir Hardie, when he addressed the 1898
STUC 'by invitation', stressed the need for a Trades Federation.
The new Parliamentary Committee was instructed to prepare and
submit a scheme at the Aberdeen congress. It differed little from the
original and the 1898 STUC voted to hear a speaker on the *Clarion*
scheme which involved funding to meet loss of earnings in disputes.
The delegates approved this scheme although later the same week
backed off doing anything about its implementation, carrying a
motion on the Previous Question by a two to one majority. In
any case the TUC called a Special Congress in January 1899 at
Manchester when the General Federation of Trade Unions came into
being. A spokesman from the GFTU, however, neither replaced the
TUC nor won acceptance from all TUC affiliates, and by this time
the shock of the famous Taff Vale judgement had boosted ideas about
an independent Labour Party in Parliament.

From the beginning the STUC supported Labour Representation
in Parliament. Keir Hardie insisted at the 1899 STUC that the
real objective was 'a new political party supported by trade union
funds and members'. Only a few weeks before, on 4 March,
representatives of the STUC, ILP and SDF met to discuss holding a
Labour Representation Conference. As the Co-operative Movement
which had over 250,000 members in some 200 individual retail
societies in Scotland was still ascertaining views on the matter,
it was decided to await the outcome. As a preliminary it was
agreed that the 1899 STUC should be asked to approve the plan
and George Carson moved the Parliamentary Committee's proposal
'That in view of the great necessity for the direct representation in
Parliament of Labour interests the Parliamentary Committee of the
Scottish Trades Union Congress invites the Congress to empower
it to take the necessary steps, in conjunction with such working-
class organisations as may be willing to co-operate, in convening
during the current year a Special Congress to decide upon united
working-class action at the next General Election'. An addendum
incorporating local authority representation was approved. Delegates
from the Bricklayers' Association and West Lothian and Renfrew
Miners wanted the term 'working-class' deleted because they
thought it narrow and difficult to define. However, their amendment
was defeated after John Kerr of the Aberdeen Trades Council argued

that it should be made clear that the STUC was 'a working-class movement'.

The Scottish Labour Representation Conference which met in Edinburgh on 2 January 1900 was the largest gathering so far held on the issue with 226 delegates from trade unions and trades councils, the ILP, SDF, and a number of Co-operative societies, and it adopted resolutions to secure 'direct working-class representation'. A twelve member Scottish Workers' Parliamentary Representation Committee was elected, comprising four STUC, two ILP, two SDF and four Co-operative nominees. A trade unionist and SDF activist, Robert Allan, became Secretary, to be succeeded in 1902 by George Carson. This Scottish initiative was soon overtaken by the establishment of the better-known Labour Representation Committee at a Special Conference convened by the TUC in London in February 1900.

The 'Khaki election' in October 1900 came too soon for the fledgling Representation Committee and its first real contest was at the North-East Lanark by-election in 1901, when Robert Smillie came third to a Liberal Unionist. In the Liberal landslide at the 1906 election only two Scottish Labour MPs were returned among the fifty-four Labour men to enter the Commons. Both were sponsored by the LRC and were General Secretaries of British unions. None of the SWRC candidates succeeded.

At the 1908 STUC, many delegates seemed to think that with the creation of a Labour Party the STUC had served its purpose. A rambling motion presented by David Palmer of Aberdeen Trades Council, questioned the need for the STUC. On a show of hands this motion was defeated by 52 votes to 51. The voting was challenged and on a recount the motion was carried by 58 votes to 50. Not surprisingly, the incoming Parliamentary Committee, which now included Palmer, decided to take no further action. At the 1910 STUC a motion from the Postmen's Federation instructing the Parliamentary Committee to confer with the TUC 'with a view towards amalgamation under the title Trades Union Congress of Great Britain and Ireland' was defeated by a large majority.

The continuing weakness of the Labour Party in Scotland worried the Party leadership and the STUC was represented at a conference in Edinburgh in 1911 by Ramsay MacDonald. It was agreed that Labour should appoint an organiser in Scotland and establish a Scottish Advisory Committee and these proposals were subsequently recommended by the 1912 STUC. Ben Shaw, who was Labour's first Scottish Organiser, conveyed fraternal greetings to the 1914 STUC. The STUC were represented at Labour's Scottish Advisory

Committee inaugural conference in Glasgow the following year by a fraternal delegate and both organisations, whilst developing in their separate ways, have exchanged fraternal delegates ever since.

The Parliamentary Committee decided that December to postpone the 1915 STUC 'in view of the unsettled conditions prevailing'. It is the one year in which the STUC has not met, although affiliation fees were requested as usual.

As an unofficial movement on the Clyde began to threaten war production targets, so the STUC's position changed. Both the British TUC and the state itself saw its value as a means of moderating unofficial militancy. Recognition was fully granted and representation was provided for it on bodies like the War Emergency Workers' Committee.

Two members on the Parliamentary Committee had enlisted for army service, one of whom, J. O'Connor Kessock, the Vice-Chairman, was killed in action and, although declaring conscription 'a violation of British civil liberties' at the 1916 STUC, the delegates were as divided over the war as the Labour Party, but generally swung behind the war effort.

In the engineering workshops the problems of dilution of labour and de-skilling of craft jobs through mechanisation were exacerbated by the conscription of craftsmen. The hands of national union leaders were tied by the Treasury Agreements with the government, whereby, for the duration of the war, they agreed to give up the right to strike and to abandon restrictive working practices and accept the introduction of dilutee labour. Grievances on the shop floor were increasingly taken over by the shop steward movement, especially over pay differentials, particularly on the Clyde where so much war production was concentrated. The STUC was not much involved in these wartime events because, of course, the ASE, the main union involved, remained unaffiliated to it.

The Russian Revolution took place a few weeks before the 1917 STUC and Congress adopted a resolution congratulating the Russian workers on 'the successful termination of their long struggle with an irresponsible autocracy'. Glasgow Trades Council showed more militancy in these years than the STUC which had an aging leadership. George Carson, now seventy, was in ill health and had already stepped down as secretary of the Glasgow Trades Council, and in 1917 the STUC Parliamentary Committee decided that he should take a back seat and Robert Allan, the retiring Chairman, was appointed Assistant Secretary. At the 1918 STUC the appointment of the pro-war Allan as Secretary was slipped through despite complaints over the procedure.

The Armistice in November 1918 brought new problems. The post-war slump hit Clydeside particularly hard and during 1918 the STUC held three joint conferences with the Labour Party Scottish Advisory Council, calling for a 40-hour and even a 30-hour week as a means of reducing unemployment. At the beginning of 1919 there was an unofficial stoppage on the Clyde among engineers over an ASE agreement to reduce the working week from 54 hours to 47. It was supported by Glasgow Trades Council and the unofficial Clyde Workers Committee and threatened to become a more general strike. The STUC Parliamentary Committee, when approached for support over this 40-hour strike, took its time to respond. The ASE subsequently settled for 44 hours, but only after a tense period during which the Riot Act was read in Glasgow's George Square. Allan told the 1919 STUC that 'the strike was the outcome of hasty and unwise action', although the Parliamentary Committee eventually supported it. After a two-day debate on the issue the delegates moved on to other business.

Few Scottish unions had been founded since 1900. The 1913 STUC voted to discourage new unions and asked the Parliamentary Committee to secure amalgamations where two or more existed in any trade or industry. The 1917 Trade Union Amalgamation Act removed several hurdles in the way of mergers and as a consequence quickened the momentum towards some Anglo-Scottish ones. This legislation facilitated the growth of conglomerates like the AEU, T&GWU and NUGMW in the twenties. As a result, more decisions in the trade union movement were to be taken in London in a period when post-war nationalisation of private capital was also removing the control of many companies from Scotland. Allan wrote to British unions stating that the STUC were anxious 'to represent the entire body of trade unionists in Scotland' and suggesting meetings to discuss affiliation. The response was mixed and particularly unsympathetic from the Shipbuilding and Engineering unions. A problem also arose over dual affiliation fees, some unions apparently paying fees to the TUC for English members and to the STUC for Scottish members.

The events on Clydeside both during and after the war no doubt helped to bring the Parliamentary Committees of the two Congresses together for the first time. There was an informal meeting in Glasgow and a further meeting took place in London in February 1920. For a time there were even joint deputations to Government Ministers although the practice of 'jaunts to London' was roundly criticised by Emanuel Shinwell, who was a delegate at the 1920 STUC. Paradoxically, STUC support for Scottish Home

Rule became more pronounced in the years when more Scottish unions were merging their identities. The 1914 STUC passed a short resolution in favour of Home Rule following Asquith's legislation on Ireland, and after seventeen years silence on the issue. A Parliamentary Committee deputation led by Hugh Lyon, of the Scottish Horse and Motormen, met Lloyd George at 10 Downing Street in 1917 and raised the Home Rule issue, while the 1918 STUC demanded Scotland's direct representation at the Versailles Peace Conference. For several years thereafter the STUC carried resolutions in favour of a Scottish Parliament and not until 1931 was a self-government resolution actually defeated.

Demands within the TUC for a more effective leadership from the centre of a 'general staff of labour', to use the wartime idiom, led to a General Council replacing the Parliamentary Committee system in 1921. The new body, elected by the whole Congress on a basis of industrial sections, also reflected a growing body of support for industrial unionism. A special STUC in January 1921 decided that the Scottish TUC should follow suit, albeit with a smaller twelve member General Council and that the secretary should be full-time and affiliation fees increased. The implementation of this scheme was, however, delayed by the 1921 STUC to see whether the TUC's scheme might include provision for a Scottish District, which it did not. Yet there were also internal problems to be resolved.

The 1922 STUC was told that a few weeks earlier the Parliamentary Committee had suspended Allan on full pay 'having regard to the unsatisfactory manner in which the duties of secretary were being discharged'. David Marshall, of the Scottish Dock Labourers, acted briefly as secretary. The unfortunate Allan suffered near fatal injuries at Carlisle railway station soon afterwards, but maintained from his hospital bed that he was a scapegoat for an abortive scheme to set up a Central Labour Institute for Scotland, which had foundered after its 1920 launch owing to declining financial support. The secretary's post was advertised and William Elger, then chairman of Edinburgh Trades Council and a member of the Clerks' Union, was appointed. The choice marked a turning point for the STUC because his organisational ability and wider interests assisted the development of a new relationship with the TUC and outside bodies in Scottish life. A special STUC in December 1922 adopted a 12-member General Council scheme as from 1923. After being little more than an annual forum throughout its first twenty-five years, the STUC, with a full-time secretary and a General Council enjoying greater continuity of membership, prepared to become part of Scotland's establishment.

The new General Council came into being as union membership
slumped from a 1921 peak of 568,000 to 226,882 in 1922 with
the sudden upsurge in unemployment. This posed the question
of what the STUC's relationship to those out of work should
be, and in 1922 the STUC agreed to hear a deputation from
the National Unemployed Workers' Committee movement which
wanted trades councils to accept unemployed workers' committees
into affiliation. No action was taken over the issue which became
a regular topic in subsequent years as the Communist-inspired
NUWM continued to press the demand. The STUC did, however,
agree to coordinate in Scotland a TUC trade union membership drive
involving propaganda meetings and the distribution of literature. A
survey of trade unionism in Scotland in 1924-25, undertaken by
W S Cormack for the General Council, estimated 536,432 union
members with 137 British unions organising 213,469 members.
Only 60 per cent of Scotland's trade unionists were affiliated to the
STUC. The trades councils should have been the recruiting agents,
but the General Council saw them primarily as political bodies. After
the Labour Party adopted its 1918 constitution local Labour parties
were set up in each constituency and quite a number operated as
joint Trades and Labour Councils, but the General Council 1924
report noted that many of the 53 Trades and Labour Councils and
four trades councils existed on paper only. By the mid-twenties the
STUC was thus more occupied with questions of organisation and
its activities were worthy if sometimes dull, and many leading trade
unionists were, of course, lost to Westminster. James Brown and
Neil McLean were joined in 1922 by Emanual Shinwell and George
Buchanan and later by Robert Smillie, James Walker and William
Leonard, yet there was remarkably little direct relationship between
the STUC and the 1924 minority government, or for that matter
with the 1929-31 Labour government.

The 1926 General Strike was Britain's largest ever sympathy strike
and once again the STUC found itself acting as agent for the TUC
in Scotland. The 1926 Congress meeting the previous month at
Inverness supported the miners' resistance to pay reductions. Elger
and the Chairman, Peter Webster, attended the Conference of Trade
Union Executives in London which agreed to call a total stoppage,
but in the bitter aftermath it was claimed by some that the General
Council's contribution did not amount to much. One delegate at the
1927 STUC accused the members of 'sitting like so many Micawbers
waiting for something to turn up from the other side of the border',
but the STUC did publish *Scottish Worker* during the nine-day
stoppage. A motion calling on the STUC to become a TUC Scottish

Advisory Committee was substantially defeated, although those who thought the STUC should dissolve itself made a further attempt at the 1928 STUC. A Scottish Trade Union Defence Committee was established by the STUC, Labour Party and Co-operative Union to combat the Baldwin government's Trades Dispute and Trade Union Bill under which, amongst other restrictions, Civil Service unions were obliged to withdraw from the STUC, but the 1928 *STUC Report* complains of public apathy towards the protest meetings arranged.

The 1927 TUC at Edinburgh considered a report on industrial unionism and effectively abandoned the pretence that it was a practical option. Nonetheless the TUC retained industrial sections for the election of its General Council. At the 1931 STUC, Joseph Duncan of the Scottish Farm Servants' Union proposed abandoning the STUC trade group system because it was impracticable with the small General Council. By the narrow margin of 57 votes to 54 the STUC voted to revert to electing the first dozen candidates, irrespective of industry and without a guaranteed seat for the trades councils. In fact both mining seats on the General Council had been vacant since 1929 due to the internal difficulties of the Scottish Mineworkers. It was 1934 before the Scottish Mineworkers resumed their affiliation to the STUC which at the same time kept out the United Mineworkers.

By 1932 one-third of Scotland's working population was jobless. The maintenance of the unemployed became a recurrent issue at the STUC, which condemned the means test and the inadequacy of transitional allowances introduced in 1931. Unemployed workers whose benefit was exhausted were thrown on to the Poor Law Relief System administered by local authorities. When Glasgow Trades Council complained at the 1931 STUC of General Council inactivity, it was criticised for not taking up places on the Public Assistance Committee. It was 1932 before the General Council brought forward model rules for Unemployed Associations under trades council auspices. Two years later only four such Associations existed. The majority of trades councils were more interested in a mass membership for the NUWM although the 1935 STUC voted not to hear an NUWM deputation. The General Council's involvement in the Scottish Council for Community service which sought to promote voluntary unpaid work for the unemployed 'in useful occupations' came in for frequent criticism at Congress.

In one sense the STUC went beyond anything attempted by the TUC in the Mond-Turner reconciliation talks following the General Strike. The STUC General Council took part in the conference

initiated by Scottish local authorities in May 1931, which led to
the establishment of the Scottish (National) Development Council
'to assist in the promotion of commercial and economic interests
of the people of Scotland'. There was no criticism of this move
at the time, although it opened up wider contacts with Scottish
industrialists which did provoke later dispute.

In 1936, Elger and Charles Gallie of the Railway Clerks joined
the Scottish Economic Council approved by the Secretary of State
for Scotland for the purpose of 'examining the possibilities of
improving conditions in Scotland'. The fact that Sir James Lithgow
was its chairman drew sharp comment, as did the government's
re-armament programme that year. Scotland was less successful than
the Midlands or London in attracting new industry and developing
consumer-based industries where transport costs and proximity to
the larger market were important. In a major debate on industrial
development at the 1935 STUC, Joseph Duncan drew attention to
Scotland's over-dependence on export trades compared with the rest
of Britain. Elger emphasised the need for location of industry policies
and for public enterprise and investment in Scotland. Even so, the
STUC made no direct submission to the Barlow Commission on the
Distribution of the Industrial Population, appointed in 1938.

Throughout the thirties international affairs could not be ignored
and the 1931 Japanese invasion of Manchuria was condemned by
the STUC, as was the rise of Nazism in Germany and the Italian
invasion of Abyssinia. Congress sponsored a food ship to Spain to
help the Spanish Republic in 1937 and ultimately gave its backing to
local Spanish Aid Committees, though these were often Communist
controlled. Broadly, the STUC followed the official Labour Party
line on international affairs against that of the ILP, which broke with
Labour in 1932, and of the Communist Party. The STUC General
Council was not often out of step with its TUC counterpart. At the
1935 STUC the General Council was bitterly attacked for sending out
'a wee black circular' to trades councils, warning them against any
involvement in the 'united front' with the Communist Party, but
'the official policy' was overwhelmingly endorsed. Foreign policy
issues, given Communist opposition to Fascism and appeasement,
could often pose organisational questions in new forms, and in 1938
the STUC General Council and Scottish Advisory Committee of the
Labour Party agreed it was essential to separate entirely the political
and trade union activities of the Trades and Labour Councils. There
was some opposition to the proposal at Girvan STUC that year
from a Communist delegate, George Middleton of the Distributive
workers, whilst other delegates complained that these joint bodies

were being used as vehicles for Communist propaganda. By the end of the year the General Council issued a Model Constitution for trades councils and a memorandum on how they should conduct their business if they wished to retain STUC affiliation.

The Chamberlain government announced conscription on the day the 1939 STUC assembled at Rothesay. In furtherance of a campaign against its introduction, a Special STUC that May called on the General Council to consult affiliated unions on the possibilities of 'industrial action'. Only one union head office later replied in favour whilst another hedged and twenty five were against. In the absence of replies from the remaining 41 unions that was the end of the matter and on the declaration of war against Germany in September, the General Council issued a Manifesto urging democrats to 'resist to the utmost the aggressiveness of Fascism'. The Manifesto was attacked at the 1940 STUC by George Middleton of the Glasgow Trades Council, who described the war as 'Imperialist'. In a General Council rejoinder, Tom Scollan, also of the Glasgow Trades council, reminded him that the Communist Party had wanted the National Government in the thirties to make a firm stand against Fascism. The delegates approved the Manifesto and the STUC continued to support the 'successful prosecution of the war' under the Churchill Coalition Government and with greater unanimity after 1941, following the German invasion of the Soviet Union in violation of the non-aggression pact.

During the war the General Council continued its attempts to curb the political activities of trades councils by casting them in the role of local agents of Congress and introducing routine visits to their meetings by members of the General Council or Congress secretariat. Less success was achieved in reducing their delegation numbers at Congress which could form one-sixth of the total. As Minister of Labour, Ernest Bevin brought trade unions into the machinery of government and the STUC was invited to nominate for a variety of wartime advisory bodies and other committees, but there were Ministry decisions, not least the transfer of women and girls to the Midlands, which the STUC found it necessary to pursue.

Like Bevin, Tom Johnston as Scottish Secretary wanted to work with the unions and brought the STUC into his Scottish Industrial Council established in 1942. In 1946 that merged with the Scottish Development Council to form the Scottish Council (Development and Industry). As attention shifted to post-war reconstruction, Johnston kept the STUC in touch with his plans to attract more industry to Scotland, and the Cabinet's 1944 White Paper on Employment Policy was seen by the STUC as a belated government recognition that maintaining full employment was the State's responsibility. The Beveridge Reports had already been endorsed by it, and in the 1945 election the General Council gave unswerving support to Labour's campaign in Scotland.

The Labour Government had the initial advantage of ready-made wartime planning controls but all the disadvantages of reconstructing a debt-ridden economy with scarce resources. Demobilisation a second time round would be better accomplished but, as the new Minister of Labour, George Isaacs, told the 1946 STUC, it had its difficulties.

When Clement Attlee addressed the fiftieth STUC in 1947 the first Labour Prime Minister to do so, affiliations at 679,862 were higher than they had ever been, thanks in no small part to the Government's policy of full-employment.

While post-war nationalisation measures were in line with past STUC policy declarations, neither the details of public ownership nor some unexpected side-effects of centralisation were ever considered in detail. The General Council joined the campaign to save the wartime Prestwick Airport as an international airport second only to London, but the first real clash over centralisation of control arose over the government's plans for BEA and BOAC. The STUC wanted a Scottish Airlines Board, but representations they made secured the appointment of a Scottish Advisory Board within BEA. This pattern would be repeated in several nationalised industries. The compensation paid to private owners was also debated. So too was the need for industrial democracy, in nationalised industries. Employee involvement usually meant the appointment of trade union officials to the Boards of the new Public Corporations. In fact three General Council members resigned their seats to fill positions in the coal, rail and electricity industries.

Scottish-based unions were now only one-fifth of the STUC's membership but motions calling for greater autonomy in Scottish affairs began to reappear after the war on STUC agendas and were often sponsored by the Communist-led Scottish Miners and Glasgow Trades Council. The Scottish Convention was gaining a broad cross-section of support in Scotland for the Covenant calling for a Scottish Parliament. In March 1947 the first of several Scottish National Assemblies took place. The 1948 STUC called for a Scottish National Planning Commission, the creation of Trade and Labour Departments at the Scottish Office and even a 'Cabinet' of Scottish Ministers. These proposals received short shrift from Arthur Woodburn, the Scottish Secretary of State, whose own White Paper on Scottish Affairs proposed more debating time for Scotland by means of the Scottish Grand Committee. The STUC also wanted direct membership on his new consultative Scottish Economic Conference. Middleton, who became STUC General Secretary in May 1949, chose to play up industrial and economic issues of importance to Scotland and had little time for nationalist sentiments, and at the 1950 STUC, John Lang of the Iron and Steel Trades, with whom he would work closely, presented a General Council motion on Scotland's Future. The delegates endorsed its view that Scotland's economic prosperity 'is inseparable from that of England and Wales and it cannot be imagined as a self supporting entity'. A Glasgow Trades Council amendment reaffirming the 1948 declaration and an amendment moved by Abe Moffat, the Scottish Miners' leader, calling for a national Parliament, were rejected. The STUC had closed the door on political devolution and would concentrate on industrial development and administrative devolution. A copy of the statement was sent to Hector McNeil, the Scottish Secretary of State, who gave it his full endorsement.

Meanwhile the Cold War increasingly polarised STUC debates between Left and Right. The government's pro-American foreign policy under Ernest Bevin came under continual attack from the Communists and Labour Left, and this was echoed within the STUC which, in 1948, had four Communists on its General Council. In the 1950 Council elections the infighting and bitterness resulted in the unprecedented defeat of the retiring chairman, William Pearson of the NUM. Matters were to come to a head following the outbreak of the Korean war in July 1950. Glasgow Trades Council had become something of a thorn in the side of more orthodox members on the General Council. The 1951 STUC endorsed the General Council's backing of the Labour Government's rearmament policy and reaffirmed support for the United Nations. In August, Glasgow Trades Council adopted a motion after the Soviet initiative calling for Five-Power Peace Talks including China along with the USA, USSR, UK and France, and copies were sent to the Prime Minister and Foreign Secretary. After much correspondence over this issue, the General Council withdrew recognition from the Trades Council arising from the 'wilful contravention' of Congress policy and advised unions to withdraw their membership. Glasgow Trades Council won an Interim Interdict preventing the General Council from entering its office and assuming control. At Glasgow Sheriff Court on 8 January 1952 an agreement was reached to permit the General Council to set up a new Trades Council but not to interfere with the existing body. A new council was established in March 1952. This litigation was an acid test for the former Communist

Middleton, who helped to break the party's grip on the Trades Council. At the 1952 STUC the General Council was accused of using 'the tactics of the sledge hammer', but the delegates rejected a reference back to the report on the issue by a two to one majority.

Foreign policy issues apart, the STUC was broadly supportive of the Labour Government and its post-war economic difficulties. A 1949 STUC emergency motion on devaluation accepted the realities after the dollar gap crisis and called for stricter government control over prices and profits, and an invitation to Aneurin Bevan to address the 1950 STUC was withdrawn following his resignation as Minister of Labour. In the October 1951 election, the STUC called for 'the continuance of Labour in power at Westminster' but quickly had to come to terms with the de-control measures introduced by the Conservative administration, which resulted in a reversal of Labour's Distribution of Industry legislation and encouraged more growth in the Midlands and Greater London. In the 1950s the STUC was again complaining of the drift south and demanding the direction of labour to narrow the unemployment gap between Scotland and the rest of the UK, which was then running at a ratio of two to one.

The STUC continued to press for distinctive treatment of Scottish economic problems, but when the Catto Report was published in July 1952, it confirmed the difficulties of unscrambling Scottish trade figures from those of the rest of the UK, but soon after a Royal Commission on Scottish Affairs was appointed. The Balfour Commission included William McGinniss of the NUGMW, a member of the General Council. The Commission's report, published in July 1954, disappointed the General Council since it did not adopt any of the three main recommendations in the STUC's written submission, but the suggested resuscitation of the Scottish Economic Conference fell on stoney ground. The Commission dismissed the idea of a regional authority for the Highlands which the STUC argued would help to regenerate that half of Scotland, a subject which had interested the Congress since the twenties. Moreover, the Commission rejected any idea of transferring Trade and Labour departments to the Scottish Office, although its recommendations subsequently resulted in the transfer of Roads and Electricity. The General Council held to their view about the transfer of Trade and Labour functions to the Scottish Office when they met James Stuart, the Secretary of State in the autumn of 1954 and his successor, John Maclay, three years later, when Middleton described Scottish controllers of these departments as 'posting boxes for London'. The STUC approach remained maximum 'administrative' devolution.

Although it came out against the US Polaris base in Holy Loch in 1960, it was on Scottish domestic issues that the STUC achieved a high profile as a campaigning body for Scotland. It is difficult to draw a line between the respective initiatives of the STUC and the Scottish Council for Development and Industry on industrial matters. Both Middleton and Lang served on the SCDI Executive. However, the STUC campaign for the fourth steel strip mill in the mid-fifties attracted much public support. The STUC lobbied Ministers at the Scottish Office and Board of Trade and generally agreed that the Ravenscraig strip mill would help Scotland to develop light industries and attract car manufacturing. For eighteen months a decision lay with the Cabinet. then Harold Macmillan announced in the Commons on 18 November 1958 that part of the production would go to Ravenscraig, he made it clear that the decision 'was a political one', since otherwise the entire project would have gone to South Wales. Macmillan met the General Council in Glasgow on 2 May 1959 before a lunch at the Conservative Club and discussed STUC concern about unemployment and Scotland's reliance on heavy industry.

The election of 1959 was something of a watershed for the STUC. The Labour Party suffered its third electoral defeat in succession but the Conservatives lost the majority of Scottish seats in the 'never-had-it-so-good' election. Henceforth the STUC began to fill a political vacuum and learned to marshal that broader spectrum of opinion which no one political party could rally in a situation where unemployment exceeded 100,000 in February 1960. During his year as Chairman, James Milne turned to Government for pressure and persuasion on car manufacturers to secure some investment in Scotland. A meeting with Scottish MPs was held in Glasgow on 2 April 1960 to discuss the car industry and unemployment and an all-party deputation subsequently met the Prime Minister in the Commons on 31 May. The announcement that Rootes Group would start small car production and the Pressed Steel Company would come to Linwood together with the decision of British Leyland to produce trucks at Bathgate were viewed as 'a mere trickle' of the jobs expected. Moreover, William Scholes, the TGWU Scottish Secretary at the 1962 STUC forewarned industrialists not to expect both cheap labour and co-operation at the same time. Unemployment dominated the STUC skyline and the General Council obtained much support from local authorities and other bodies for its series of 'Jobs for Scotland' conferences throughout the country. In a memorandum to the Prime Minister at the end of 1962, the General Council called for a Scottish Development

Authority with financial and industrial functions and for the revival
of the Scottish Economic Council. Macmillan gave a delegation to
London a sympathetic hearing in January 1963, one of several
meetings between the STUC and Prime Ministers in the early 1960s.

The initiative of the SCDI in appointing the Toothill Committee
of Enquiry into the Scottish Economy had been welcomed at the
1960 STUC. The Committee's main findings, however, ran counter
to STUC demands for the direction of industry into unemployment
blackspots, since it called instead for a concentration on 'growth
points' including the New Towns. Under James Jack, who
succeeded George Middleton as General Secretary in 1963, the
General Council worked hard to make a distinctive Scottish case
for more investment and direction of industry.

Conservative Governments under Macmillan and Sir Alec Douglas
Home were belatedly seeking to redress the economic imbalances
which had developed within the UK and published two White
Papers on Regional Development. The White Paper on Central
Scotland — A Programme for Development, noted the importance
of suitable infra-structure if industry was to be attracted and
designated eight growth points including the New Towns, but
when the 1964 STUC debated a motion on Scotland's economic
development, the White Paper was brushed off as 'a pre-election
statement' of good intentions.

Following the narrow election of a Labour Government in October
1964, the STUC had high hopes of action based on its policies
for planned economic development in Scotland. The Labour and
Trade Union movements are often said to speak the same language;
it is their priorities which cannot always be the same. With a
slender Commons majority, another election loomed for the Wilson
Government, already dogged by the inherited massive balance of
payments deficit and speculation against the pound.

At the 1965 STUC, George Brown, as First Secretary of State
and Minister for Economic Affairs, spoke about the Government's
economic strategy and the importance of trade union co-operation
in regional planning. His newly-created Department of Economic
Affairs published a National Plan and early in 1966 the Scottish
Office published their strategy, *The Scottish Economy: A Plan for
Expansion 1965-70*, which included a target of 130,000 new jobs
by 1970 to offset losses in declining industries and stem emigration.
During the 1965 STUC debate on Scotland's Economy, James Jack
referred to press speculation on whether Congress would be 'as
vigorous in their demands' upon a Labour Government. In fact, the
STUC proved to be more demanding because it expected more. The

Scottish Economic Planning Council, set up by the Secretary of State for Scotland early in 1965, had Middleton as its Vice-Chairman. Alex Kitson of the SCMU, one of four STUC nominees on the SEC, likened the Council to a 'puppet appendage' of the Civil Service. The Industrial Development Act 1966 designated the whole of Scotland (except Edinburgh) a Development Area, with investment grants and tighter control over Industrial Development Certificates intended to steer new projects away from Non-Development Areas in the UK. Not entirely satisfied with this legislation, the STUC nonetheless repeatedly asked the Government to include Edinburgh, where the local trades council complained industry was being lost to surrounding areas.

The STUC General Council's posture was one of support for specific projects in Scotland, and the Pulp Mill at Fort William, the Prototype Fast Reactor at Dounreay and the Aluminium Smelter Plant at Invergordon came to fruition, as did the Highlands and Islands Development Board in 1965. Inevitably, STUC concentration turned to Central Scotland where the declining fortunes of coal, steel, shipbuilding, engineering and railway industries were eroding employment. The mining unions constituted nearly one-tenth of STUC membership in the mid-fifties, but with increasing competition from imported oil and pit closures, their numbers were cut by more than half by 1970. The General Council regularly canvassed Government on the industry's behalf for a national fuel policy and had demanded that Longannet should be a coal-fired power station. Addressing the 1964 STUC, Lord Robens, the NCB Chairman, did accept that Scotland's higher productivity figures had tipped the scales for Longannet and won 10,000 jobs, but to the displeasure of the miners' delegation, he warned that productivity could not end up exclusively in the miners' pay packets and would have to be shared with the community.

Shortly after obtaining an apparently decisive majority at the 1966 election, Wilson told an unreceptive Aberdeen STUC that a prices and incomes policy 'is a necessary condition of obtaining full employment'. The Government's growing intervention in pay bargaining began to take up more time in STUC debates. Yet, no matter the result of STUC card votes on prices and incomes resolutions in the late sixties, there was little Congress could do. Even the TUC General Council, which became involved in incomes policy machinery and vetting, had problems in obtaining consensus because affiliates were autonomous. STUC debates more often became rehearsals for September TUC decisions, with many union General Secretaries travelling to Scotland to have their say in front of the television cameras.

The 1966 Budget brought in Selective Employment Tax, which the STUC complained would hit service employment, particularly in the Highlands and Borders. As a result, James Callaghan, the Chancellor, got a poor reception when he addressed the 1967 STUC. Although his Regional Employment Premium to help private manufacturing employers in Development Areas was welcomed, the STUC believed that it ought to be extended to the public sector as well. The Chancellor in that year of devaluation acknowledged that, whilst trade unions were in business to gain rising living standards for their members, the Government's job was to do this on behalf of the nation as a whole.

After the thirteen 'wasted years' there was a growing impatience in Scotland. Labour lost the by-election at Hamilton in November 1967 to the SNP, and at the 1968 STUC there were two motions on the agenda in response to the nationalist upsurge. The Scottish Miners wanted the establishment of a Parliament for Scotland, but not separation. Their leader, Michael McGahey, said his union was 'a national union operating in a nationalised industry which miners would never allow to be destroyed'. An AEUW Foundry Workers' motion rejected 'total devolution' and demanded that the STUC repudiate the nationalist movement outright. The wording of these motions was embarrassing to the General Council and in a prepared statement, James Milne asked that they be remitted for consideration in detail. The Miners agreed and after a card vote the Foundry Workers' motion was remitted too.

William Ross's response as the Scottish Secretary, was to scold the 1968 STUC for not being more constructive. He warned delegates not to become 'the Scottish Trades Union Congrouse' or take refuge 'in the quicksands of nationalism', but later that year his Government proposed the appointment of a Royal Commission on the UK Constitution. An interim statement by the General Council which was endorsed by the 1969 STUC rejected separation, yet saw advantages in providing a Scottish legislative assembly. William Hutchison of the AUEW explained the General Council's difficulty in producing a sensible plan for structural change instead of a slogan about devolution. This wariness was backed by Alex Donnet of the G&MUW who maintained that 'although Scotland did have its economic problems, separation from the rest of the UK would not solve these difficulties', and there were others who argued that real devolution of power to people in their communities could be better achieved by local government reform. The STUC presented substantial written and oral evidence to the Wheatley Commission on Local Government in Scotland which was largely reflected in the report by the Royal Commission.

Relations with the Wilson Government deteriorated, however, over the plans of the Employment Secretary, Barbara Castle, to reform industrial relations with a bill which, among other things, would have required union ballots, a cooling-off period before strikes, and fines for certain forms of unofficial action. At the 1969 STUC the otherwise unanimous condemnation of the 'package' from the floor was broken by Dan Crawford of the Painters union, who questioned how the unions would 'put their house in order' and their willingness to leave reform to the TUC. The Employment Secretary vigorously defended her proposals from the platform and reminded delegates that unions did not achieve all that they wanted through collective bargaining alone. In face of strong opposition amongst Labour MPs and divisions in his Cabinet, the Prime Minister withdrew the Bill's contentious sections after an agreement with the TUC General Council over a 'solemn and binding undertaking' by which they agreed to strengthen TUC machinery for handling industrial disputes and inter-union problems. The 1970 STUC made corresponding amendments to its constitution.

Despite this episode, the 1964–70 period brought the STUC closer than at any time in its history to Government Ministers and the Civil Service machinery and there was still much in the Government's record to commend it to the STUC. By 1970, Britain's balance of payments position had turned around into surplus, while William Ross was able to tell the Oban STUC that public expenditure in Scotland had doubled in the five years ending 1970. By this time the ranks were closing and the Congress President assured the Prime Minister when he addressed the STUC for a third time that the movement would be behind him in the coming election, though hopes of Labour becoming the natural party of government were unexpectedly dashed that June.

The Heath Government was not long in office before it began to retreat from its election rhetoric of not subsidizing "lame duck" industries. Rolls Royce, to STUC approval, was taken into virtual public ownership, and when Upper Clyde Shipbuilders faced closure in 1971, the General Council was prompt to intercede with Ministers for financial support. By 14 June, however, John Davies, the Trade and Industry Secretary, told the Commons that no further financial aid would be given and that UCS would go into voluntary liquidation. Shop stewards at UCS set the pace over the resistance on Clydeside to more unemployment. The initiative of a "work-in" immediately captured the public mood and attention of the media. In responding to the crisis, the General Council met the Prime Minister in London on 21 June to plead the case against closure of the yards. Action like this, as well as a Special STUC convened in Glasgow on 16 August, was vital in transforming the UCS workers' battle into a symbol of national self-assertion against a government with no Scottish mandate. An independent three-man Committee of Inquiry was appointed to examine the social consequences for West Central Scotland. The TUC too showed concern and in addressing the Special STUC in August, Victor Feather, General Secretary, called for the establishment of a Clydeside Development Authority. The Government accepted the report of its own Advisory Committee under Lord Robens and Govan Shipbuilders Ltd was established in 1971.

The UCS work-in dominated the 1972 STUC. There were five composite motions on the Scottish Economy on the agenda and, moving an AUEW-TASS motion, Bill Noven called for resistance to closures and contended that the real fight had taken place "at the gates of shipyards in Govan and John Brown's" and not at Downing Street or St Andrew's House. He queried if the STUC were not becoming "a paper tiger" but the majority of his colleagues on the General Council did not share that view despite their support for what the UCS workers had achieved.

By this time the highly complex Industrial Relations Act of 1971 was in force. Drawing from American experience, the Act sought to treat trade unions as corporate bodies which could be held responsible for their members. Non-collaboration was seen as the most effective method of making the Act impotent. The STUC followed TUC advice to affiliated unions that they should not register under the Act or enter into legally enforceable agreements with employers. The vast majority of unions deregistered. During the Private Session at the 1973 STUC a decision was taken to expel unions remaining on the Register of Trade Unions after 31 July 1973. Six unions, including the newly-affiliated Educational Institute of Scotland, were later excluded. The subsequent repeal of the Industrial Relations Act resolved this difficulty and permitted their re-entry. Nor was the STUC disposed to the Government's incomes policy and anti-inflation legislation. The 1973 STUC opposed the introduction of Value Added Tax, necessitated by membership of the EEC, and criticised "the stringent limitations on wage increases while prices and rents are allowed to soar". The objection to incomes policy was deep-seated, but another motion moved by

David McGibbon of USDAW, opposing any statutory control whilst calling for a voluntary incomes policy if prices, rents and dividends were controlled, was rejected.

The demoralising rise in unemployment led the General Council to promote a Scottish Assembly on Unemployment in February 1972. Attended by over 1,500 representatives from all walks of life in Scotland, this Assembly funnelled something of the growing frustration in Scottish affairs at the time. STUC Chairman, Raymond Macdonald of the T&GWU, later chaired the seventeen member Standing Commission appointed by the Assembly, which submitted a Charter of Proposals to the Prime Minister on industrial and economic measures to improve matters. The Second Scottish Assembly held in January 1973 had less impact, and James Jack publicly accused the SNP, with 148 of the 953 delegates present, of exploiting the occasion, but politically the STUC came in for Nationalist criticism for appearing to be "subservient" to the TUC "in London".

The long-awaited Kilbrandon Report on the Constitution published in October 1973, raised the temperature on the issue of Devolution, but its proposals for a legislative Scottish Assembly were submerged in the "Who Governs ?" election of February 1974 which was fought in the midst of the "three-day week" energy crisis. It was Edward Heath's handling of the second miners' pay dispute, coinciding with the OPEC oil price increases following the Arab-Israeli conflict, which precipitated the two elections of that leading to a minority Labour Government and a formidable SNP vote.

The 1974 STUC's response was to come out strongly in favour of Kilbrandon and legislative devolution within a British framework. In a report to the 1975 STUC on its submission to the Prime Minister on the subject, the General Council called for "a meaningful Scottish Assembly which will not simply degenerate into a talking shop". Harold Wilson, in furtherance of his special relationship with the STUC, travelled to Scotland with half the Cabinet for two days of talks with the General Council on 27-28 February 1975. Discussion included Devolution, the setting up of the Scottish Development Agency and a National Enterprise Board, the establishment of the Offshore Supplies Office and the British National Oil Corporation to benefit from North Sea oil developments, and also the problems of the coal and steel industries.

As the effects of public expenditure cuts imposed at the behest of the International Monetary Fund began to bite, however, the STUC found it harder to maintain its rapport with the government.

Strikes in the winter of 1978-79 involved public sector workers in Scotland as elsewhere and put under acute pressure the concept of any "social contract" between government and organised labour. Despite its biggest ever affiliated membership of 1,054,000 and its commitment, admittedly sometimes an uncertain one, to Scottish devolution, the STUC was able to play only a marginal role in the abortive referendum of March 1979.

The referendum debacle brought down the Callaghan Government and exposed trade unions in Scotland, as in Britain as a whole, to a brutal decade of de-industrialization and legislation calculated to break the collective strength of organized labour. Yet in 1979 the STUC was, as it has remained, the collective focus for trade unionism in Scotland, and it is still the Scottish TUC. In Wales the only comparable body is known as the Wales TUC. The difference between a noun and an adjective can be overplayed, but it still symbolizes something more, for the Welsh body is akin to a regional council of the TUC, with little power to initiate anything independently of London. The Scottish TUC, on the other hand has, since its foundation, been an autonomous body with policies and priorities which echo Scottish needs and a Scottish identity.

This was personified by the man who was its General Secretary, Jimmy Milne, at the time when this book was being prepared though, sadly, he died in September 1986. Milne, a skilled pattern maker from Aberdeen, was the first Communist to occupy this position and when he took office in 1975 there were those who predicted a collision course between him and the General Council. STUC history gave some substance to such fears, for some of his predecessors had invested much effort in seeking to neutralize Communist influence both at Congress and in the Trades Councils.

Jimmy Milne, while never compromising on his own political beliefs, managed to work well within a tradition created by William Elger, George Middleton and James Jack, whose concern was always to secure and maintain for the STUC the status they felt to be its due in relation to all public and private sector decisions affecting the labour force in Scotland. This became a harder task after 1979 as old industries began to go to the wall and virtually all Scottish unions, apart from the EIS, were absorbed into bodies with a remit to act for members on a United Kingdom basis, but Jimmy Milne never flinched from it and, moreover, worked effectively to strengthen the STUC's commitment to a Scottish Parliament with real powers.

He was a man of charm and culture and in February 1986, partly in recognition of his work in widening the unions' contacts with the arts, the STUC commissioned a special orchestral work in his honour. This was performed in Glasgow by the Scottish National Orchestra, and was given as its title "Sunset Song" in acknowledgement of Jimmy Milne's roots in Scotland's North-East. The title of the work was all too prophetic given the untimely death of a man who embodied so many of the broad Labour movement's best Scottish traditions. Reports, however, to borrow a phrase, of the death of Scottish trade unionism are greatly exaggerated. That this is so owes everything to Jimmy Milne and the men and women who went before him in creating and nurturing the STUC since 1897.

9

Labour 1979 to 1988

JAMES NAUGHTIE

Black Friday, St David's Day, 1979, was the end of one nightmare for Labour and the start of another. The referendum result, with its miserable and technically insufficient Yes majority, was declared after a campaign which had been dull and ill-tempered from the start and which lacked any fire. Labour and the SNP had found it impossible to work together; the No campaign found it easy to unify behind a banner of nervous resistance to change; the electorate seemed to enjoy tip-toeing back from the brink and then sulking when life lost its excitement. For many Labour folk it later seemed to have been inevitable, because the political horrors of the previous five years, under the shadow of the Nationalist threat, seemed unlikely ever to end happily. But on March I, as the embryonic establishment of a 'new' Scotland wallowed in its gloom, another and even more fearsome nightmare was about to begin.

A little more than two months later, Mrs Thatcher was in Downing Street. From the moment of the Callaghan Government's defeat by one vote in the Commons on the night of March 28 it was clear that the game was up. Party professionals believed overwhelmingly that Callaghan's decision not to call an election the previous Autumn, and to put his faith in the trade union leadership for the winter had always been a hopeless gamble. Devolution was the instrument of his defeat in March, but the election turned on the economy and from the start of the campaign a pervasive scent of death began to settle on the Labour campaign. We know now from those who sat in Downing Street at the time that Callaghan never believed he could win it: he saw it as a Last Hurrah for Labourism against the economic culture that we had not yet come to know as Thatcherism. But it was in Scotland that that message was best received.

It had been a Labour crisis there — the party's inability to cope with the SNP — which had helped to bring Callaghan down but it was in Scotland that Labour could still claim to be a popular bastion against Conservatism. The 44 seats won brought the party back to its 1970 level and its vote, 41.2 per cent, was almost exactly 5 per cent up on October, 1974. The party could argue that the SNP had been put in its place (down to 17 per cent from 30 per cent in October, 1974) but the 1979 election was the start of a new battle against Mrs Thatcher's British mandate.

In the early days it seemed little more than an old-fashioned party political fight. The wheel had turned, the Tories were in, but soon th؟y would be gone again. In particular, the nationalists could be ignored, so the argument went. They had lost all but two seats and had been humiliated by what seemed to have been an enormous misjudgment in forcing an election on the referendum issue. Labour had recognised the truth of the referendum result and had concentrated on the economy in the Scottish campaign. The campaign was lost, but there was some bitter-sweet satisfaction in Keir Hardie House that Labour in Scotland had recovered its position and was ready, once again, to prepare for Government. It was a miscalculation, of course. The ebb and flow of the constitutional question was to sap the party more than some of its leading figures imagined, and the strength of Mrs Thatcher in the south was to prove far more potent than anyone in Scotland could be expected to understand in early days after the election and, indeed, in the course of the first economic hurricane under her leadership.

How much patience would the party have with a Conservative Government telling Scotland what to do, and how would the frustration show? It was obvious early on to the more far-sighted that such feelings would be hard to control. Donald Dewar, who was later to be charged with controlling them, said shortly after the election: 'It may be that many who did vote No, or who abstained, may come to regret the indecisive result of the referendum as Mrs Thatcher's shock troops ride roughshod. . .over Scotland.' Anyone who believed that life under Mrs Thatcher was to be politics as usual — as it had been before the devolution upheavals of the seventies — was wrong. In the Labour Party it was obvious that the Callaghan years were over and that preparations had to begin for something new. What it was, however, was not yet clear. The air was thick with confusion and gloom.

Foot's election by the Parliamentary party, in the last exercise of its power alone to choose the leader, was evidence of that confusion. His leadership was no more than an uncomfortable interlude and for

all the affection felt for him in the party in Scotland that is how it was
always seen. There, a young Left-leaning group was beginning to
control the party's direction, conscious that they were preparing for
whoever would follow Foot. A year or so into his leadership, when
Mrs Thatcher was fighting her opponents inside the Conservative
Party over unemployment and Sir Geoffrey Howe's notably hard-
line 1981 Budget, it was already obvious that any future Labour
Government was going to be quite different from its predecessors.

The Left's success in forcing constitutional change on a battered
party ushered in a period of agony for Foot in England, where he
began the demeaning and debilitating struggle with the hard Left
and Militant which contributed so obviously to the 1983 general
election defeat and his own inevitable departure soon afterwards. In
Scotland, however, the scene was quite different. In the devolution
arguments the young Labour Left had started to prepare for power,
because they could hardly imagine that some kind of Assembly
was not eventually going to be established in Edinburgh. The old
guard, Right and Left, was much more anxious and divided over
the Assembly. Among Parliamentarians the lack of enthusiasm on
the part of many of those campaigning for a Yes vote had been one of
the embarrassing themes of the referendum campaign. Behind them,
however, there was a phalanx of talented and ambitious Labour
figures — many of whom were to gather under the umbrella of the
Labour Coordinating Committee — who had taken the Assembly
seriously and were ready to mould the party in their own image.
While in England the landscape wasted with the debris of intra-party
warfare, the Scottish scene looked calm by comparison. But an
enormous shift in party attitude was taking place, nonetheless.

The defeats of 1979, culminating in the European election in
which Labour won only two of the eight seats (Glasgow and
Strathclyde West), were seen as the end of an era. The new
Scottish group in the Commons had twelve newly-elected members
and its tone changed quickly. It was younger, more irreverent,
more impatient, brighter. In the constituencies, the Left made
advances and it was no coincidence that in 1983 when Neil Kinnock
became the first leader elected under the new party rules involving
constituencies and unions as well as the Parliamentary Party, he did
especially well in Scotland. There was an irony, of course, in the
depth of his support among those who were devolutionists, because
he had argued against the scheme from the start, but he soon
began to make his committment to an elected Assembly so public
so often that the doubts were dispelled. Moreover, his popularity
among constituency activists in Scotland (which had been cultivated

assiduously in the previous three years or so) was symptomatic of an important victory which had been won by the so-called soft Left against the others after 1979.

The high tide of what became known as Bennism had passed in Scotland by the end of 1982, and at its height it had not matched the equivalent movement's impact in the south.

It was the emergence of the soft Left in the period before the 1983 that established the character of the post-referendum party. Looking back after the 1987 election, when fifty Labour MPs were elected in Scotland, the picture is quite clear: the Scottish party solved its internal problems much more quickly than was done in England. The challenge had always been strikingly different from the one which the ailing party in the south confronted — it was the difficulty of handling power in Mrs Thatcher's Britain. Labour's grip on Strathclyde alone (45.8 per cent of the vote in 1982 and 79 out of 103 seats) gave it still the feeling of being Scotland's established party and the problem for the leadership was how to handle its power through the local authorities in confronting a Government elected with a much smaller share of the vote in Scotland than Labour's. The first phase of the argument over strategy in the party was effectively solved by the Lothian affair of 1981.

The innocently-titled Local Government (Miscellaneous Provisions) (Scotland) Act 1981 was the instrument by which the Government intended to force more stringent financial disciplines on local authorities. Later there was to be similar, and tougher, legislation for England and Wales and ministers saw the first confrontation under the Scottish Act as a useful indicator to the political battles which were sure to arise later. It was, for them, a happy one: they won the fight with Lothian Regional Council. For Labour it was a turning point, a moment at which the power of central Government, deliberately enhanced with the help of a healthy majority in the Commons for legislation to tame Left-wing spending councils, had to be acknowledged.

In the summer of 1981 George Younger, the Secretary of State, decided that Lothian was guilty of 'excessive and unreasonable' expenditure of £53 million. Labour councillors protested and their campaign became the centrepiece of the fight against the Government's policy to local government. But they lost. By mid-September, the Labour group was in chaos and the trade unions involved were making it clear that they were unwilling to face the consequences of a last stand against St Andrews House. Younger and Malcolm Rifkind, then a mere Parliamentary under-secretary, insisted that the cuts had to be made and, although they made some

minor concessions on the scale of the budget changes, they got their
way. The episode established the Government's determination to
risk confrontation with Labour authorities, and it revealed the deep
misgivings in the party about the tactics adopted by the Lothian
councillors. A watershed had been reached.

It was clear that Mrs Thatcher's Government was not at all nervous
about its policy to local government, just as it showed, after the purge
of the 'wets' in 1981, that the long-term assault on public spending
was going to continue. In fighting this policy Labour was aware, not
least because of the Lothian experience, that a strategy of resistance
would be costly and would usually lead to defeat. Thousands
marched through the streets of Edinburgh at one moment in
the Lothian campaign to support the rebelling councillors, but
such flashes of public sympathy for hard-line resistance had little
impact elsewhere and when the end of the affair came it surprised
no-one. The revolt had, however, produced something new: a group
of younger councillors, perhaps more ideological by temperament
than their predecessors, who saw themselves in the vanguard of
opposition to Thatcherism. It was seen, not altogether unreasonably
given the polling evidence, as alien to most people in Scotland. A
number of them went on to slip effortlessly, it seemed, into the
party mainstream which they had found so unattractive when they
were fighting their battle with Younger and Rifkind. The Lothian
experience reminded Labour of the difficulties of direct action
against a Government with a comfortable majority but did help
to produce the next generation of leaders with local government
experience, inside Lothian and elsewhere, who were wiser and
cannier for the experience.

To imply, however, that these years were happy and a time of
advance for Labour in Scotland would be absurd. Although the
Scottish party was less of an irritation to Foot than in England
and even Wales, there were some celebrated difficulties. George
Galloway, as party chairman in 1981, produced a damning criticism
of Foot from the Scottish executive on the eve of a trip to Glasgow
by the leader and caused a furore (not his last) as a result.
But after 1982 in Scotland the Left-Right squabbles were not
of the same kind as elsewhere. For example, not a single Scots
MP was deselected in the first round of contests after the rules
changed (although the eccentric Right-winger Willie Hamilton in
Central Fife came close) and the party's difficulties did not have,
in general, the vicious character which was disfiguring so many
constituencies in England. The political outlook, however, was
still bleak.

Roy Jenkins's victory for the SDP over the Tories in the Hillhead by-election in March 1982 was an infuriating one for Labour. Although the seat was later won (by Galloway in 1987) with the help of earlier boundary revisions, the sight of the hated Jenkins and his one-year-old party marching into central Glasgow and winning 33.4 per cent of the vote with no established organisation and no significant Liberal tradition to help them was a grim one for Labour. The consolation was that the SDP's victory had come about because of Tory unhappiness with Thatcherite economic policy and the ready availability of an acceptable protest candidate with whom they could safely flirt.

It could therefore be presented as some more evidence of the unpopularity of Mrs Thatcher in Scotland but it took only eight days for the effect of that by-election to be wiped out: the Falklands were invaded and within 48 hours a task force had been assembled and was on its way to the South Atlantic. After that bizarre campaign, when the Argentinians finally raised a white flag over Port Stanley, Mrs Thatcher must have felt that she could hardly lose the 1983 general election, and she was probably right. Opinion surveys demonstrated that the war had been popular and her brand of leadership was very favourably compared in the minds of most voters with the amiable unpredictability of Foot. There had been considerable public unease about the Falklands campaign in its early stages, of course, and some fierce opposition, but even in Scotland, where feelings were noticeably less fevered and jingoistic than in the south, there was no popular movement against the war. Tam Dalyell, the Labour MP for Linlithgow, became a kind of cult figure for his defiance of the received national opinion, but it did little good. By the time Foot came to fight Mrs Thatcher in June 1983 Labour had sunk to a pathetically low level. The David Steel–Roy Jenkins deal in the Liberal-SDP Alliance was not altogether convincing to the electorate but convincing enough to help produce Labour's worst result — in terms of share of the vote — for more than half a century.

In Scotland the vote slumped to 35.1 per cent (and 41 seats) and although the performance compared to that elsewhere allowed the party to claim that it was still dominant, the reaction to defeat produced a natural bout of introspection. In particular, it raised the national question again. It was seen as the most important strategic — and indeed, ideological issue — facing the party and it was the cause of considerable unease in the shadow cabinet in London because it was recognised as an exceptionally dangerous tinder-box. Put bluntly, the question was: how long could Scottish

Labour voters be expected to vote loyally for a party which could not deliver what they wanted because it was handicapped by the millstone of a party of long-term losers in the south? Against the background of the catastrophic scale of the 1983 defeat it was a question which could not be wished away. Moreover, it had been anxiously discussed throughout the first term as the scale of Mrs Thatcher's ambitions became clear.

With the Criminal Justice Act, the Education Act, the Tenants Rights Act and the Local Government Act, ministers had simply ignored their position in Scotland and had successfully placed on the statute book a series of controversial and far-reaching reforms, largely thanks to the skills and combativeness of Rifkind as the junior minister in charge. The frustration of Labour MPs, particularly those who had not experienced the difficulties of Parliamentary opposition before, was considerable. Shortly after the election a group of them began to try to force the pace on strategy. What happened next was of immense importance to the party's Parliamentary performance thereafter.

The wild boys in Parliament who wanted to play a much harder game against their English (and Welsh) colleagues, led by George Foulkes, John Maxton, Dennis Canavan and John Home Robertson, all of whom had been getting progressively angrier since 1979 through the hapless meanderings of the Scottish Affairs Select Committee — which never recovered from a rebel Tory effort to wreck it from the start and was too partisan to be effective, despite the efforts of Donald Dewar in the chair — and the progression of controversial Government bills. But their anger was leading them dangerously close to an argument for a Scottish mandate, a case which the Scottish leadership believed correctly would offer an enormous opportunity to the SNP. When a Scottish mandate was accepted, where was the case against separation? More immediately, could any Labour Government legitimately run England on the basis of seats won in Scotland? Without accepting the nationalist case it was obviously a nonsense, and the hierarchy duly panicked.

Foulkes infuriated his colleagues by submitting to the party in Scotland and to the unions a number of ideas for disruption, including non-cooperation between Labour authorities and the Scottish Office. Bruce Millan, the former Secretary of State, was in his last year as leader of the front bench team and he was incensed. The countermove was organised, significantly, by the two new MPs in the 1983 intake, Gordon Brown, who could use his power base as Scottish chairman to give him authority, and Norman Godman, MP for Greenock and Port Glasgow. They proposed a much more measured campaign, aimed at persuading English colleagues of the inevitability of devolution under a Labour Government. It suggested a number of Parliamentary manoeuvres designed to press the devolution case, and to highlight it in the press, but stopping well short of a disruptive effort to claim the Scottish mandate. It was discussed at a long and ill-tempered meeting of the Scottish group at which the most important speech was made — somewhat to the surprise of some of his colleagues — by John Smith, the former minister of state at the Privy Council Office who steered the Scotland Act through the Commons. He was more enthusiastic for the Brown-Godman approach than some had suspected he might be. It certainly helped to outflank the mandaters, who lost decisively. From then on their efforts were occasionally embarrassing — and sometimes helpful to the SNP — but not serious. Canavan, in particular, could be easily portrayed by the leadership as a maverick who had gone slightly off the rails on the issue.

That tactical decision, early in Mrs Thatcher's second term, was important in setting the tone. The SNP soldiered on in the Commons with Donald Stewart and Gordon Wilson as their only MPs" but they were effectively isolated by Labour's growing committment to a specific Assembly scheme. Even No campaigners like Robin Cook were accepting the drift: it seemed that the argument was settled and that the more dangerous — and nationalistic — argument had been cut off. By publishing an Assembly Bill and attempting to answer many of the lingering criticisms of the 1979 Act — principally because of the omission of taxation powers — the campaign was seen to be practical and to be geared to some future *British* election victory rather than some Scottish coup d'état organised in an unspecified way with a popular national front.

It also established the kind of pragmatic leadership which was being promoted under Donald Dewar, as Millan's successor on the front bench team. Dewar, of course, was a kenspeckle figure in the party, having been MP for South Aberdeen as early as 1966 (he was beaten by Iain Sproat there in 1970 but won a celebrated victory over the SNP in the by-election in Garscadden in 1970). To his colleagues his characteristics have always been an equal and enormous capacity for hard work and for gloom. Given his somewhat lugubrious appearance, his gatling-gun delivery and his restless physical energy he has always been able to present a formidable spectacle as an opposition attacker in full flight against the Government. As a front-bench performer he has always been of high quality. Conservative carping at his relentless questioning has been a defensive reaction as much as anything else. On form, he has always given Rifkind a hard run, and only Smith and Cook among his colleagues could have made the same boast after the 1983 election. Dewar was the figure around whom the mainstream of the party could congeal quite happily. But it was not at first a relationship which was entirely peaceful.

He was an effective figure in reflecting a broad strand of Scottish opinion, for example on the perpetual problems afflicting Ravenscraig or the close of Scott-Lithgow or Gartcosh, but he did find some difficulty during the miners strike, cause célèbre for so much of the Labour movement in the eighties. Dewar, although his view of Ian MacGregor, the Coal Board chairman of the time, was as fierce as that of any of his colleagues, was deeply unhappy at some elements of what we came to know as Scargillism and found it acutely unsettling to be drawn into the kind of 'direct action' which a number of his colleagues were encouraging. Kinnock's eventual public break with Scargill, which had been a private fact much earlier, was a welcome development to Dewar who faced criticism from the Left for alleged softness on this as on other issues.

He sprang, of course, from what we used to call the Right and had voted for Denis Healey as leader in 1980 and for Roy Hattersley in 1983 against Kinnock. But in time he became a Kinnock ally. The leader's line in the miners' strike helped him, in the midst of what was an extraordinarily emotional public campaign in support of the National Union of Mineworkers across central Scotland, and later he found himself at one against dissident elements in his ranks over the tactics which being used by local authorities in resisting spending curbs (a throwback to Lothian days) and, more pressingly, on Labour's atttitude to the poll tax, the latest Government Act to be tried on the familiar Scottish test-bed while being prepared for fullscale implementation in England and Wales. His emergence as a unifying figure, surrounded by Tribunites and even the occasional member of the hard Left Campaign Group, was a remarkable achievement, given the depth of his argument with some colleagues over tactics. He was in some ways the model Kinnockite — drawn towards the 'new realism' of the leadership from a different tradition in the party but committed to it absolutely. Like many shadow cabinet colleagues he entertained doubts from time to time about Kinnock's leadership, and certainly about the party's chances of victory at the end of Mrs Thatcher's term, but he was the loyalist in the Commons and his work in the country seemed never-ending.

As he surveyed the scene after the 1983 election, he could reflect that the devolution issue, while not settled, was less dangerous than it had been. After a period of nervousness in the aftermath of the referendum embarrassment, the party had reasserted its demand for an Assembly with economic powers and was never likely to retreat from it. Backing that pledge, and ready to defend it fiercely, was a group of emerging Labour figures who had been blooded in the battles of the seventies and who were certainly seen at Westminster — as in Scotland — as an improvement on their predecessors. By 1983 that process had come to fruition. The intake of that year — including Brian Wilson, Henry McLeish, John McAllion, John Reid and Sam Galbraith among others — was notably talented and forceful and schooled in the politics of the post-referendum era. Moreover, with former local councillors in the group like Alistair Darling and Nigel Griffith sitting for Edinburgh seats the link with the party in Scotland was closer and much more constructive than it had been before. With only a few exceptions, the day of the time-serving political hack rewarded for alleged good (and long) conduct had gone. Under Dewar's leadership, the bulk of the Parliamentary party felt happy with the strategic approach. There were grumbles from the hard Left, most awkwardly on the poll tax, but the Scottish party at Westminster could claim at the start of the third term to be in better shape that at any time since 1979.

This impression was confirmed by Labour's progress after the 1983 election to its highest level in popular esteem in Scotland for decade. The 1984 European election produced a share of the vote of 41 per cent and five seats (adding Fife and mid-Scotland, the Lothians and Strathclyde West to Glasgow and Strathclyde East) and by mid-1985 the regular surveys by MORI for *The Scotsman* and System Three for the *Glasgow Herald* were showing support just below (and in one or two instances, just above) fifty per cent. Despite Kinnock's difficulty with elements of the party, there appeared to be no doubt that in Scotland the reaction to six years or so of Thatcherism was increased support for Labour. This kind of support led to another confrontation with the Government over council spending which threatened to embarrass the Westminster leadership of the party but which, in the end, subsided.

Edinburgh and Stirling district refused to comply with default orders from Younger as Secretary of State and had a partial victory in securing from the party's Scottish executive a statement outlining 'a strategy for non-compliance' which sat rather unhappily beside Dewar's oft-repeated opposition to any action which broke the law. On this, the issue which was to continue to trouble the hierarchy at Westminster, the problem was eventually resolved in a way which allowed the two councils to claim political victories while implementing some unwelcome increased charges and seemed to do little to change the party's general standing. It neither encouraged a nationalist revival through a fight with the Government, nor seemed significantly to damage the recovery which had been evident in the polls since the disaster of 1983.

This recovery was highlighted in the 1986 regional elections, in which Labour won a vote across the country of 43.9 per cent (45.6 per cent if the results of the 'non-partisan' regions are omitted) and won an absolute majority in four regions (Fife, Lothian, Central and Strathclyde), becoming the largest single party in two others (Grampian and Tayside). It meant that the electoral setbacks of the 1982-83 period could be safely forgotten, or so it seemed, and preparations made for the coming general election.

The problem, of course, was the old one. The party in the rest of Britain was not ready for an election and would not be when it was called in summer 1987. Kinnock's determination to wrestle his hard Left and Militant opponents to the ground had won him some support outside for bravery but not much extra public support. The defence controversy rumbled on and there were signs from time to time that the old problems which had seemed intractable under Foot were indeed that, and could never be solved. In a campaign which was designed by the Conservatives to illustrate the message of coming prosperity, even the glitter of the Kinnock campaign could do little. But in Scotland, fifty seats were won. The result exceeded the expectation in Keir Hardie House and produced a euphoric reaction in the Scottish party.

But to what end? The old problem had not been solved. The Scots MPs arrived to find themselves on thinly-populated opposition benches again, and facing a surging sea of Tories across the chamber. Mrs Thatcher, after some minor jitters in the campaign, was in domineering mood, talking about the radical cutting edge which was to be sharpened for the third term. So it was. Privatisation was to be extended to electricity, water, British Rail and even — in preparation for the fourth term — to the sacred territory of the minefields. There was to be no letting up, and of course to Labour nationally the sense of impotence was enormous. For new MPs, particularly arriving from the council chamber perhaps, it was a truly shocking sight, which seemed to leave them almost bereft of speech. The problem, however, was not simply at Westminster, but at home.

The SNP had lost Stewart (Labour winning the Western Isles, to recover long-lost land) and Wilson in Dundee East. But along with the retread Margaret Ewing (once, in an earlier incarnation, Bain) and Andrew Welsh they had produced Alex Salmond, a shrewd strategist and the man given the task of attacking Labour for its alleged inability to translate its election 'victory' into action. He began by calling them 'the feeble fifty' and producing on every occasion of any importance evidence of their inability to change the Government's mind. Labour's difficulty in this, of course, was that he was right: even the meagre band of twelve Scottish Tories — so meagre and short of talent that Rifkind as Secretary of State had real difficulty in staffing his ministerial team adequately — were bent on more radical legislation at the Prime Minister's behest. Here was the 1979 problem on a much grander scale. The mandate argument was crude, and in Labour's view constitutionally destructive, but it was bound to have increasing resonance in a Scottish population perhaps getting tired of voting Labour (or Alliance or SNP) and ignoring the Conservatives in large numbers, but getting nothing for it.

Cheered by opinion polls suggesting that independence as an eventual option was beginning to win more support, the SNP began to campaign hard. Its chosen ground was the poll tax debate. Scotland's preparations for the introduction of the tax, flat-rate on all adults, were a year ahead of those in England and Wales and the SNP strategy was simply to outflank Labour by promoting a campaign of non-payment, the 'Scottish resistance'. There was some Labour unhappiness on the hard Left and in the unlikely figure of Dick Douglas, the MP for Dunfermline West and an old-fashioned Right-winger who resigned the chairmanship of the Scottish group of MPs on the issue, undertook a sponsored run to Buckingham Palace from Fife to petition the Queen and voted for Tony Benn in the leadership election as a snub to Kinnock. For a time, Dewar was embattled again.

But a special party conference in Govan in September/settled the matter. Support for a strictly legal campaign of resistance, as advocated by Dewar and Kinnock, was overwhelming and the leadership had surmounted another hurdle. Moreover it appeared that poll tax registration figures suggested little public support for the SNP campaign. The episode, however, sent another tremor through the party. Dewar had a difficult summer and as if the fates were conspiring against him he found himself facing a by-election in Govan after the resignation of Millan to become a European Commissioner in Brussels. The constituency party promptly dumped the potential candidate who had leadership support and chose Bob Gillespie, an official of Sogat 82 who had supported non-payment. As the campaign began he moderated this line — saying he would not encourage other individuals to withhold payment — and Dewar found himself able to pronounce him 'a first-class local candidate'. But there was a ghost at the feast, Jim Sillars. As a wayward Labour MP he had broken with the party a decade earlier to found his own Scottish Labour Party — soon to fold having made little public impact — and later to join the SNP, where he tried to edge it towards a harder nationalist-socialist position. Govan, where his wife Margo MacDonald had held the seat for the SNP for nine heady months in 1974, was to be the scene of an argument about the fundamentals of Left-wing politics in Scotland.

On the night of Nov 10, the old nightmare came back. Sillars swept away the Labour majority of about 19,500 and turned it into an SNP majority of 3,500. Nothing so horrible had happened to Labour in a Scottish by-election since Winnie Ewing won Hamilton in 1967. In his moment of victory, Sillars said that she had lit a candle then: the voters of Govan had now lit a bonfire. His bravado and heady overstatement was understandable, if premature. But his win was a thunderclap in Scottish politics. The Tories began to redefine their unionism (demonstrating immediately that they would reveal old party divisions), and Labour began a familiar exercise in agonised self-criticism, and London journalists began to queue again for their shuttle flights north. *The Scotsman* started the 'Govan Debate' and the atmosphere quickened. Everyone began to say that they did not know what would happen next, and that it was a long time since they had found themselves saying that.

Labour's defeat in Govan could be explained partly by the performance of a weak candidate, Bob Gillespie, who had been selected after some farcical factional struggles in the local party and who been forced to modify his 'won't pay' poll tax position under pressure from the hierarchy. The implications, however, were serious and long term, as a gloomy Dewar admitted. A break-through by the SNP with an avowedly left-wing candidate — arguing for an independent Scotland inside the European community — was bound to increase Labour's worries, stirring up all the old nationalist fears and guilty feelings, perhaps in equal measure. There would probably be no doubt about the policy — an assembly with tax raising powers — but the tone was likely to change. Of all the possible beneficiaries of Govan, Sillars was the least welcome to Labour.

As a reminder to the party that the national question will never go away, it could hardly have been better-timed. Here was an even bigger Parliamentary group from Scotland than in

1945, the landslide year, and yet still there was a panic over
the SNP and the electorate's reaction to enforced impotence in
Parliament. Labour's response was clear — that established policy
on an Assembly with tax-raising and economic powers was the
kernel of a realistic and radical policy, and was now built into
the party as a bulwark. That was beyond question — even among
the No campaigners there was now scarcely a whimper about
the policy — but how could the weakness of the British party
be ignored?

At Westminster it was becoming ever more obvious that Labour
depended disproportionately on its Scottish MPs. In the shadow
cabinet Gordon Brown was carving out an enviable niche as
everyone's coming man (and in some dreamy eyes, a future
leader), Robin Cook was performing in sparkling fashion, and
John Smith (whose heart attack in Autumn, 1986, seemed
unlikely to keep him out of politics for too long) was the ballast
behind Kinnock. Their difficulty was the extent to which they
could ever depend on a national Labour victory to produce the
Assembly they wanted in Edinburgh and the jobs they wanted in
Whitehall. While Kinnock's modernisation plan unfolds — Brown,
for example, had been influential in pressing on the leader his
ideas for the creation of a genuine mass-membership party — they
are committed to it. But what does a talented generation from
Scotland decide to do when it finds the road to power in
London blocked?

It is a depressing thought for some of them who have lived
through a turbulent decide which, in Scotland, has been successful
for the party, despite the horror of Govan. Local government has
worked — Mrs Thatcher is even forced to cite Strathclyde as model
of public enterprise willing to help private interests in creating
jobs and running communities — and Labour has succeeded in
maintaining an updated model of the world which the Thatcher
Governments have been pledged to destroy. Much legislation has
changed Scottish life, but Labour dominance has meant that the
social assumptions have changed less radically north of the border
and have been a hurdle which even Rifkind has not wanted to leap
over. There have been party arguments — and bitter disputes over
the best way to challenge the Government — but a generation of
politicians has been produced from the devolution maelstrom which
is aching for power. It is ideologically united compared with the
position before 1979; it is gradually shedding the remnants of rusty
machine politics which disfigured it for so long; it is an opposition
which has had plenty of practice for Government.

It is all, however, useless without power at Westminster. But for the moment the southern route is only one which can be contemplated, because the quagmire of nationalism has sucked down too many in the past. They hope that they will never have to confront it again, but many of them suspect that they will. For the moment they can look back on a decade of achievement in the party — and try to stop asking themselves what it has brought them.

References

Chapter 1

1. On the general British background see appropriate references to chapters. Labour historiography is extensive but includes the following recent publications: K.D. Brown (1982) *The English Labour Movement 1700 - 1951*; C. Cook and I. Taylor (1980) *The Labour Party: An Introduction to its History, Structure and Politics*; J. Hinton (1983) *Labour & Socialism: A History of the British Labour Movement 1867 - 1974*; R. McKibbin (1974) *The Evolution of the Labour Party 1910 - 1924*; R. Moore (1978) *The Emergence of the Labour Party 1880 - 1924*; B. Pimlott (1977) *Labour and the Left in the 1930s*; J. Jupp (1982) *The Radical Left in Britain 1931 - 1941*.
2. T. Gallagher (1987) *Glasgow — The Uneasy Peace*; J. Holford (1988) *Reshaping Labour: Organisation Work and Politics — Edinburgh in the Great War and After*.
3. On specifically Scottish developments see: G. Brown (ed) (1975) *The Red Paper on Scotland*; M. Keating and D. Bleiman (1979) *Labour and Scottish Nationalism*; W. Knox (1984) *Scottish Labour Leaders 1918-39: A Biographical Dictionary*; I. MacDougall (ed) (1978) *A Catalogue of Some Labour Records in Scotland*, and (1978) *Essays in Scottish Labour History*; W.H. Fraser 'The Labour Party in Scotland' in K.D. Brown (ed) (1985) *The First Labour Party 1906 - 1914*. On the devolution debate, see J. Bochel, D. Denver and A.Macartney (eds) (1981), *The Referendum Experience, Scotland 1979*

Chapter 2

1. Election statistics in this chapter are derived from F.W.S. Craig (1980) *British Electoral Facts, 1900-79*; David Butler and Ann Sloman (1979) *British Political Facts, 1900-79*, and G.D.H. Cole (1941) *British Working Class Politics, 1832-1914*.
2. The major works involved in this debate are Paul Thompson (1967) *Socialists, Liberals and Labour, 1884-1914*, Peter F. Clarke (1971)

Lancashire and the New Liberalism, Jay Winter (1974) *Socialism and the Challenge of War, 1912-18*, and Ross McKibbin (1974) *The Evolution of the Labour Party, 1910-24*.

3. Iain McLean (1975) *Kier Hardie* p 28.
4. Martin Haddow (1943) *My Sixty Years* p 32.
5. T. Graham (1948) *Willie Graham* p 39 ff.
6. J. Hamilton Muir (1901) *Glasgow in 1901* p 188.
7. Harry McShane and Joan Smith (1978) *No Mean Fighter* p40.
8. Robert Keith Middlemass (1965) *The Clydesiders* p 43.
9. Tom Johnston (1909) *Our Scots Noble Families*.
10. Ross McKibbin (1974) *Evolution of the Labour Party* p 24.
11. *ibid*. p 1.
12. John Paton (1935) *Proletarian Pilgrimage* pp 170-173.
13. *ibid*. p 191.
14. For this argument see G. Stedman Jones (1975) *Outcast London* pp 337-349.
15. Quoted in McLean (1975) p 56.
16. Muir (1901).
17. Quoted in Iain McLean (1971) *The Labour movement in Clydeside politics 1914-22* Oxford D. Phil. Thesis, p 157.
18. *ibid*. pp 149-151.
19. McShane (1978) pp 12-13.
20. John McNair (1955) *James Maxton, Beloved Rebel* p 49.
21. Recorded by Lord Brockway, 26 November 1983.
22. For Labour's 1918 reorganisation see Henry Pelling (1961) *A Short History of the Labour Party* pp 40-45.
23. Gordon Brown (1981) *The Labour Party and Political Change in Scotland 1918-29* unpublished Edinburgh PhD Thesis, p 104.
24. Jennie Lee (1963) *This Great Journey* p 22. The future ILP MP and wife of Aneurin Bevan was the daughter of a Fife miners' agent.
25. R.E. Dowse (1966) *Left in the centre* p 57; Iain McLean (1983) *The Legend of Red Clydeside* p 205.

Chapter 3

1. R.K. Middlemass (1965) *The Clydesiders* pp 111-13; J. Paton (1936) *Left Turn* pp 143-444; E. Shinwell (1955) *Conflict without Malice* pp 76-77. References to the Scottish Council of the Labour Party are drawn from its reports, deposited in the National Library of Scotland.
2. E. Shinwell *op.cit*.
3. J. Paton *op.cit*. p 150.
4. R. McKibbin (1974) *The Evolution of the Labour Party*.
5. J. Scanlan (1932) *The Decline and Fall of the Labour Party* p 29.
6. J. McNair (1955) *James Maxton, The Beloved Rebel* p 91.
7. R. McKibbin *op.cit*. pp 70-1.

8. R. Jenkins (1964) *Asquith* p 486.
9. *Times* 28 December 1922.
10. *ibid.*
11. W.H. Miller (1981) *The End of British Politics? Scots and English Political Behaviour in the Seventies*; J.G. Kellas (1976) 'The Political Behaviour of the Working Class' in *Social Class in Scotland* ed. A.A. McLaren pp 145-6.
12. I.S. Wood (1980) 'John Wheatley, the Irish and the Labour Movement in Scotland' *Innes Review* XXXI.
13. M. Keating and D. Bleiman (1979) *Labour and Scottish Nationalism.*
14. *ibid.* pp 102-8.
15. A. Dewar Gibb (1930) *Scotland in Eclipse* p 54.
16. J.D. MacCormick (1955) *The Flag in the Wind* p 51.
17. R.E. Dowse (1964) *Left in the Centre* p 105.
18. J. Paton *op.cit.* p 335; also R E Dowse *op.cit.* pp 37-40.
19. D. Marquand (1977) *Ramsay MacDonald* p 392.
20. R.E. Dowse *op.cit.* p 40.
21. D. Marquand *op.cit.* pp 430-3.
22. I. MacDougall (1981) *Militant Miners* pp 138-43.
23. *ibid.* p 145.
24. Lord MacMillan (1952) *A Man of Law's Tale* p 91.
25. Quoted in A. Gamme (1931) *From Pit to Palace: the Life Story of the Rt Hon James Brown* p 125.
26. T.N. Graham (1948) *Willie Graham* pp 161-2.
27. W. Bolitho (1924) *Cancer of the Empire* p 16.
28. E. Wertheimer (1929) *Portrait of the Labour Party* pp 184-5.
29. See I.S. Wood above, also Sheridan Gilley (1980) 'Catholics and Socialists in Glasgow 1906-12' in *Immigrants, Hosts and Minorities* ed. K. Lunn.
30. *Forward* and Wheatley's own *Glasgow Eastern Standard* carried many articles by him on the strike and lock-out, along with reports on his work in support of the miners.

Chapter 4

1. For the general background see R. Skidelsky (1967) *Politicians and the Slump*; J. Stevenson and C. Cook (1977) *The Slump. Society and Politics During the Depression*; B. Pimlott (1977) *Labour and the Left in the 1930s*; C. Cook and I. Taylor (1980) *The Labour Party: An Introduction to its History, Structure and Politics.*
2. D. Aldcroft (1979) *The Inter-War Economy; Britain, 1919-1939*; N. K. Buxton (1975) 'The Role of the New Industries in Britain during the 1930s: A Re-interpretation' *Business History Rev.* XLIX.
3. G.C.M. McGringle and J. Kirby (1936) *Poverty and Public Health* pp 190-193.
4. C. Cook and J. Ramsden (1973) *By-Elections in British Politics* pp

109-117.
5. Labour Party (1931) *Two Years of Labour Rule* pp 24, 48-51.
6. *ibid.* pp 5-12.
7. Data compiled from F.W.S. Craig (1971) *British Parliamentary Election Statistics 1918-1970* and Scottish Conservative and Unionist Party *Year Book for Scotland 1966* pp 135-238.
8. See Stevenson and Cook pp 100-106 on the New Party's election performance.
9. *Year Book for Scotland 1936.*
10. C. A. Oakley (1975) *The Second City* p 24.
11. Glasgow University Library, Broady Coll. B22, Text of Speech at Bridgeton 21.10.36.
12. Broady Coll. A64, J McInnes (1949) *Glasgow's Housing: Labour's Achievements and Future Policy*; H6, Glasgow Corporation Housing Department (1949) *Review of Operations 1919-1947.*
13. Stevenson and Cook p 115.
14. Cook and Ramsden p 170.
15. R.E. Dowse (1966) *Left in the Centre: The ILP 1892-1940* pp 152-202 on the disaffiliation and decline of the ILP. Pimlott pp 100-101 gives further details on the SSP and relations with the Communist Party.
16. *DNB 1922-1930* (1937) pp 904-905.
17. *Who Was Who 1929-40* p 8.
18. J. McNair (1955) *James Maxton: The Beloved Rebel* pp 200-201; A.J.B. Marwick (1964) 'James Maxton: His Place in Scottish Labour History' *Scottish Hist. Rev.* XLII; G. Brown (1986) *Maxton: A Biography.*
19. Labour Party (1937) *Central Scotland: Report of the Labour Party's Commission of Enquiry into the Distressed Areas* pp 1-2, 22-24.

Chapter 5

1. Paul Addison (1975) *The Road to 1945* p 25.
2. National Library of Scotland (NLS): Arthur Woodburn MSS: Autobiography, p 145.
3. NLS: Woodburn MSS: Autobiography p 114.
4. Speech quoted in *Forward* October 27 1945.
5. This version is James Margach's (1979) *The Anatomy of Power* p 25. Another, even briefer, runs: 'Cos you weren't good enough. Goodbye.'
6. Robert MacKenzie (1955) *British Political Parties* p 645.
7. *ibid.* p 532.
8. Jean Mann (1962) *Women in Parliament* p 23.
9. NEC Organisation SC, Memo from Taylor, 28 January 1942.
10. Woodburn MSS: Shepherd-Woodburn, 25 August 1939.
11. R.B. McCallum and Alison Readman (1947) *The General Election of 1945* p 4 state that the Unionists totally disbanded their organisation; this is contradicted by reports in the *Conservative Agents' Journal*

January 1940 ff.
12. Paul Addison interview 14 November 1983.
13. Johnston (1952) *Memories* p 147.
14. Addison, interview, and Sir G S Harvie-Watt (1980) *Most of my Life* pp 75-6.
15. Herbert Morrison (1960) *An Autobiography* p 199.
16. Interview with Mrs N Tomter (formerly Fraser) joint secretary of the Scottish Reconstruction Committee.
17. Angus Calder (1971) *The People's War* pp 401-5.
18. Addison (1975) p 225.
19. In *Studies in the Problems of Sovereignty* (1917) p 208.
20. George Pottinger (1979) *The Secretaries of State for Scotland* p 104.
21. Alan Sked and Chris Cook (1979) *Post-War Britain* pp 31-5.
22. John MacCormick (1953) *The Flag in the Wind* p 115.
23. A. Woodburn *Scottish Demands for Home Rule or Devolution* p 2.
24. *ibid.* pp 6, 10.
25. *ibid.* p 5.
26. *Glasgow Herald* 30 January 1948.

Chapter 6

1. C.A.R Crosland (1956) *The Future of Socialism*.
2. D. Butler and D. Stokes (1969) *Political Change in Britain*.
3. Speech at Town Hall, Birmingham, 1 January 1964 reprinted in (1964) *The New Britain: Labour's Plan* p 9.
4. M. Keating and D. Bleiman (1979) *Labour and Scottish Nationalism*.
5. G. McCrone (1965) *Scotland's Economic Progress, 1951-60. A Study in Regional Accounting* pp 28-9.
6. Keating and Bleiman, p. 56.
7. W.L. Miller (1981) *The End of British Politics, Scots and English Political Behaviour in the Seventies*.
8. *ibid.* p 130.
9. *ibid.* p 29.
10. Butler and Stokes, *op.cit.*
11. I. Budge and D.W. Uriwn (1966) *Scottish Political Behaviour*.
12. Butler and Stokes, *op.cit.*
13. M. Keating (1975) *The Role of the Scottish MP* PhD Thesis CNAA.
14. *ibid.*
15. R.M. Punnett (1972) *Government in Opposition* PhD Thesis University of Strathclyde.
16. Keating and Bleiman, *op.cit.*
17. S.G. Checkland (1977) *The Upas Tree, Glasgow 1875-1975*.
18. These are described in M Keating and A. Midwinter *The Government of Scotland* (forthcoming).
19. R.H.S. Crossman (1977) *The Diaries of a Cabinet Minister* Vol 3 p 48.

Chapter 7

1. *Evening News and Dispatch* 28 September 1964.
2. J.G. Kellas (1975) *The Scottish Political System* pp 40, 156.
3. R.H.S. Crossman (1976) *The Diaries of a Cabinet Minister* Vol 2 p 550.
4. H.M. Drucker (ed) (1982) *John P MacKintosh on Scotland* p 140.
5. LP Report 1968.
6. M. Keating and D. Bleiman (1979) *Labour and Scottish Nationalism* p 157.
7. *ibid.*
8. T. Dalyell (1977) *Devolution: The End of Britain?* p 94.
9. *ibid.* p 99.
10. Keating and Bleiman p 165.
11. *The Scotsman* 19 August 1974.
12. On the history of the SLP see H M Drucker (1977) *Breakaway: The Scottish Labour Party*.
13. *The Scotsman* 19 January 1979.
14. *Morning Star* 21 February 1979.

Chapter 8

1. A. Tuckett (1986) *The Scottish Trade Union Congress: The First Eighty Years* p 32.
2. See *TUC Annual Reports* which contain a list of affiliated bodies.
3. *STUC Report 1898* p 32.
4. Sydney and Beatrice Webb (1894) *The History of Trade Unionism* appendix.
5. See. *TUC Annual Report 1895* and also B.D. Roberts *History of the Trades Union Congress 1868-1921*.
6. *The Scotsman* editorial 8 September 1896.
7. See *TUC Annual Reports*.
8. See European Community's Trade Union Information Series on Trade Unions in Member countries of the EEC.
9. *Labour Leader* 1 September 1895.
10. *Dundee Advertiser* 11 November 1895.
11. Andrew Boyd (1972) *The Rise of the Irish Trade Unions 1720-1970* p 51 et seq.
12. See *The Labour Gazette* monthly reports 1895-96 also Eric Wigham (1973) *The Power to Manage — A History of the Engineering Employers' Federation*.
13. *Falkirk Herald* 29 April 1896.
14. *Labour Leader* 19 September 1896, which contains the Scottish Trades Federation Scheme.

Contributors

Jim Craigen, Labour and Co-operative MP for Glasgow Maryhill, February 1974-1987, was assistant to STUC General Secretary, James Jack, 1964-68. A trade unionist since leaving school, he has worked as a compositor, industrial relations assistant and assistant secretary of SCOTBEC. He is presently Director of the Scottish Federation of Housing Associations.

Dr Ian Donnachie is Staff Tutor and Senior Lecturer in History at The Open University in Scotland and has also taught in several Australian universities, notably Deakin University, Vic. and the University of Sydney. With interests in modern social and economic history his most recent publications include: *A History of the Brewing Industry in Scotland*; *Industrial Archaeology in the British Isles* (with John Butt); and *Scottish History, 1560-1980* (with George Hewitt).

Professor Christopher Harvie holds the Chair of British Studies at the University of Tübingen, West Germany, having previously taught at The Open University. He publishes widely on modern British and Scottish history and his books include; *The Lights of Liberalism; University Liberals and the Challenge of Democracy 1860-86; Scotland and Nationalism: Scottish Society & Politics 1707-1977*; an *No Gods and Precious Few Heroes: Scotland 1914-1980*.

Dr Michael Keating is a Professor of Political Science at the University of Western Ontario, having previously held posts at the University of Strathclyde, and the University of Essex. His numerous books on politics and government include: *Labour and Scottish Nationalism; The Government of Scotland; Labour and the British State; Regions in the European Community*; and *Remaking Urban Scotland*.

James Naughtie presents 'The World at One' on BBC Radio 4, and was formerly Chief Political Correspondent of *The Guardian* and *The Scotsman*.

Frances Wood is an honours graduate in politics of Edinburgh University. She has been a Labour Party activist and member since 1974. Formerly a full-time District Councillor in Edinburgh she is now a Staff Development Officer with the Institute of Housing in Scotland.

Ian S Wood is a Lecturer in History at Napier Polytechnic, Edinburgh, a tutor with the Open University, and was editor of the Scottish Labour

History Society Journal 1974-87. A regular contributor to *The Scotsman* on political and historical themes, he is also working on a biography of John Wheatley.

Index